GOVERNING THE ISLAND OF
MONTREAL

A publication of the Franklin K. Lane Memorial Fund, Institute of Governmental Studies, University of California, Berkeley

The Franklin K. Lane Memorial Fund takes its name from Franklin Knight Lane (1864–1921), a distinguished Californian who was successively New York correspondent for the San Francisco *Chronicle*, City and County Attorney of San Francisco, member and later chairman of the United States Interstate Commerce Commission, and Secretary of the Interior in the cabinet of President Woodrow Wilson.

The general purposes of the endowment are to promote "better understanding of the nature and working of the American system of democratic government, particularly in its political, economic and social aspects," and the "study and development of the most suitable methods for its improvement in the light of experience."

Lane Studies in Regional Government:

New York: The Politics of Urban Regional Development, by Michael N. Danielson and Jameson W. Doig

Governing the London Region: Reorganization and Planning in the 1960s, by Donald L. Foley

Governing Metropolitan Toronto: A Social and Policy Analysis, by Albert Rose

Governing Greater Stockholm: Policy Development and Urban Change in Stockholm, by Thomas J. Anton

Metropolitan Winnipeg: Politics and Reform of Local Government, by Meyer Brownstone and T. J. Plunkett

GOVERNING THE ISLAND OF MONTREAL

Language Differences and Metropolitan Politics

Andrew Sancton

Published for the Institute of Governmental Studies
and the Institute of International Studies
University of California, Berkeley

UNIVERSITY OF CALIFORNIA PRESS
BERKELEY   LOS ANGELES   LONDON

University of California Press
Berkeley and Los Angeles, California

University of California Press, Ltd.
London, England

1   2   3   4   5   6   7   8   9

Library of Congress Cataloging in Publication Data

Sancton, Andrew, 1948–
    Governing the Island of Montreal.

    (Lane studies in regional government) (A Publication
of the Franklin K. Lane Memorial Fund, Institute of
Governmental Studies, University of California,
Berkeley)
    "Published for the Institute of Governmental
Studies and the Institute of International Studies,
University of California, Berkeley."
    Includes index.
    1. Montréal Metropolitan Area (Québec)—Politics and
government. 2. Biculturalism—Québec (Province)
3. Montréal Metropolitan Area (Québec)—Languages—
Political aspects. I. University of California,
Berkeley. Institute of Governmental Studies.
II. University of California, Berkeley. Institute of
International Studies. III. Title. IV. Series.
V. Series: Publication of the Franklin K. Lane Memorial
Fund, Institute of Governmental Studies, University
of California, Berkeley.
JS1761.3.A8S26   1985   306'.2'0971428   84-23922
ISBN 0-520-04906-3

To my mother and father
Mary Alice Bain Sancton
John William Sancton

Contents

Tables and Maps

Foreword

This book is about language and related intergroup conflicts in the Montreal metropolitan area and how they have affected attempts to provide health, education, and several other public services. Andrew Sancton analyzes and documents these factors—with particular attention to language differences—viewed both as fact and as symbol of other deep and pervasive sources of discord. He considers the influence of conflict on the structure of local government—whether general-purpose municipalities or special-purpose school or health care agencies—and shows the relation of such communal influences to local inhabitants' expectations of governmental response and performance. Perhaps most significant is his demonstration of the intimate link between the local and the provincial polities. Events in Montreal, as in many other metropolitan areas of the world, were, of course, also subject to national and even international influences. These Montreal developments occurred simultaneously with Quebec's transformation into a modern welfare state and the reassessment of its role in Canadian federalism.

In this foreword we suggest some ways in which other metropolitan regions share the kinds of communal divisions that characterize the Montreal region. We believe this may be helpful in understanding the complexity of metropolitan governance. Some important forms of such conflict, of course, are not rooted in language differences (e.g., in strife-ridden Belfast everyone speaks English). Even where language conflicts are most notable (e.g., Montreal, Brussels, and to a much lesser extent Jerusalem), language is only one of the factors that cause conflict. To illustrate this, we take brief looks at Belfast, Brussels, and Jerusalem.

In addition, we are especially interested in examining similar conflict phenomena in the United States. As Sancton suggests, the spatial segregation of blacks in the central cities and in a few of the suburbs of most metropolitan areas of the United States sets the stage for continued suspicion and even hostility between the central city and its suburbs. Such influences can work against local governmental consolidation or other boundary changes as well as against the creation of a limited-purpose, second-tier metropolitan government, or indeed against any concerted cooperation among jurisdictions.

Although Hispanic Americans and Spanish-speaking immigrants are not as tightly segregated as blacks, they are much more segregated than whites. We inquire briefly into their present and possible future role in the governance of metropolitan areas, especially because the rapidly growing Hispanic population is intensifying important cultural and linguistic conflicts that until recently received little attention.

Finally, the structure of the Montreal Urban Community, as a federal-confederal organization of municipalities, offers the opportunity to contrast and compare it with the widespread councils of governments (COGs) in the United States, which resemble the Montreal structure in some important ways, although they are much weaker.

In discussing the COGs we raise the question whether a confederal approach under statutes or joint agreements would provide an effective means of cooperation. Some people would argue that such a metropolitan confederation could be the best of both worlds: reorganizing metropolitan governance without eliminating local "sovereignty." In any event, we conclude that in most U.S. regions the achievement of any more authoritative and comprehensive form of metropolitan government seems unlikely.

Conflict Management: An Emerging Goal of Metropolitan Governance

In many metropolitan regions, the reduction or containment of intergroup conflict has recently become a more noticeable and talked-about objective of government. In contrast, 30 years ago, or in many places as little as 15 years ago, questions of financial equity, housing, transportation, and the provision of other large-scale services were seen as the uppermost issues.

This shift in the metropolitan agenda is grounded, at least partly, in profound demographic changes. Throughout the world, large-scale population movement has characterized the era since World War II. Everywhere, people have flocked from the countryside into the city and the suburbs. Much movement is also attributable to the international flight of refugees as well as to the temporary (and permanent) movement of foreign "guestworkers" traveling long distances in search of employment. Many, if not most, of the world's metropolitan regions are steadily becoming more heterogeneous—racially, ethnically, economically, and in other ways. Moreover, the heterogeneous elements are usually segregated residentially.

The political awareness and activism of many of the "newcomers" and of "oldtimers" who occupy niches as second-class citizens have clearly been on the rise. The Quiet Revolution of francophones in Montreal is an excellent example. Analogous influences have undoubtedly done much to raise the level of intergroup conflict in many metropolitan regions.

The service and finance issues that until recently were the principal concerns of many would-be metropolitan reformers are still quite important, but in many metropolitan regions they have been overshadowed by a variety of ethnic, linguistic, cultural, and economic conflicts. There is often intense competition among groups for improved status and for a greater share of resources. In responding to these pressures, public policy and governmental processes are employed in efforts to manage and moderate the conflicts. Consequently, changes in governmental policy or structure require careful, sensitive consideration of their effect on intergroup relationships.

In looking at urban governance, we see how these conflicts raise two principal questions. First, how do they affect efforts to reorganize services and governments in metropolitan areas? Second, how do the new structures attempt to deal with conflict?

Reorganization Resisted in Montreal

While Andrew Sancton treats both questions in this book, he focuses principally on the first. His study of Montreal shows how language and other social, cultural, and economic differences associated with language can compound the other tensions in a large urban region, making it especially difficult to find acceptable formulas for governance.

In effect, no significant governmental reorganizations or other major policy decisions—especially those affecting education, health, and police—can be taken in Montreal without considering their impact on French-speaking and English-speaking residents as well as on other ethnic, religious, cultural, and economic interests. The policies and organization of government in the Province of Quebec, and on the Island of Montreal, have been used to protect and redistribute both symbolic and material goods of anglophones, francophones, Protestants, Catholics, and Jews and to respond to the needs of an upwardly mobile majority as well as to challenge minorities that are still economically powerful. The book tells a fascinating and instructive story of traditional local governments adapting to the changing scale of urban activities and collaborating across divisions of language, religion, and lifestyle to form alliances, resisting what Sancton calls the imperatives of the rational organization of the metropolis.

Whereas the language differences that deeply divide the Montreal region, especially the Island of Montreal, have militated against reorganization, it has been a different story in some other Quebec areas. Thus on Île-Jésus, immediately north of Montreal, where there are no dominantly anglophone municipalities, the 14 municipalities were successfully consolidated in 1965 into the "uni-city" of Laval. Also, in the Quebec Urban Community, consolidation has reduced the number of municipalities from 26 to 13, and in the Outaouais Regional Community, centered across the river from Ottawa in Hull, from 32 to 8.[1]

In sharp contrast is the language-divided Island of Montreal, where 27 of 28 suburban municipalities have survived the creation and development of the Montreal Urban Community.[2] As Sancton clearly demonstrates, linguistic, cultural, and economic differences parallel and reflect the segregation of the population into a series of enclaves organized as municipalities. Of course Montreal municipalities also display the "typical" kinds of local resistance in addition to those based on language and other associated differences. Anglophone suburbs resist amalgamation with other anglophone suburbs, and francophone suburbs with francophone suburbs, and both types resist absorption by Montreal and provincial efforts to regroup them.

Thus, we see how local governments can be tough and persistent organizations, especially when bolstered by the kinds of influences noted here. In local-regional and local-central struggles, a basic protective response is to form coalitions of local governments. These coalitions can put up powerful resistance to changes they do not like, as has happened in many places, e.g., in France, British Columbia, the United States, and Montreal (among both anglophone and francophone municipalities).

The struggle for workable and acceptable governing formulas is universal and, as emphasized here, can be especially difficult for metropolitan communities in which language differences and other divisions spark quiet antipathies or overt antagonism. The result can be stalemate, withdrawal of the opposing sides into relative isolation, domination of the weaker by the stronger under more-or-less peaceful circumstances, or open civil strife and outright warfare. In such regions the success of reform efforts depends largely on devising approaches to metropolitan governance that respect the constraints of local autonomy while at the same time capitalizing on any opportunities for collaboration.

1. These developments are similar to the formation of Toronto's Metro and subsequent reforms elsewhere in Ontario. Altogether, the number of lower-tier municipalities in Ontario has been reduced from 201 to 85. T. J. Plunkett, "Canada: Ontario," in *International Handbook on Local Government Reorganization*, ed. Donald C. Rowat (Westport, Conn.: Greenwood Press, 1980), p. 13.

2. One suburban municipality, Pointe-aux-Trembles, has recently been annexed by the City of Montreal. (See footnote to Table 5.)

Virtually everywhere we find metropolitan communities divided by language, race, religion, class, customs, lifestyle, and national aspirations.[3] These diversities always pose difficult challenges of conflict resolution, accommodation, and governance. The skill, ingenuity, and effectiveness with which the challenges are met can help determine the conditions of life in a multicultural society as well as its very fate. The stakes are raised and the challenges heightened when the polyglot populations live within the same local region and when there is greater visibility of socioeconomic differences and more intense competition for resources.

In extreme cases conflict can become so severe that agreement on the reorganization of a region, or perhaps even its basic governance, becomes very difficult if not virtually impossible. Excellent examples of such extreme tensions are found in three Old World regions renowned for their persistent communal conflict: Brussels, Belfast, and Jerusalem. Admittedly, Montreal seems far from such a pass, as conflict in all three is more intense than in Montreal, and all lack structures of governance as accommodative of interest conflicts as are found in Montreal today. Nevertheless, we have chosen to use these three examples to highlight the divisive roles that such tensions can play. Afterward we will draw comparisons and contrasts involving metropolitan regions in the United States where conflicts among racial, ethnic, economic, and cultural divisions combine with certain peculiarly American constitutional features and political ideologies to make governmental change extremely difficult.

3. "Ethnic politics should not be viewed as a parochial phenomenon ... for there are few places on earth where ethnicity is not presently of political import. Even if we confine our attention to those distinctions that exist principally within national boundaries ... we are left with an imposing list: Afrikander v. Bantu, Kikuyu v. Luo, Yoruba v. Ibo, Bahutu v. Watusi, Kurd v. Iraqim, Moslim v. Hindu, Ukranian v. Great Russian, Great Russian v. most Eurasian groups, Mongolian v. Chinese, the overseas Chinese v. most of Southeast Asia, the overseas Indians v. most of eastern and southern Africa, Turk v. Greek Cypriot, Arab v. Jew, Ladino v. white Spanish, Welsh v. English, Walloon v. Flemish, Czech v. Slovak, Christian v. Jew, Protestant v. Catholic, Catholic v. Buddist, black v. white, and on we go; this list merely scratches the surface. One can even discern conflicting subgroups within opposing groups (thus orthodox v. reform Jews, Afrikans-speaking v. English-speaking whites, Ulster v. Celtic Irish), particularly in Africa and the Middle and Far East." Edgar Litt, *Ethnic Politics in America* (Glenview, Ill.: Scott, Foresman and Co., 1970), p. 6. Matthew Holden observes that "the problem of overcoming Madisonian faction is not merely a United States problem of race, but one that can be found repeatedly in the confrontations of French-speaking and English-speaking Canadians; or of Serbs, Croatians, Macedonians and others in Yugoslavia; or of Hindus and blacks in Guyana; or of Walloons and Flemings in Belgium; or of Melanesians and Indians in Fiji; or of Indians and whites in countries of Latin America." *The White Man's Burden* (San Francisco: Chandler Publishing Co., 1973), pp. 203–4. See also Nathan Glazer and Daniel P. Moynihan, eds., *Ethnicity: Theory and Experience* (Cambridge: Harvard University Press, 1975).

Brussels: An Ethnic Battleground

Three distinct ethnic groups share Belgium's capital region: the Dutch-speaking population, who identify with the Flemish; the French-speaking Walloons; and other French-speaking inhabitants who "tend to view themselves as 'Belgian' or Bruxellois rather than Walloon or Flemish."[4] These differences have prevented effective agreement between Dutch-speaking and French-speaking inhabitants as to the appropriate area, organization, and operation of Greater Brussels. This contrasts sharply with what has happened in the unilingual Walloon and Flemish areas outside the Brussels region, where since the beginning of constitutional reform in 1971 the reorganization of Belgium's territory into a "federal [regime] along ethnic lines"[5] has largely been accomplished. But the Brussels region remains an ethnic battleground that defies reorganization.[6]

The conflict over Brussels is being fought at the national level by Walloons and Flemings, whose national leaders have "struck a bargain," agreeing to parity between them in staffing the Brussels execu-

4. Martin O. Heisler, "Managing Ethnic Conflict in Belgium," American Academy of Political and Social Science, *Annals* 433 (September 1977): 34.

John Fitzmaurice reports that "Brussels, which is physically in Flanders, is now over 80 percent French-speaking with variation between boroughs from 72 to 92 percent, but retains a significant Flemish minority. In the Flemish *Communes* surrounding Brussels, a French-speaking population of commuters, typical 'suburbanites,' has grown up, 'drowning' the French population, and in some *Communes*—Kraainem and Tervuren, for example—increasingly represents the majority.

"In the last decade a large number of immigrant workers have come to Belgium, mostly from the Mediterranean and North Africa. At present these immigrants number about 850,000. In some Brussels boroughs they represent close to one third of the population." *The Politics of Belgium: Crisis and Compromise in a Plural Society* (London: C. Hurst and Co., 1983), p. 57.

5. Ibid., p. 41.

6. "Indeed, Brussels may be said to constitute the 'war zone,' a theatre of confrontation where the two societies interact most vigorously. From an ethnic perspective, one may say that Brussels is the embodiment of the Belgian drama, the constant struggle for territorial imperatives." Henri J. Warmenhoven, "In the Hurricane's Eye: Recent Local Government Reform in Belgium," in *Local Government Reform and Reorganization: An International Perspective*, ed. Arthur B. Gunlicks (Port Washington, N.Y.: Kennikat Press, 1981), p. 55. See also Martin O. Heisler, "Institutionalizing Societal Cleavages in a Cooptive Polity: The Growing Importance of the Output Side in Belgium," in *Politics in Europe*, ed. Martin O. Heisler (New York: McKay, 1974), p. 217. Governments have fallen over the Brussels issue, for example, the Martens government in April 1980. See Eugeen Roosens, "The Multicultural Nature of Contemporary Belgian Society: The Immigrant Community," in *Conflict and Coexistence in Belgium*, ed. Arend Lijphart (Berkeley: Institute of International Studies, University of California, 1981), p. 87. For a detailed description of the conflict over regional and communal reform for the past two decades, see Fitzmaurice, *The Politics of Belgium*, pp. 111–38. The national compromise of 1980 was made possible only by postponing agreement on Brussels.

tive and the Belgium cabinet. Despite the "bargain," the conflict continues in Brussels itself and in the remainder of the capital region as well as at the national level.

Belfast: Religious and International Strife

Like all Northern Ireland, the metropolitan region of Belfast is torn by intense local conflict far more violent than the language conflicts in Montreal. Belfast's religious differences closely parallel class differences and become virtually indistinguishable from differences in national aspirations, thus being intimately entangled with international conflicts.[7]

Northern Ireland is small, with an area of 5452 square miles and a population of about 1.5 million. It can be considered a proper area for regional governance, and in fact this was the direction taken by the local government reforms of 1971–73. The former system comprised 2 county boroughs for Belfast and Londonderry; 10 borough councils for the other, more urbanized portions; and for the remainder, 6 county councils overlying 24 urban district councils and 31 rural district councils. This structure was replaced by 26 district councils, and most of the important functions were transferred to the central boards, government departments, and area boards dominated by the central government. The district councils, including the one for Belfast, were left only with responsibility for

> minor environmental and recreational activities. . . . In the new administrative structure the main public services have been removed from the local government sphere and are administered regionally as the responsibility of the central government. There are no longer all-purpose authorities for geographical areas but a distinct and separate administrative structure for each group of related services.[8]

7. Richard Rose, in *Governing Without Consent: An Irish Perspective* (London: Faber and Faber, 1971), uses history, political analysis, and survey research to explore the problem of authority in a regime of religious and national antagonisms. See especially Chapter 10 on the structure of communalism. See also Ian Budge and Cornelius O'Leary, *Belfast: Approach to Crisis* (London: MacMillan Press, 1973) for a comparison of Belfast and Glasgow with "broad institutional resemblances" and "social similarities" between the two cities. Not having to deal with the international complications that confront Belfast, and not having groups with conflicting national identities, Glasgow has been able to compromise on religious differences.

8. Derek Birrel and Alan Murie, *Policy and Government in Northern Ireland: Lessons of Devolution* (Dublin: Hill and Macmillan, 1980), p. 175.

There was much talk during the 1960s about the need to simplify the structure of local government to increase "efficiency, expertise, specialization and impartiality."[9] It was hoped, however, that reorganization of the early 1970s would also lead to a more representative participation on ad hoc bodies of "public-spirited citizens of all religious persuasions," people who had been excluded from local government councils or who had even refused to participate in them. Moreover, it was expected that "the removal of central or major services from local government [would end] claims and disputes about religious discrimination and sectarian bias in housing allocations, housebuilding, planning, employment and other matters."[10]

These expectations were not fully realized, although there seems to be general agreement that the provision and allocation of public housing by a centralized board is largely impartial. In any event, many of the disputes continued after the transfer of authority and responsibility to the central government.[11] Moreover, experience in Belfast demonstrates how, when intercommunal conflict becomes the instrument of international conflict, "efficiency of public and municipal services, including the preservation of law and order, and the impartiality and fairness toward the minority, including its political representation, have a fairly marginal impact on the severity of the intercommunal confrontation."[12]

Jerusalem: Religion, Nationality, Language, History, International Politics

Jerusalem is another example of a divided metropolis—riven by religion, language, history, and clashing national aspirations—in search of a system of governance. Its future fate, like that of Beirut and Belfast, will largely be decided in extralocal and extranational arenas. One cynical (or perhaps realistic) survivor of the American metropolitan reform struggles has even suggested that Jerusalem's 1967 unification by Israeli arms in the Six-Day War illustrates one of the few successful methods of achieving the governmental unification of a large heterogeneous metropolis, i.e., force.

As seen by many in Israel, the problem of governing Jerusalem is maintaining Israeli authority over the unified city while also accom-

9. Ibid., p. 177.
10. Ibid., p. 179.
11. See ibid., pp. 191–92, for an evaluation of centralized planning, housing, social security, education, health, and social services.
12. Emanuel Gutman and Claude Klein, "The Institutional Structure of Heterogeneous Cities: Brussels, Montreal and Belfast," in *Jerusalem: Problems and Prospects*, ed. Joel L. Kraemer (New York: Praeger, 1970), pp. 193–201.

modating the needs of diverse ethnic, religious, and political cultures of Arabs, Christians, and Jews.

Arabs participate informally in governance of the city and its environs, although they refuse to acknowledge Israeli sovereignty by accepting public office or otherwise participating "openly in the city's elected government."[13]

Although they maintain that minorities in Jerusalem, including Arabs, have never been more sympathetically and equitably governed than since 1967, Elazar, Gutman, and Klein and Jerusalem's Mayor Kollek nevertheless conclude that the present ad hoc relationships and institutions should eventually be succeeded by more formal arrangements. The time for such steps will depend on international developments as well as on relationships between Israelis and Arabs and especially on their responses to the situation in Jerusalem. Mayor Kollek envisions

> a future structure in Jerusalem under which the city would be governed through a network of boroughs. Each borough would have a great deal of autonomy over its own municipal services and its lifestyle. It would decide its own needs and priorities. It would be modeled not on the boroughs of New York but on those of London, which have their own budgets and a great deal of independence.
>
> Of course, the borough idea is not a panacea. The Arabs will want the Temple Mount to be in their borough, and no Jew would agree to that. But the proposal does suggest an approach under which many of the aspects of everyday life can be delegated to local authorities and the people of the various neighborhoods can feel some increasing control over their own lives and the decision-making process.[14]

13. Ibid., p. 8. See Uzi Benzinian, "Israeli Policy in East Jerusalem after Unification," in *Jerusalem*, ed. Kraemer, pp. 100–130, for a description of means used by the city government "to legalize the modes of behavior peculiar to East Jerusalem, . . . to solve legal entanglements by means of administrative regulations, . . . and to overlook legal infringements." The bilateral policy of "mutual nonrecognition" also governs relationships between the city and the Supreme Muslim Council. Israeli authorities regard the council "as a representative body possessing great influence over the inhabitants of East Jerusalem." Daniel J. Elazar points out that for many centuries conflict among heterogeneous populations in the Middle East was managed or suppressed under systems of autocratic imperial rule. Today the problem is managing such conflict in freer, more democratic systems that allow all groups to participate in governance. Daniel J. Elazar, "Local Government for Heterogeneous Populations: Some Options for Jerusalem," in *Jerusalem*, ed. Kraemer, p. 209.

14. Kraemer, *Jerusalem*, p. 9. Kollek, in *Jerusalem*, ed. Kraemer, p. 217, rejects the federated-city model: "For Jerusalem's purposes the federated city arrangements have less utility than the various county-based arrangements because they require more symmetry of size and population among units. Jerusalem's situation, on the other hand, is essentially asymmetrical in the size of its neighborhoods, in the composition of their populations, and in their fundamental interests. Jerusalem as a 'county' embracing 'cities' of different sizes, shapes, and scope would do better to accommodate these asymmetries."

Obviously, no single model could be transplanted to solve Jerusalem's problems of governance, but Elazar clearly envisions some variation of areawide jurisdiction (county or capital district), with authority also shared with asymmetrical second-tier units, supplemented by contractual arrangements and functional authorities. Undergirding the institutional order would be a consociational orientation among the leaders of the heterogeneous groups. He does not tell us, however, how elites at the local level can successfully negotiate compromises to maintain the regime in the absence of elite bargaining at the national level. Moreover, it is not clear that such a structure can address the class division between Arabs and Jews or between the "oriental" and "western" Israelis.

In any event, the difficulty of developing the kind of consideration and forebearance needed for such arrangements to work—in Jerusalem as well as in other deeply divided regions (e.g., Brussels and Belfast)—emphasizes how ethnic and religious groups may simply refuse to accept a system of *tolerance*. Where such intransigence characterizes a severely split region, mutual accommodation among contending groups will prove far more difficult:

> Under uncommonly auspicious circumstances or particularly well-contrived dispositions, such as fastidious adherence to equal treatment and strict observance of minority . . . an intercommunal situation [like that in Belfast, Brussels, Jerusalem, or Montreal] may be contained for a while and a mutually acceptable status quo . . . worked out. . . . Such experiences seem to point, however, to the ineluctable conclusion that *even the most equitable and judicious of municipal services and administration cannot rectify what are in the eyes of one side, if not both, . . . political, that is, "national wrongs. . . ."* [Emphasis added]
>
>   In Jerusalem . . . because of unique international aspects and the diametrically conflicting claims of sovereignty . . . no mutually acceptable solution has been forthcoming.[15]

Experience in the United States: Segregation, Race, and Metro Government

Montreal and many urban regions in the United States share the kind, though not necessarily the intensity, of "communal" divisions found in Brussels, Belfast, Jerusalem, and many other metropolitan areas around the world. Sancton recognizes the similarities of metro-

---

15. Kraemer, *Jerusalem*, pp. 203–4.

politan politics in Montreal and American metropolitan regions. He states in his introduction:

> Despite major differences between black-white relations in American cities and French-English relations in Montreal, some evidence suggests that the two kinds of cleavages have similar inhibiting influences on metropolitan reform. . . .
>
> In short, racially divided American cities provide an unfavorable environment for metropolitan reform in terms of both legal and sociopolitical factors, and in both respects the environments in Toronto and Winnipeg were much more favorable. The environment of metropolitan Montreal has been favorable in terms of legal-institutional structures but much more difficult socially and culturally.[16]

In the United States, the growth of racial and linguistic minorities and their segregated pattern of settlement in central cities and in some suburbs provide fertile grounds for estrangements similar to those noted in other metropolitan regions, including metropolitan Montreal. These estrangements influence the structure of intergovernmental relations in much the same way as in Montreal. Moreover, certain pervasive features of American government, especially the division of powers and heavy reliance on "direct democracy" (popular referenda), strongly predispose the system against the acceptance of organizational reform, and these features lend strength to the other influences that tend to work against change.[17]

The centrifugal forces at work are highlighted by viewing the modern metropolis as a network of spatially specialized settlements, each sharing particular values. For example, we note Oliver P. Williams's explanation of the process of specialized location on the basis of perceived needs to share lifestyle values. He suggests that to fortify such values, governmental fragmentation may be encouraged or perpetuated.

> Those life-style values which depend upon location for their realization are the major sources of metropolitan politics. Local government in its various manifestations is the governmental

---

16. For a more extensive discussion, see Sancton's essay "Canadian City Politics in Comparative Perspective," in *City Politics in Canada*, ed. Warren Magnusson and Andrew Sancton (Toronto: University of Toronto Press, 1983), pp. 299–305. Differences between the United States and Canada are recognized by Sancton as well as by us. See also John Porter's discussion of differences in "Ethnic Pluralism in Canada," in *Ethnicity*, ed. Glazer and Moynihan, pp. 267–70.

17. This point is discussed in more detail in the foreword of another Lane volume: C. James Owen and York Willbern, *Governing Metropolitan Indianapolis: The Politics of Unigov* (Berkeley: University of California Press, in press).

level which has primary control over the immediate physical and social environment of any given social-spatial unit. . . .

One of the important strategies commonly pursued by socio-spatial units in maximizing their possibilities for realizing life-style values is homogeneous and complementary group-ings. . . . Following the logic of this strategy, a decentralized (sub-urbanized) metropolitan governmental pattern appears to be superior to a centralized (consolidation) . . . for the enhancement of life-style values. Under the former arrangement, diverse groups need not constantly compete in the same political arena, a situation characteristic of heterogeneous units, such as the core city (particularly as it has existed traditionally). The more . . . the suburb specializes, the easier it is, politically, to maintain the primacy of the values prized by the dominant type of socio-spatial unit.[18]

Why would a suburb consent to consolidate with others that have different values and lifestyles? Race and ethnic origins are only two of the many factors that can differentiate communities in metropolitan areas, but the visibility of color and the audibility of language give them powerful salience. This is increased by the relative segregation of blacks in central cities and, within central cities, in a relatively few census tracts. A quarter of a century ago, Morton Grodzins identified the metropolis as a "racial problem," and his interpretation is still persuasive, despite the subsequent social and legal changes in the relationship between U.S. blacks and whites.[19]

The surge of black migration to metropolitan areas that started during World War II has continued throughout the period since. This migration, along with high rates of natural increase, has resulted in a rapid and continuing rise in the proportion of blacks living in metro-

18. Oliver P. Williams, "Life-Style Values and Political Decentralization in Metropolitan Areas," in *Community Structure and Decision-Making: Comparative Analyses*, ed. Terry N. Clark (San Francisco: Chandler, 1968), p. 432. See his earlier formulation in Oliver P. Williams et al., *Suburban Differences and Metropolitan Policies: A Philadelphia Story* (Philadelphia: University of Pennsylvania Press, 1965). Brett W. Hawkins, however, finds that our "measure of segregation, the weak simple correlation coefficients and other explorations indicate that it is not a strong explanatory variable" of the vote on city-county consolidation in 15 city-county consolidation referendums between 1949 and 1964. Brett W. Hawkins, "Life Style, Demographic Distance, and Voter Support of City-County Consolidation," *Social Science Quarterly* 43 (December 1967): 329–37.

19. Morton Grodzins, *The Metropolitan Area: As a Racial Problem* (Pittsburgh: University of Pittsburgh Press, 1958). For a view one decade later, see Charles Tilly, "Race and Migration to the American City," in *The Metropolitan Enigma*, ed. James Q. Wilson (Cambridge: Harvard University Press, 1968), pp. 135–58.

politan areas. Thus, in 1940 some 43 percent of blacks in the United States lived in metropolitan areas, whereas by 1980 the proportion had risen to 81 percent, an increase of 38 percentage points in 40 years. In the same period, the proportion of nonblacks living in metropolitan areas also rose, but at a substantially lower rate, up only 21 percentage points: from 54 percent in 1940 to 75 percent in 1980.

The pattern of black settlement is almost universally segregated. Banfield and Grodzins had predicted this, and now the only significant change needed to make their 1958 projection current is to replace their word *Negro* by the word *black*: "It is highly probable that within thirty years Negroes will constitute from 30 to more than 50 percent of the population in at least ten of the fourteen largest central cities . . . the general picture is clear: large Negro concentrations, in some cases, majorities, in the largest central cities; large white majorities, with segregated Negro enclaves, in the areas outside."[20]

In one out of five U.S. metropolitan areas in 1980, over 90 percent of the blacks lived in central cities. Among the 427 central cities, nine out of 10 had a disproportionately large black population, and in only one out of 10 was the proportion of blacks roughly comparable to their share of the population of the entire metropolitan area. In short, Hispanics are also substantially segregated, though somewhat less so than blacks. The Hispanic population was disproportionately high in seven out of 10 of the 427 central cities and proportionate in only three out of 10.[21]

In contrast, the 1980 distribution of whites was roughly proportionate in over four out of five of the central cities. Moreover, less than 1 percent of the central cities contained an overrepresentation of whites. These few "white-segregated" central cities, all of them in Virginia, are small, census-designated central cities in multicity metropolitan areas.

20. Edward C. Banfield and Morton Grodzins, *Government and Housing in Metropolitan Areas* (New York: McGraw-Hill, 1958), p. 29. Sancton uses almost the same words that we use in commenting on the timelessness of the Banfield and Grodzins analysis. He wrote in Magnusson and Sancton, *City Politics*, p. 299, that "twenty years later little has changed, apart from the fact that blacks are no longer referred to as 'Negroes.' " See also Robert C. Weaver, "The Impact of Ethnicity Upon Urban America," in *Ethnic Relations in America*, ed. Lance Liebman (Englewood Cliffs, N.J.: Prentice-Hall, 1982), pp. 66–100.

21. According to Robert C. Weaver, "Two circumstances shaped urban residential patterns for Mexican-Americans in a mold somewhat different from that of blacks or Puerto Ricans. In many cities of the Southwest, Mexicans were among the original founders and thus had access to desirable areas. Also, in recent years cities in the Sunbelt often grew by annexation, and the areas annexed frequently included traditionally Mexican settlements. In short, residential segregation of Mexican-Americans, while often the pattern, has never been as prevalent or as rigid as that of blacks and Puerto Ricans." Robert C. Weaver in Liebman, *Ethnic Relations*, pp. 75–76.

The Hispanics[22] comprise the most rapidly growing minority group in the country; they increased by approximately 61 percent between 1970 and 1980. Hispanics can thus play an important and growing role in many metropolitan areas. They constitute 20 percent of the population of New York City, 28 percent of Los Angeles, 56 percent of Miami, 54 percent of San Antonio, 47 percent of Corpus Christi, 84 percent of Brownsville, and 93 percent of Laredo.

Clearly, southwestern states and parts of New York and Florida already face linguistic and cultural conflicts resembling those of Montreal. Acrimonious conflict has risen in California over the desirability of bilingual educational programs and of mandatory bilingual ballots.[23] Even though some Hispanic leaders insist that a "knowledge of English is essential for all Californians," they maintain that bilingualism and biculturalism is a right under the Treaty of Guadalupe. Moreover, complete immersion in English language and Anglo-American culture, especially in early school years, is considered self-defeating by many, because it increases the likelihood of educational failure that will affect the Hispanic child's adult future. "Hispanic leaders strongly resent the idea that speaking Spanish is somehow unamerican, or that being unable to read English is evidence of illiteracy. They even more strongly resent the idea that speaking Spanish or being unable to read English indicates that a Hispanic is an 'illegal alien.' "[24] On the other hand, non-Hispanic business leaders and local public administrators have adamantly opposed bilingual education and use of Spanish in business. "They saw any retreat from English as divisive and destructive. They would fight any government regulation forcing them to do business in Spanish. English is the historically dominant language which all immigrants have had to learn—regardless of what language they speak at home—and to give that up would be unthinkable to them."[25]

22. The census term is "persons of Spanish origin or descent." Some blacks and whites, as well as persons of American Indian ancestry, are also counted in the Spanish origin category.

23. The United States government, through legislation and/or judicial action, has played a more important role than the states in encouraging or requiring bilingual education, multilingual ballots, the desegregation of schools, and the protection of equal voting rights. It is still too early to know whether the Canadian government will develop a similar role under the Charter of Rights and Freedoms of its new constitution. For a discussion of changing perceptions of appropriate national policies, see Martin Kilson, "Blacks and Neo-Ethnicity in American Political Life," in *Ethnicity*, ed. Glazer and Moynihan, pp. 248–51, 266.

24. William C. Grindley and Shirley Hentzell, *California Hispanics: A Report from the Near Horizon Symposia* (Menlo Park, Calif.: SRI International, 1981), p. 32.

25. Ibid., p. 31. For a position generally supportive of bilingual education programs but calling for more evaluative research, see Pastora San Juan Cafferty, "The Language Question: The Dilemma of Bilingual Education for Hispanics in America," in *Ethnic Relations*, ed. Liebman, pp. 101–27.

American metropolises with large concentrations of Hispanics, many of them recent immigrants, have not yet reached face-to-face combat over language and lifestyles, although distinctive conflicts are seen that reflect the kinds of communal divisions we have observed in Montreal, Belfast, Jerusalem, and Brussels. In addition, conflicts over economic issues such as jobs, housing, and schools have been exacerbated by the Reagan administration cutbacks and the recession. Some conflict has emerged between ethnic minorities, especially blacks and chicanos. With good will, intelligent policies, and prudent negotiation, perhaps in time these sources of division can be reconciled, but certainly they will not simply go away. We have seen elsewhere, and from historical evidence, that often such conflicts cannot be assuaged solely by largess and nondiscrimination in the administration of services. Both blacks and Hispanics in the United States complain, sometimes bitterly, about both their second-class status and what they consider degradations of their culture. Here as elsewhere the battlegrounds—or the arenas of accommodation—will be the metropolis and its communities, and the negotiations will also be statewide and national in scope. The attempts to deal with such issues in the Montreal region through provincial and municipal action will have considerable meaning for Americans.[26]

Nathan Glazer ("Politics of a Multiethnic Society," in *Ethnic Relations*, ed. Liebman, p. 149) warns us that the "melting pot is attacked not only on the empirical ground that it really did not melt that much or that fast, but on the normative ground that it should not have been allowed to do so. And on the basis of this attack, Americanization becomes a dirty word, and bilingualism and biculturalism receive government support.

"I doubt that this is wise.... One can still see the virtue of forging a single society out of many stocks and can still see that this process deserves some public guidance.... [T]here is still, or should be, an ultimate goal which should guide us. Insofar as we have one, it seems to be first, that every group must match every other group in economic resources, occupational status, political representation, and *distribution through cities and metropolitan areas to boot*, and second, that every group must be maintained, insofar as it is in the public power to maintain it, through an educational system that supports its language and its culture. That, it strikes me, is a recipe for conflict. We will have to do better, and one way of doing so is to explore whether the much maligned goal of assimilation does not still have much to teach us." [Emphasis added]

26. See Charles B. Keely's comment on the difference between Quebec and the American states with large concentrations of Hispanics. "The worst case scenario ... is a breakdown of civic culture itself, a loss of agreement on basic values, and a contest of interests that cannot be accommodated within the political system. This, I might add, is different from the case of Quebec, and lack of a territorial base of Hispanics makes the comparison with Quebec not a particularly useful guide. Yet the threat to system maintenance is also greater, since the territorial base provides a basis of accommodation and problem management in Canada that is absent in the United States." Charles B. Keely, "Immigration and the American Future," in *Ethnic Relations*, ed. Liebman, p. 32.

In any event, the bifurcation of U.S. metropolitan areas into predominantly white suburbs and heavily black central cities (plus a few black suburbs) has contributed to attitudes toward metropolitan governance that resemble those Sancton associates with the linguistic, cultural, class, and nationalistic divisions on the Island of Montreal. Reinforced by central-city media accounts, residents of the segregated suburbs hold stereotyped views of central cities—based in some degree, of course, on real evidence—seeing them as crime ridden, welfare dependent, culturally deviant, and perhaps machine controlled. Whatever their merits, such views do not facilitate either suburban-central city cooperation or large-area political integration.

Suburban whites are not alone in being dubious about closer suburban-central city relations. In some cases moves toward metropolitan government found many black leaders viewing it as far from benign. For example, in 1969 Mayor Richard Hatcher of Gary, Indiana, commented: "Black political power today is most visible and most meaningful in urban America. Yet in the cities, where black power is important, the realization of black political hope is threatened by a two-pronged attack. By cutting away territory where black people have gained some measure of reasonable influence, or by adding territory around the black center, the opponents of change seek to weaken whatever momentum black political action can generate."[27] (Significantly, Mayor Hatcher was attacking "Metro Government, Uni-Gov or whatever euphemistic label is locally popular" at the very time the Indiana legislature was considering the creation of Unigov for the state capital region by consolidating the City of Indianapolis and Marion County.)[28] Hatcher acknowledged that there is a persuasive case for metropolitan government and referred to "the proliferation of tax districts without contiguous boundaries . . . [and] the confusion these many overlapping authorities can cause." He also recognized the legitimate concerns for "overall planning in the megalopolises" and for the "larger community." Nevertheless, he reiterated the view from the ghettos, where "it still looks as if whitey is trying to mute black voices by diluting the vote of these new huddled masses."

27. Richard G. Hatcher, "The Black Role in Urban Politics," *Current History* (November 1969); reprinted in Gussner Wikstron, Jr., and Nelson Wikstrom, *Municipal Movement, Politics and Policy* (Washington, D.C.: University Press of America, 1982), pp. 437–41.

28. See Owen and Willbern, *Governing Metropolitan Indianapolis.* See also Dale Rogers Marshall, "Metropolitan Government: Views of Minorities," in *The Governance of Metropolitan Regions: Minority Perspectives,* ed. Lowden Wingo (Washington, D.C.: Resources for the Future, 1972), pp. 9–30, for a review and evaluation of studies of racial attitudes toward metropolitan government and of its impact on blacks. See also Nand Hart-Nibbrig, "The Attitudes of Black Political Leaders Toward Regional Governance in the San Francisco Bay Area: A Case Study of Black Activists in Berkeley, California." (Ph.D. diss., University of California, 1974).

When Detroit's Metropolitan Fund sponsored a 1973 series of discussions and debates of regional issues facing the metropolis, the question of what a metropolitan government would mean for blacks and for suburban whites was argued at almost every one of the 12 panel discussions held during that year. In commenting on a paper by Los Angeles Mayor Tom Bradley,[29] A. J. Dunmore, manager of urban affairs, Chrysler Corporation, warned: "you're going to have as big an assignment of selling blacks that the good of the total community is important to them, and won't deprive them of privileges, as you are having to sell the suburbs . . . [on] giving up some of . . . what they feel is newly gained freedom in their little lily white enclaves."[30] Other panelists echoed these views but also emphasized the need to find ways the groups could work together.

Black leaders also affirmed the need to try to cooperate rather than "stonewall." Agreeing that the exercise of "black power" alone would not adequately protect the interests of blacks, Mayor Hatcher commented:

> Black political awareness must be protected *now*. At the same time, the call for intergovernmental cooperation must be heeded, lest the problems it would confront grow so monumental as to defy solution. Black leaders must join efforts to answer those difficulties. . . . If they do not join in seeking honest answers while protecting emerging black power, supragovernments will be formed around them. . . . With or without black contributions, intergovernmental cooperative ventures will be developed. They must not be developed in a closet.[31] [Emphasis added]

Writing in 1982, Robert C. Weaver, the first black member of the president's Cabinet, also concluded that: "Ethnicity among minorities, for all it does to compensate for their having been deprived in many brutal ways and as much as it may do for their ego status, serves to impede coalitions among them and with others. Also, it delays effective action to deal with urban problems, since some in minority groups fail

---

29. Thomas Bradley, "Regional Governance and Racial and Ethnic Minorities," in *The Regionalist Papers*, ed. Kent Mathewson (Detroit: Metropolitan Fund, 1974), pp. 163–78.

30. Ibid., p. 120.

31. Richard G. Hatcher, "The Black Role," pp. 440–41. Hispanic leaders have not been as articulate as black leaders in expressing doubts and fears that metropolitan government would dilute "minority power." In interviews conducted by Hispanic students at the University of California, Berkeley, in 1975, metropolitan government was much less salient than state and national policies with respect to education and employment. Nevertheless, one would expect responses similar to Mayor Hatcher's in central cities that have Hispanic mayors.

to face up to the fact that their fate is inextricably linked both to the industrial world and to American cities."[32]

Although racial and ethnic factors are powerful influences on suburban separatism, they are only part of the explanation. Thus, even if blacks were not largely absent from much of suburbia and were not concentrated in central cities, suburban-central city suspicions and often downright hostility would still be facts of urban public life. In the nineteenth century, before the great growth of the nonwhite population, suburban-central antagonism was already present in New York, Philadelphia, and Boston and has been a continuing factor through the present century. Class and lifestyle differences exist even without the reinforcement of race, language, and religion, and in fact may be even more basic in explaining attitudes. Race and language may be important partly because they help make the other differences more *visible*.

Governmental Structure for a Divided Metropolis

It should be quite clear from Sancton's book and from our analysis of other metropolitan areas with similar conflicts that a complete unification of a region's local government could be accomplished only by overriding some of the value differences of heterogenous populations. One way to organize a metropolitan structure, short of such arbitrary consolidation, is to create a governing body comprising representatives of local governments. This may at least provide a forum in which leaders of otherwise antagonistic organizations may "counsel and reason together" about common problems of regional scope.

Andrew Sancton has shown that the Montreal Urban Community has been able to do this, despite the sharp linguistic divisions among the inhabitants of the Island of Montreal. Of course, the provincial government of Quebec has been involved, sometimes decisively, but without abolishing the municipalities as centers of authority and influence.

It is important to recognize the two-tier, constituent-unit federation or confederation such as the Montreal Urban Community, the Quebec Urban Community, the Outaouais Regional Community in Quebec, the Greater Vancouver Regional District and the Capital Regional District (Victoria) in British Columbia, and the hundreds of regional councils of governments (COGs) in the United States. Their formal structures are quite different from a *consolidated* metropolitan government, or even from a separate, independent, directly elected upper-tier metropolitan government (e.g., the Greater London Council).[33]

32. Robert C. Weaver in *Ethnic Relations*, ed. Liebman, p. 100.
33. They should also be distinguished from the much more authoritative governments of metropolitan Toronto and other metropolitan regions of Ontario, even though their governing bodies consist of certain elected officials of constituent municipalities.

There are a multitude of reasons why most metropolitan areas in the United States continue to have many general-purpose and special-purpose local governments. As noted earlier, the American system of government with its division of powers, localized and undisciplined party system, strength of belief in home rule, and frequent resort to the impediments of direct democracy (referendums, etc.) is quite different from government in Canada. Sancton shows that the provincial government of Quebec has frequently acted to change governmental structure and the distribution of authority and responsibility between provincial and local governments.

Yet the Montreal Urban Community, different as it is in the source of its authority, its taxing authority, and its responsibility for police and transit, bears some important resemblances to the only form of regional governance that is now widespread in the United States. The governing body of the Montreal Urban Community, like the regional councils of government (COGs) in the United States, consists of elected officials selected by the elected officials of counties, cities, and, in a few instances, special-purpose bodies.

Despite the plenary power of the parliamentary legislative bodies in both Montreal and British Columbia, local elected officials have been able to maintain the identity of their municipalities and to function as both lower-tier and upper-tier governors. Furthermore, because in both provinces such two-tier organizations have gone far beyond COGs in voluntarily—or under compulsion—assuming responsibility for direct administration of many regional services, they may suggest one way in which COGs could develop in the United States.

Following a relatively slow startup of the COGs in the 1960s, they proliferated across the country in the 1970s, responding to federal policies that both encouraged their formation and required the kinds of regional planning COGs could provide. Undoubtedly, a key explanation of their spread lies in the fact that their formation did little to alter existing power relationships. By 1977 more than 600 COGs had been created, mostly through the initiative of local governments themselves (though a few were created under special state statutes). Local officials refer to COGs as "voluntary associations" of local governments, as "forums" in which local officials can discuss common problems and perhaps agree on common policies, and as "advocates" of regional positions before state or national bodies.

Most COGs have developed "comprehensive" (i.e., multifunctional land-use) plans for their regions—again in response to federal requirements. Despite the rapid growth and large number of COGs, and their assumption of a seemingly important planning responsibility, their success is nevertheless clearly limited. Fewer than five of the 600 or so COGs have any authority to *implement* regional plans or require that local plans conform to regional plans. Most commentators would also agree with Elazar that "efforts to promote metropolitan planning have had only minimal success."[34] Furthermore, critics maintain that their review of grant applications has been only a pro forma exercise.

On the other hand, they can be effective *voluntary associations, forums,* and *advocates* without having more than "minimal success" *as authoritative regional governments.* The COGs have helped thousands of local officials to understand the effects of local actions upon their regions. These officials have also gotten a better grasp of the ways their neighboring local governments and the entire region, as well as the state and national governments, can affect their own communities. The persistence of COGs is actually rather remarkable, given several recent adverse developments such as withdrawal of most federal assistance, the dismantling of the federally required review and comment process, the Reagan administration's move to take the federal government out of such substate regionalism, and the failure of most state governments to recognize COGs or to use them in developing and executing state-local policies or provide them with financial support. Despite all this, only a score or so of the 600 COGs have disbanded in the last three years of relatively tough sledding.

Obviously, it is much too early for long-term judgments on the durability and effectiveness of COGs as regional governmental institutions. But under the adverse circumstances noted, their very continuance as formal organizations is significant. Currently they are indeed much alive, and most are reorienting themselves to emphasize provision of technical assistance for their member governments.

Confronted with both the racial-ethnic divisiveness noted and such well-known obstacles to reform as the referendum requirement, COGs may be this country's only realistic alternative to (1) state-controlled regional authorities or (2) special districts with some or little (frequently little) local popular responsibility. To be an effective alternative, however, the COGs in the United States would have to develop into limited regional governments wielding some real authority, probably with close structural ("federal") linkages to existing county and municipal governments.

34. Daniel Elazar, "The Federal Government and Local Government Reform," *National Civic Review* 72 (April 1983): 193. Elazar attributes the minimal success to "a well-nigh nationwide local reluctance to accept them, if not downright opposition. In such cases, local governments, realizing that they must at least superficially conform to the federal requirements, go through the motions while arranging matters among themselves in such a way as to assure that the review processes are all form and little or no substance."

The Outlook for Montreal

Montreal's experience with this type of metropolitan government may be especially instructive for the United States in its efforts to devise systems of intergovernmental arrangements that are not only constitutionally and politically feasible but also able to deal effectively with large-area issues. Sancton's work on Montreal is in part a case study of the development of such a "federal" (some would say "confederal") metropolitan government—the Montreal Urban Community—with many constituent units, a few provincially mandated functions, and protection for the interests of both suburbs and the central city built into the structure.

Sancton's book tells a story not only of governmental reorganization (and attempted reorganization) but also of continuing and even growing communal conflict, especially religious and linguistic. He also shows how public and private institutions have developed a way of working together, even when in conflict. Both immediately and in the long run this may be Montreal's most important lesson. The reorganizations and other changes affecting local services discussed by Sancton were implemented before the "new militancy" of the 1960s and 1970s reached its recent peak. The provincial language legislation that resulted drove home to the anglophones a full realization of their fundamental weakness.

Sancton suggests that *future* reorganization and boundary-change proposals are much more likely to meet with fervent opposition than in the 1960s and early 1970s. Until then, the sources of potential conflict were largely submerged and in fact seemed comparatively invisible to English speakers. Previously the two cultures, with their different languages and religions, coexisted on the same metropolitan island, but in substantial isolation. It was possible for an anglophone to get along quite well in most businesses and many neighborhoods in Montreal, virtually oblivious to the fact that most of the population was French speaking. Moreover, for a variety of reasons, anglophones clearly were much better off economically than francophones. Immigrants to Montreal were understandably much more likely to learn English than French. In contrast, the "other side" (francophones) grew more and more acutely aware of the sources of conflict, although until then the French-speaking population had not directly challenged the economic dominance of the anglophones nor contested the predominance of English as the language of commerce.

Then came the Quiet Revolution, which may have seemed sudden but whose roots went far back, resulting from developments such as modernization and responses to it that were in progress during most of this century. French language and culture were championed overtly and vigorously, and the relatively comfortable linguistic isolation and self-sufficiency of the anglophones came under strenuous challenge.

The ancient policy of leaving the English speaking to govern themselves was no longer accepted. A new militancy emerged whose leaders were bent on effecting significant social change and especially on improving the francophones' political and economic position, using strong measures, even to the point of advocating outright separation from the Canadian federation.

The new language law (Bill 101) seemed to have as its ultimate goal making Quebec a solely French-speaking province. In any event, it represented a major assault on the prevailing use of English in preference to or alongside French. Mayor Drapeau was quoted as saying "Bill 101 was an exercise in revenge against the English." Moreover, Sancton observes that "many provincial politicians and bureaucrats committed themselves, consciously or unconsciously, to dismantling Montreal's dual French-English system of local institutions."

In broad outline, we see how the emerging francophone militancy quickly undermined a longstanding but basically unstable *modus vivendi* between the two groups. This arrangement had depended on a grudging acceptance by the side that understandably harbored smoldering resentments. With the old practices challenged, the institutional machinery available to the threatened group—anglophones—quickly seemed even more precious than before. This helps explain the durability of the 29 suburban municipalities as well as the agreement to in effect divide up the community ("sectorize" it) in welfare administration and to retain the separate school systems fundamentally unchanged by going through partially cosmetic reorganizations.

In his closing pages, Sancton seems to pose two alternatives: (1) continued severe conflict and pressure from the francophones, who could use their political preponderance to force the creation of a completely French-speaking province (perhaps even politically separate from English-speaking Canada), or (2) a more limited kind of conflict, moderated by a leadership able to negotiate its way toward some new accommodation that, while recognizing the predominance of the French language, would still protect the interests of linguistic, religious, and cultural minorities.

Sancton clearly sees the second alternative as far more desirable, although he acknowledges the difficulties of achieving it. He also emphasizes how essential provincial and national developments and conflict-resolution are to such a desirable solution for Montreal. Our fascination with Sancton's Montreal story is heightened by our awareness of the complexity and volatility of the circumstances and the magnitude of the stakes, which go far beyond Montreal. In any event, the recent, more moderate postures of leaders in Montreal and the Province of Quebec now appear to make the outlook more sanguine for Sancton's preferred alternative.

Stanley Scott
Editor, Lane Fund
Publications

Victor Jones
Coeditor, Lane Studies in
Regional Government

Berkeley, California   April 1984

Acknowledgments

This book has been in the making for more than 10 years. Not being the most meticulous record keeper, I now find it impossible to list all the librarians, civil servants, politicians, educators, social workers, and others who gave of their time and expertise at various stages in the research. I am fortunate in that I know many would prefer not to have their assistance publicly revealed. I hope that most who are still interested will recognize their contributions in the pages that follow and will realize that, without their assistance and cooperation, this book would not have been possible.

Others have helped by reading all or part of the manuscript at one stage or another and providing me with valuable encouragement, advice, and warning. My list of readers and advisers is, I think, complete and follows in roughly chronological order: L. J. Sharpe, Elizabeth Cahill, Thomas J. Plunkett, Kenneth Newton, Jacques Léveillée, James Mallory, Frank Smallwood, Terry Copp, Henry Milner, Daniel Latouche, Robert Cournoyer, D'Arcy Coulson, and Allan O'Brien. Stanley Scott and Victor Jones, the coeditors of this series, have not only encouraged the project from the very beginning but have also admirably performed their duties by being the most demanding readers of all. Everybody is thanked; no one is held responsible for what has finally emerged.

Financial assistance for research has been provided by a Canada Council doctoral fellowship in 1973–74 and by an Institute of Public Administration of Canada research grant held in 1980–82. From 1974 to 1977 Marianopolis College provided an excellent environment in which to study the city it has served so well. Since 1977 the University of Western Ontario has provided me with another pleasant place to work, with much appreciated secretarial services, and with small research grants to help with incidental expenses.

Permission to use parts of my own previously published work has been granted by the Institute of Public Administration of Canada, which in 1979 printed my article "The Impact of Language Differences on Metropolitan Reform in Montreal" in its journal, *Canadian Public Administration*, and by the University of Toronto Press, publisher in 1983 of *City Politics in Canada*, which included my brief account of city politics in Montreal.

Pamela Sancton has been with me in this project from the very beginning; first by helping me comb old Montreal newspapers, then by providing criticism, advice, and encouragement.

I was brought up in a home where public discussion of public issues was always encouraged. Such was the beginning of my fascination with politics. For this—and many other reasons—this book is lovingly dedicated to my Mother and Father.

Andrew Sancton
London, Ontario
November 1983

Abbreviations

BNA	British North America
CMA	Census Metropolitan Area
CMSM	Conference of Montreal Suburban Mayors
FLQ	*Front de Libération du Québec*
ICC	Intermunicipal Co-ordinating Committee
MCSC	Montreal Catholic School Commission
MIS	*Mouvement pour l'intégration scolaire*
MUC	Montreal Urban Community
MUCTC	Montreal Urban Community Transit Commission
PQ	*Parti québécois*
PSBGM	Protestant School Board of Greater Montreal
PSC	Public Security Council
RIN	*Rassemblement pour l'indépendance nationale*
RN	*Ralliement national*
UN	*Union nationale*

1

Introduction: The Environment for Metropolitan Reform

Canada is a country with two official languages and two founding cultures. The City of Montreal is their main point of contact. Founded in 1642 by Paul de Chomedey, Sieur de Maisonneuve, as an outpost for zealous French missionaries, Montreal soon displaced Quebec City as the metropolis of Canada. Since the British conquest of Montreal in 1760, however, the city's dominant economic group has traced its origins to the British Isles.[1] This group also comprised a numerical majority for a brief period in the mid–nineteenth century but has been a minority for well over one hundred years. Noting this and other factors, J. R. Mallory concluded in 1955 that "Montreal is an extremely difficult city to govern. Within it the two major races in Canada, aloof in their two solitudes, must somehow live together."[2] This book is about how these living arrangements have evolved and how they have been disrupted since 1960 by the often complementary objectives of organizational reformers and French-Canadian nationalists.

Before 1960 the French and English in Montreal formed two distinct societies that seldom came into contact with one another. The English used Montreal as the base from which they managed much of the Canadian economy. For the French elite, Montreal provided a vital setting for professional and cultural pursuits. More important, however, the city provided thousands of manufacturing and service jobs for the growing number of ordinary French Canadians who could no longer be accommodated on the farms. Part One of this book describes the way various local government institutions in Montreal both reflected and perpetuated the mutual isolation of the two major linguistic groups.

1. Complete histories of Montreal can be found in a number of works, the most useful English ones being William Henry Atherton, *Montreal: 1535–1914* (Montreal: S. J. Clarke, 1914), 3 vols.; and John Irwin Cooper, *Montreal: A Brief History* (Montreal: McGill-Queen's University Press, 1969). Cooper's book is mainly concerned with the period since 1800.

2. "Montreal: Problem Metropolis," *Community Planning Review* 5 (1955): 4. The term "two solitudes" was originally coined by the novelist Hugh MacLennan.

Starting in the 1960s, French Quebec experienced a massive social and political modernization, known as the Quiet Revolution. Whether the aggressive nationalism bred by the Quiet Revolution will eventually bring fundamental changes in the constitutional relationship between Quebec and the rest of Canada is still uncertain.[3] But it is clear that in Quebec the Quiet Revolution fundamentally changed the patterns of French-English relations in Montreal. Part Two describes this process. The French-speaking majority was no longer willing to accept the superior economic position of the English, nor were French political leaders willing to allow English local institutions to remain in complete isolation from the province's wider political environment.

The book's remaining chapters analyze the impact of the French-English cleavage on attempts since 1960 to reorganize local institutions in Montreal to create reformed networks of metropolitan institutions for three sets of activities: municipal government, education, and social services. The literature that describes the assumptions, objectives, and accomplishments of the metropolitan reform movement is voluminous.[4] Readers familiar with the literature may find this book's discussion of metropolitan reform in the context of school boards and social service facilities unusual. In many jurisidictions, including Quebec's, these matters are not normally included in the purview of municipal government. They are included here for two principal reasons: (1) to demonstrate and emphasize that local government and politics encompass more than municipal government, taking in all local institutions that govern the delivery of public services and that are subject to a degree of direct local control; and (2) to facilitate in-depth analysis of the political effects of Montreal's linguistic cleavage, studying its impact in a variety of local institutional settings.

Part Three shows how modern Quebec nationalism has been an elusive but important factor in aiding the efforts of those promoting reform and rationalization of Montreal's complex local government systems. Such reforms, even if motivated only by the same forces that brought institutional modernization to other Canadian cities, have also had inevitable language-related side effects. They have reduced the extent to which the English-speaking minority in Montreal is able to control its own schools, hospitals, social services, and municipali-

3. As a result of a 1981 agreement between the Canadian federal government and all provinces except Quebec, the British Parliament in 1982 approved a new Constitution Act for Canada. Henceforth, all constitutional changes can be made entirely in Canada. Whatever the virtues of the new arrangements might be, they have not resolved the controversy about Quebec's future role in relation to the rest of Canada.
4. It is well summarized and documented in John C. Bollens and Henry J. Schmandt, *The Metropolis: Its People, Politics, and Economic Life,* 4th ed. (New York: Harper and Row, 1981), especially Ch. 3.

ties. These local institutions have increasingly been integrated into large organizations controlled by the French-speaking majority, in both Montreal and the province of Quebec as a whole. From the point of view of many Quebec nationalists, who see Quebec as a French society that should be governed by the principle of "majority rule," this seems a desirable objective. Consequently, such nationalists have tended to support reforms that, at least on the surface, have had more to do with organizational efficiency than with language.

Alliances of Convenience

Just as the forces of Quebec nationalism have tended to reinforce the drive for metropolitan integration—at least since 1960—the desire of English-speaking Quebeckers to maintain a degree of local autonomy has been a counterforce. Montreal's English-speaking population, probably because of its ethnic and religious diversity and past orientation toward the marketplace rather than politics, has been remarkably inarticulate in expressing coherent policy positions reflecting its interests as a linguistic minority in the new Quebec.[5]

Nevertheless, English-speaking suburban mayors, school board members, and social service administrators have been surprisingly effective in protecting themselves against the onslaught of the organizational reformers. Rather than rushing to the public platform to mobilize English-speaking citizens in defense of abstract notions of collective minority rights, they have worked quietly behind the scenes to further their interests. Before Quebec's Quiet Revolution, these subtle accommodations were made in private by powerful English-speaking businessmen and French-speaking politicians.[6] But now, in French Quebec at least, this kind of interaction is widely considered distasteful evidence of the province's squalid political past.

Consequently, the new defenders of Montreal's English-speaking institutions have sought alliances with local French-speaking groups whose apparent short-term interests happened to coincide with those of the English speakers. In this way the political defense of Montreal's English-speaking institutions—rarely publicly articulated in terms of language rights—has generally been protected from the usual glare of publicity that otherwise invariably accompanied public discussion of language-related issues in Quebec. In the municipal sphere, French- and English-speaking suburban mayors have formed a powerful alli-

5. For an explanation of this, see Sheila McLeod Arnopoulos and Dominique Clift, *The English Fact in Quebec* (Montreal: McGill-Queen's University Press, 1980), especially Ch. 3.

6. For example, see Conrad Black, *Duplessis* (Toronto: McClelland and Stewart, 1977), pp. 603–24.

ance that carefully avoids the potentially explosive linguistic questions. In education, language issues have never escaped public attention, but English-speaking Protestants concerned with language-group
autonomy have benefited greatly from the fact that their interests generally coincide with those of the French-speaking Catholics who are
still fervent defenders of a Catholic confessional school system.

Although it is still too early to judge whether these semiprivate
alliances of convenience serve the long-term interests of the groups
involved, they have obviously been fairly successful in attaining their
immediate objectives. This book does not attempt any systematic comparative analysis of different cities; however, the writer maintains that
linguistic cleavage explains why Montreal has experienced limited
local institutional change, far less than Toronto and Winnipeg, the
two other Canadian cities already treated in this series of Lane books.[7]

This contention has recently been confirmed by Harold Kaplan's
massive study, *Reform, Planning and City Politics: Montreal, Winnipeg, Toronto.* Because Kaplan uses a variant of the social systems
theory developed by Talcott Parsons as the framework for his description and analyses, his work has a focus quite different from this
book's. Nevertheless, Kaplan does claim that "throughout most of the
twentieth century Montreal remained the least reformed and least developed of the three municipal systems."[8] His work contains no explicit explanation for this, but his emphasis on the importance of the
linguistic cleavage clearly implies that he considers it to have been a
major retarding factor.

Comparisons with the United States

In the federal systems of Canada and the United States, the establishment of local government institutions is a responsibility of the
provinces and the states, respectively. Explanations of the metropolitan reformers' generally greater success in Canada usually cite at least
two relevant factors that distinguish Canadian provincial governments
from their American equivalents. First, Canadian provinces have a
parliamentary system of government in which executive leaders,
backed by disciplined legislative majorities, find it easier to implement comprehensive political programs over the objections of particu-

7. Albert Rose, *Governing Metropolitan Toronto* (Berkeley: University of California Press, 1972); and Meyer Brownstone and T. J. Plunkett, *Metropolitan Winnipeg:
Politics and Reform of Local Government* (Berkeley: University of California Press,
1983).

8. Harold Kaplan, *Reform, Planning and City Politics: Montreal, Winnipeg, Toronto* (Toronto: University of Toronto Press, 1982), p. 312. Despite its publication date,
the book does not treat events that occurred after the end of 1970.

lar interest groups. Second, in their control over local government institutions, Canadian provinces are not restrained by constitutional "home-rule" provisions or by a political culture that dictates referenda and local citizen approval of most significant changes in local institutions. There is no dispute that these factors go far toward explaining why the Toronto and Winnipeg experience with metropolitan reform looks much more significant than the experience of most U.S. metropolitan areas.

Racial issues are another reason that metropolitan reform has been difficult in the United States. Suburban whites have opposed both municipal and school board consolidations, seeing both as devices that would open the suburbs to center-city blacks.[9] From the black perspective, some proposals for metropolitan government have been seen as attempts "to mute black votes"[10] by enlarging the political arena to create a white majority. It is not surprising that this environment of mutual suspicion and distrust works against structural change. Despite major differences between black-white relations in American cities and French-English relations in Montreal, some evidence suggests that the two kinds of cleavages have similar inhibiting influences on metropolitan reform. In contrast, although Toronto and Winnipeg are remarkably heterogeneous in ethnic makeup, neither has the deep cleavage of two major groups separated by race or by language.

In short, racially divided American cities provide an unfavorable environment for metropolitan reform in terms of both legal and sociopolitical factors, and in both respects the environments in Toronto and Winnipeg were much more favorable. The environment of metropolitan Montreal has been favorable in terms of legal-institutional structures but much more difficult socially and culturally. This combination of influences makes Montreal a fascinating subject for students of metropolitan politics.

Political Will

Even in cities like Toronto and Winnipeg, where the main prerequisites for metropolitan reorganization seem to have been in place, the achievement of structural change depends on another essential ingredient: political will. The government that has the power to implement substantial change must also be committed to such change.

9. Michael N. Danielson, *The Politics of Exclusion* (New York: Columbia University Press, 1976).

10. This statement was made by Richard Hatcher, the black mayor of Gary, Indiana. It is quoted in Bollens and Schmandt, *The Metropolis,* p. 387.

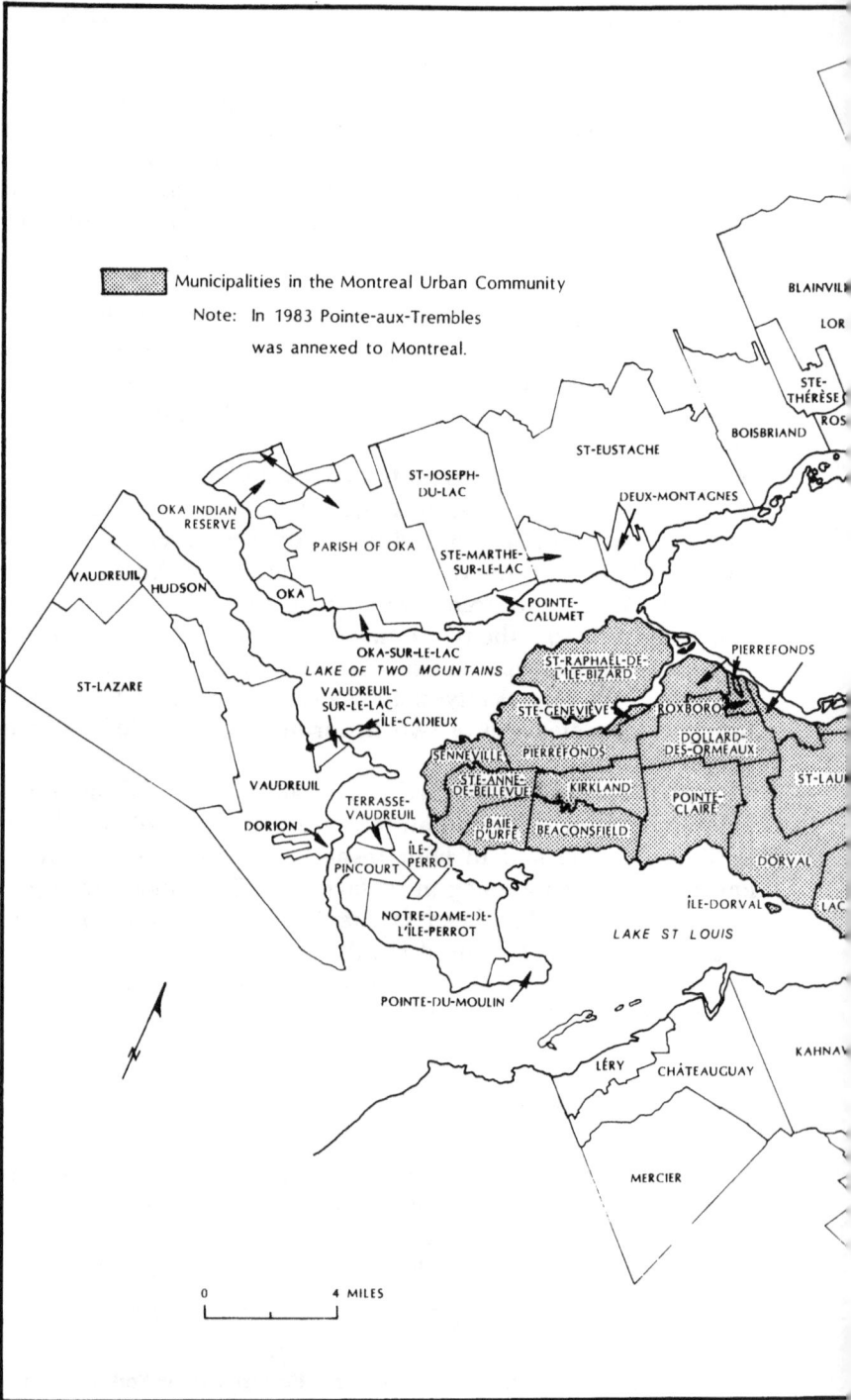

Municipalities in the Montreal Urban Community

Note: In 1983 Pointe-aux-Trembles
was annexed to Montreal.

BLAINVILI

LOR

STE-
THÉRÈSE

ROS

BOISBRIAND

ST-EUSTACHE

ST-JOSEPH-
DU-LAC

DEUX-MONTAGNES

OKA INDIAN
RESERVE

PARISH OF OKA

STE-MARTHE-
SUR-LE-LAC

VAUDREUIL

HUDSON

OKA

POINTE-
CALUMET

OKA-SUR-LE-LAC

PIERREFONDS

LAKE OF TWO MOUNTAINS

ST-RAPHAËL-DE-
L'ÎLE-BIZARD

ST-LAZARE

VAUDREUIL-
SUR-LE-LAC

STE-GENEVIÈVE

ROXBORO

ÎLE-CADIEUX

DOLLARD-
DES-ORMEAUX

SENNEVILLE

PIERREFONDS

ST-LAU

VAUDREUIL

STE-ANNE-
DE-BELLEVUE

KIRKLAND

POINTE-
CLAIRE

TERRASSE-
VAUDREUIL

DORION

BAIE-
D'URFÉ

BEACONSFIELD

DORVAL

ÎLE-
PERROT

PINCOURT

ÎLE-DORVAL

LAC

NOTRE-DAME-DE-
L'ÎLE-PERROT

LAKE ST LOUIS

POINTE-DU-MOULIN

N

LÉRY

CHÂTEAUGUAY

KAHNAW

MERCIER

0   4 MILES

Map 1

The Census Metropolitan Area of Montreal, 1981

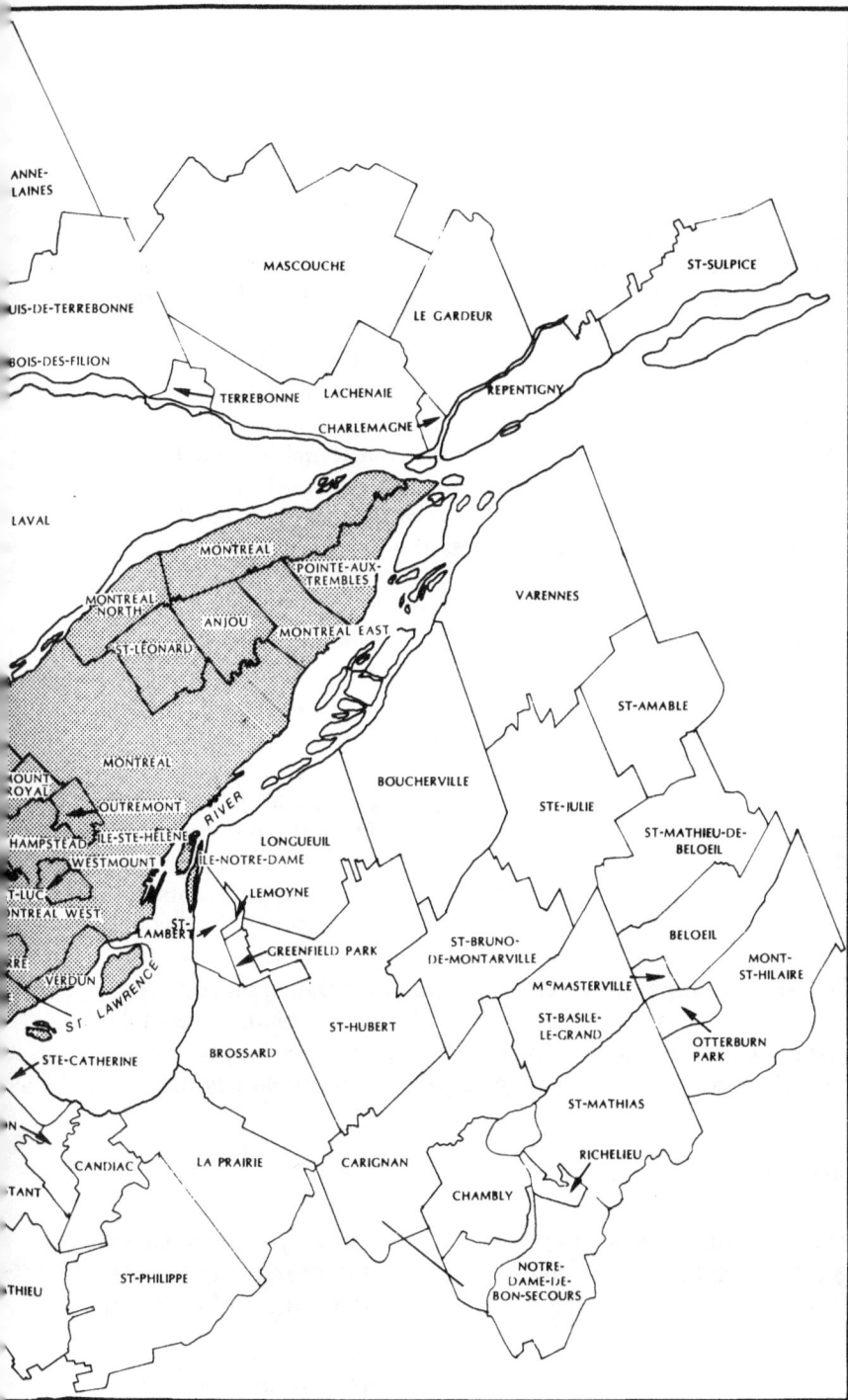

ANNE-
LAINES

MASCOUCHE

ST-SULPICE

UIS-DE-TERREBONNE

LE GARDEUR

BOIS-DES-FILION

TERREBONNE

LACHENAIE

REPENTIGNY

CHARLEMAGNE

LAVAL

MONTREAL

POINTE-AUX-
TREMBLES

VARENNES

MONTREAL
NORTH

ANJOU

MONTREAL EAST

ST-LÉONARD

ST-AMABLE

MONTREAL

BOUCHERVILLE

STE-JULIE

MOUNT
ROYAL

OUTREMONT

ILE-STE-HÉLÈNE

LONGUEUIL

ST-MATHIEU-DE-
BELOEIL

HAMPSTEAD

ILE-NOTRE-DAME

WESTMOUNT

LEMOYNE

ST-
LUC

ONTREAL WEST

ST-
LAMBERT

GREENFIELD PARK

ST-BRUNO-
DE-MONTARVILLE

BELOEIL

MONT-
ST-HILAIRE

RE

McMASTERVILLE

VERDUN

ST. LAWRENCE

ST-HUBERT

ST-BASILE-
LE-GRAND

OTTERBURN
PARK

STE-CATHERINE

BROSSARD

ST-MATHIAS

N

CANDIAC

LA PRAIRIE

CARIGNAN

RICHELIEU

TANT

CHAMBLY

THIEU

ST-PHILIPPE

NOTRE-
DAME-DE-
BON-SECOURS

RIVER

The governments of Ontario and Manitoba were committed to the Toronto and Winnipeg reforms.

In contrast, the situation has been substantially different in Vancouver, Canada's third-largest city. The government of British Columbia has established a relatively weak body (by Canadian standards, at least) known as the Greater Vancouver Regional District but carefully has not referred to it as a new tier of government. Existing municipal functions and boundaries have scarcely been altered.[11] The regional district cannot be equated with the Municipality of Metropolitan Toronto or the post-1971 City of Winnipeg. British Columbia's major governing party, Social Credit, appears to have been much more influenced by American ideas on the sanctity of existing municipalities than by the other Canadian provinces' more interventionist approaches.

Part Three shows how since 1960, the declared intentions of Quebec's various provincial governments with regard to local structural change in Montreal have followed the general Canadian norm, that is, highly interventionist. One characteristic of Quebec's Quiet Revolution has been to question "everything," and this has certainly included the organization of municipal government, school boards, and social service facilities in metropolitan Montreal. Many possibilities for reform have been explored by numerous government reports, and at one time or another many quite drastic plans for change have been adopted as official government policy. Later chapters discuss the political forces resulting from the language cleavage that helped determine how and to what extent these policies were implemented.

When a government fails to do what it said it would do, some critics always claim that the government was never really committed in the first place. No doubt, many policy proclamations of Quebec's governments concerning institutional changes in Montreal were little more than declarations of preference or intent rather than firm commitments. On the other hand, before a significant change can take place a provincial government must at least declare its support for the change. Quebec has done this, whereas British Columbia has not.

Natural Boundaries

This introduction has tried to show how in every respect except language, Montreal's environment for structural change since 1960 has been highly favorable. Geography is yet another unique factor that

---

11. Paul Tennant and David Zirnhelt, "Metropolitan Government in Vancouver: The Strategy of Gentle Imposition," *Canadian Public Administration*, vol. 16 (1973): 124–38. See also British Columbia, Ministry of Municipal Affairs and Housing, *Report of the Regional District Review Committee* (Victoria, B.C.: 1978).

is particularly helpful to those advocating metropolitan institutions for Montreal. The City of Montreal is located on the Island of Montreal (see Map 1), the location of about 62 percent of the population of the census-defined metropolitan area of Montreal.[12] Moreover, the island contains almost all the east-west axis of metropolitan Montreal's urban development. In short, the island itself forms a natural territorial unit, largely resolving one of the big problems for metropolitan reformers in many other areas: where to draw the boundaries of metropolitan government.

Admittedly, numerous claims have been made that the heavily urbanized areas north and south of the island should be included in any projected metropolitan institutions. It is often suggested that these built-up areas beyond the island are more significant than the relatively undeveloped areas on the island's eastern and western tips. But such sophisticated claims have easily been beaten back by the commonsense notion that river shorelines defining the island represent more politically acceptable boundaries than the calculations of urban geographers and planners.

12. This figure is derived from the 1981 federal census. (See Table 2 of this book.) The 1971 figure was 71 percent. The recent trend to off-island urbanization is perhaps the most dramatic feature of Montreal's recent development. See pages 130–31 for more details.

I

French and English in Montreal prior to 1960

2

The Emergence of the "Two Solitudes"

A full account of the institutional structures underlying language-group autonomy in Montreal would include the organization of the metropolitan area's businesses, religious institutions, media, universities, and a host of cultural and voluntary groups. Because this is a study of local government, its focus is restricted to institutions at the local level that provide public services, allocate public resources, or make legally enforceable regulations. Part One describes the historical development of municipal government, school boards, and social services in Montreal prior to 1960. The main feature of this development was the emergence of separate networks of institutions for the French and the English. Before looking at these institutions, however, the historical evolution of Montreal's unique pattern of French-English relations is described briefly.

British Control

The history of the French in North America is "the story of the ceaseless struggle of a minority group to maintain its culture in the face of all manner of conscious and unconscious pressures to conform to the dominant civilization of other ethnic groups and other cultures."[1] French has been the dominant language on the shores of the St. Lawrence River for more than 350 years. French has survived for more than 200 years in almost complete isolation from the political and social influences of France, the original colonizing power. From 1760 until 1960 the French language and culture in Quebec were protected mainly by the Roman Catholic church. French-speaking politicians, with the blessing of their spiritual leaders, were successful in keeping the control of educational, social, and cultural institutions under the church itself or in the hands of governmental

1. Mason Wade, *The French Canadians*, rev. ed. (Toronto: Macmillan, 1968), vol. 1, p. xiii. See also Susan Mann Trofimenkoff, *The Dream of Nation* (Toronto: Macmillan, 1982).

institutions controlled by the church's faithful adherents. But they were not able to control the economy.

Immediately after the British occupation of Montreal in 1760, the mainly Scottish merchants who accompanied the army seized control of the valuable fur trade. They quickly formed a mutually profitable partnership with expert French-Canadian traders who, unlike the departing officials of the French government, had little choice but to remain. This partnership lasted until 1821, when the Montreal-based North West Company was absorbed by the Hudson's Bay Company. This marked the end of the sole private commercial venture in which British entrepreneurs in Montreal relied on special French-Canadian skill and expertise not obtainable elsewhere. Later, French-Canadian society "turned inward upon itself and poured its brains and energy into the professions, the church, the petty trades, and agriculture."[2]

Meanwhile, British capitalists in Montreal accumulated large fortunes and great power through the development of the timber trade, steamships, canals, and railroads.[3] In the second half of the nineteenth century they brought the industrial revolution to Montreal. The city became known across the country for its clothing, textile, tobacco, and leather-processing factories. In virtually all instances the British were the bosses, and the French and recent immigrants from Ireland were the workers.[4] This was the beginning of a pattern that still persists, with both class and ethnic cleavages coinciding.

Montreal's Ethnic Balance

Since the early nineteenth century the relative size of Montreal's various ethnic groups has been carefully monitored. Despite the growing importance of British immigration, the high birth rate of French Canadians and their continued immigration from the rural hinterland had reestablished their numerical superiority on the Island of Montreal by the mid–nineteenth century. Table 1 shows changes in the strength of the major ethnic groups between 1871 and 1981. The table shows the French holding a remarkably steady majority of about 60 percent on the island for more than a century. Meanwhile, the British lost more than half of their relative strength because of the rise of "others." By 1961 the "others" outnumbered the British.

2. D. G. Creighton, *The Commercial Empire of the St. Lawrence* (Toronto: Ryerson, 1937), p. 154.

3. See Gerald J. Tulchinsky, *The River Barons: Montreal Businessmen and the Growth of Industry and Transportation, 1837–53* (Toronto: University of Toronto Press, 1977).

4. An ethnically mixed, working-class neighborhood in the center part of the city was described in a fascinating book first published in 1897. See Herbert Brown Ames, *The City Below the Hill* (Toronto: University of Toronto Press, 1972).

Table 1– *Principal Ethnic Groups on the Island of Montreal, 1871–1981*

Ethnic Group	1871	1881	1891	1901	1911	1921	1931	1941	1951	1961	1971	1981
					(total population in thousands)							
	144	193	277	361	555	724	1004	1117	1320	1748	1955	1678[b]
					(percentage distribution)							
French	60.3	62.1	—	63.9	62.7	60.7	60.2	62.6	63.8	62.0	59.0	58.9
British[a]	38.1	35.2	—	33.7	26.2	27.3	26.3	24.2	22.2	18.2	17.0	13.8
Others	1.6	2.7	—	2.4	11.1	12.0	13.5	13.2	14.0	19.9	24.0	27.3

Source: The data for 1871–1951 come from Norbert Lacoste, *Les caractéristiques sociales de la population du grand Montréal* (Montréal: Les presses de l'Université de Montréal, 1958), p. 77. The 1961 data come from Norbert Lacoste, "Les traits nouveaux de la population du 'grand Montréal,'" *Recherches sociographiques*, vol. 6 (1965), pp. 265–82; 1971 data from Canada, Statistics Canada, *1971 Census of Canada* (Ottawa: Information Canada, 1973), Cat. 92–723. 1981 data from Canada, Statistics Canada, *1981 Census of Canada* (Ottawa: Minister of Supply and Services, 1983) Cat. 95–942 (vol. 3.—Profile Series B).

[a] Includes English, Scottish, Welsh, and Irish.

[b] Includes only those reporting a single ethnic origin. In 1981, for the first time, census respondents were allowed to report multiple ethnic origins. On the Island of Montreal in 1981, 60,000 people categorized themselves in this way. Prior to 1981 ethnic origin was supposed to be based on one's paternal ancestry.

If members of the "other" ethnic groups had undergone any significant assimilation by the French majority, the relative strength of the French group would have been greatly increased. This did not happen, partly because most immigrants throughout Quebec's history have learned English before they learned French.[5] This is hardly surprising, given the economic dominance of the British in Montreal and the economic strength of the English language in North America. Moreover, until quite recently the French made no effort to assimilate immigrants, preferring instead to keep their culture relatively free of outside influences. As long as their birth rate was one of the highest in the western world, the natural increase of the French offset the effect of virtually all the immigrants who chose English. But when the birth rate of the French plunged dramatically in the 1960s, they could no longer be so complacent about retaining their majority position.

Ethnic Diversity Without Conflict

The main feature of French-English relations in Montreal has been the city's remarkable freedom from overt communal conflict despite the potentially explosive situation. According to Lewis Coser's well-known analysis of social conflict, this should not be surprising. He points out that "unequal distributions of privileges and rights may lead to sentiments of hostility, but they do not necessarily lead to conflict."[6] Conflict occurs only when the deprived group develops "the awareness that it is being denied rights to which it is entitled. It must reject any justification for the existing distribution of rights and privileges."[7] In other words, conflict will not break out if the position of the privileged group is seen as legitimate.

Throughout most of Quebec's history, the British role seemed to have the necessary legitimacy, mainly because French Quebec's most important institution, the Roman Catholic church, did not encourage its members to become entrepreneurs and because it raised no objection to British political rule as long as the church's rights and privileges were respected. The most serious threat to Montreal's social peace came during the Rebellion of 1837, but then the rebels were still in a clear minority, even among French Canadians.[8] Furthermore, most of the sporadic fighting in Lower Canada did not take place

5. Jacques Henripin, "The Demographic Dilemma of French-Canadian Society," in *Quebec Society and Politics*, ed. Dale C. Thomson (Toronto: McClelland and Stewart, 1973), p. 157.

6. Lewis Coser, *The Functions of Social Conflict* (Glencoe, Ill.: Free Press, 1956), p. 137.

7. Ibid.

8. For the best account in English, see Fernand Ouellet, *Lower Canada 1791– 1840: Social Change and Nationalism*, trans. Patricia Claxton (Toronto: McClelland and Stewart, 1980).

within Montreal. Later in the nineteenth century a number of serious violent incidents occurred, resulting from perceived insults to religious beliefs rather than from demands by French Canadians for more political or economic power.

In the first half of the twentieth century the main sources of communal conflict were events taking place in Europe. In 1917 there were serious riots in Montreal when French Canadians protested the enforcement of military conscription aimed at bolstering Canada's contribution to the European trenches. French Canadians generally resented the English-Canadian enthusiasm to subsume Canada's particular interests within those of the British Empire. Isolated in Canada for more than a century and a half, French Canadians felt few direct ties with people in any European country (including France), and they consequently saw no reason to force young Canadian men to fight in European wars. One of the most dramatic incidents in the agitation against conscription was an unsuccessful attempt in 1917 to dynamite the home of Sir Hugh Graham, the pro-conscription proprietor of *The Montreal Star*.[9]

In the late 1930s many French-speaking university students took to the streets to support Spanish fascism. Franco's fervent Catholicism, support for corporatism, and opposition to secular trade unions were all seen as attractive elements in his position. Like their colleagues elsewhere, English-speaking intellectuals in Montreal supported the Spanish Republic. Public meetings on the Spanish Civil War were often explosive occasions. At the same time, Jewish shopkeepers in Montreal found their businesses physically attacked by small groups of French-speaking anti-Semitic vandals.[10] Primarily due to the delicate political maneuvering of Prime Minister MacKenzie King, there were no conscription riots in Montreal during World War II. Although there was still profound disagreement between the French and English communities on the conscription issue, it was virtually all contained within the normal political process.

From 1944 until his death in 1959 the internal affairs of Quebec province were carefully controlled by Premier Maurice Duplessis.[11] The former leader of the Quebec Conservative Party first became premier in 1936, at the head of a new political party called the *Union nationale*, an alliance between Conservatives and Liberals who were disenchanted with the corrupt and obviously pro-business Liberal re-

9. J. I. Cooper, *Montreal: A Brief History* (Montreal: McGill-Queen's University Press, 1969), p. 147.

10. Ibid., p. 170.

11. For accounts in English of Duplessis's career, see Pierre Laporte, *The True Face of Duplessis* (Montreal: Harvest House, 1960); Conrad Black, *Duplessis* (Toronto: McClelland and Stewart, 1976); and Herbert Quinn, *The Union Nationale*, 2d ed. (Toronto: University of Toronto Press, 1979).

gime that had ruled Quebec since 1896. Duplessis was out of office between 1940 and 1944, but after returning to power he presided over a period of massive economic growth in Quebec that was accompanied by remarkably little change in the province's political practices.[12] The *Union nationale* built an impregnable electoral base in rural Quebec by skillfully manipulating the use of local patronage, drawing on the support of traditional elements in the Roman Catholic church, and making emotional appeals to ethnic loyalty.

Despite his reputation as a French-Canadian nationalist, Duplessis as premier, like his predecessors, proved very accommodating to British, American, and English-Canadian businessmen who wanted to invest in Quebec's plentiful natural resources. Although he never received the votes of English-speaking Montrealers, Duplessis did nothing to endanger their independent local institutions or their unlimited legal right to use the English language. Duplessis would attack the English-language business interests in public, but in private he took great pleasure in associating with their leaders. In short, the only English-speaking Montrealers who had major complaints about the Duplessis regime were those with an unusually highly developed sense of political morality. When opposition to Duplessis mounted in the 1950s, most of it came from French-Canadian intellectuals rather than English-Canadian businessmen.

Evidence of English Dominance

The dominance of English-Canadian business interests in the economic life of Montreal was first studied at McGill University in the 1930s and 1940s. Working under Professor Everett C. Hughes, various graduate students in sociology documented the extent to which linguistic and class cleavages coincided.[13] Hughes himself made substantial contributions to our understanding of French Canada. Within the Montreal context he viewed French Canadians as playing a unique auxiliary economic role. After claiming that the English of Montreal controlled "half a continent," he pointed out that:

> The French of Montreal enter into these nationally dominant institutions in minor and less specialized roles ... [T]he very presence of the numerous French allows the English to be more

12. Kenneth McRoberts and Dale Posgate, Quebec: *Social Change and Political Crisis,* 2d ed. (Toronto: McClelland and Stewart, 1980), Ch. 5.

13. See particularly S. M. Jamieson, "French and English in the Institutional Structure of Montreal" (M.A. thesis, McGill University, 1938); Everett C. Hughes and Margaret L. McDonald, "French and English in the Economic Structure of Montreal," *Canadian Journal of Economics and Political Science,* vol. 7 (1941): 493–505; and D. L. C. Rennie, "The Ethnic Division of Labour in Montreal" (M.A. thesis, McGill University, 1953).

specialized and more devoted to control functions than they could be if Montreal were a purely English city. Those of the French who are in dominant positions are concentrated in institutions which have for their hinterland, not the continent, but merely the province.[14]

Hughes was careful to distinguish between the economic and social roles of the Anglo-Saxons and the Jews. Jewish businesses tended to be smaller than Anglo-Saxon ones and therefore were more visibly in direct competition with those of the French Canadians. This, according to Hughes, helps explain why some of the economic frustrations felt by French Canadians in the 1930s were manifested through various forms of anti-Semitism.[15]

Most of the significant recent research on class and language in Montreal has been government sponsored. In the mid-1960s the federal Royal Commission on Bilingualism and Biculturalism paid special attention to Montreal when studying the impact of ethnic and linguistic factors in the workplace.[16] Volume III of the royal commission's report presents the most systematic analysis yet undertaken of Anglo-Saxon dominance in Montreal's economic life. In these blunt sentences, the commission summed up its findings for metropolitan Montreal:

In relation to those of British origin, those of French origin fare better on the occupational scale in Canada as a whole than they do in the one province where they form a majority of the population; and they fare better on the occupational scale in Quebec as a whole than they do in the industrial centre of the province, Montreal. For those of British origin the converse is the case. The increasing disparity, however, is not due to a lower position for those of French origin, since in these terms they fare a little better in Montreal. Rather it is the result of the fact that those of British origin fare far better in Montreal than anywhere else in the country.[17]

14. Everett Hughes, *French Canada in Transition* (London: Kegan, Paul, Trench, Trubner and Co., 1946), pp. 207–8.

15. Ibid., p. 218.

16. Five of its research studies were specifically devoted to this topic. See Jacques Dofny, *Les ingenieurs canadiens-français et canadiens-anglais à Montréal,* Documents de la Commission royale d'enquête sur le bilinguisme et le biculturalisme, no. 6 (Ottawa: Information Canada, 1971). The other four studies have not been published. They are E. C. Hughes, "Career Patterns of Young Montrealers in Certain White Collar Occupations"; Stanley Lieberson, "Linguistic and Ethnic Segregation in Montreal"; McGill University, Department of Geography, "Montreal Population: A Study in Four Volumes"; and J. Porter and P. C. Pineo, "French-English Differences in the Evaluation of Occupations, Industries, Ethnicities, and Religions in the Montreal Metropolitan Area."

17. Canada, *Report of the Royal Commission on Bilingualism and Biculturalism* (Ottawa: Information Canada, 1969), vol. 3, pp. 42, 45.

The commissioners also looked at 1961 income figures. They found an average difference of $1898 in the annual labor income of Montrealers of French and British origin. After detailed statistical analysis, they concluded that 45.1 percent of this difference could be attributed to differences in the educational achievements, and hence the occupational positions, of the two groups. Other factors were age, which accounted for a further 5.9 percent of the difference (the Anglo-Saxon professionals tended to be older than the French); type of industry, 4.2 percent (Anglo-Saxons worked in higher-paying industries); and differential impact of unemployment, 6.3 percent. Together these factors explain only 61.5 percent of Montreal's difference, whereas in Ottawa they explain 89.9 percent of the difference ($1496) and in Toronto, 77.6 percent of the difference ($1093).[18] It is true that Montreal French Canadians were much less likely to be bilingual than those in Ottawa and Toronto, but in Montreal, French is the majority language, and consequently one should expect English to be less necessary. The only possible conclusion from these figures is that Montreal's English-speaking employers consciously or unconsciously discriminated against French Canadians, simply because of their ethnic origin or language.

Another disturbing fact discovered in the 1961 census data was that in metropolitan Montreal bilingual people of British origin were not likely to have incomes as high as those who were unilingual. This was true even when education and occupation were held constant. Stanley Lieberson explains this apparent anomaly as follows: "British bilinguals earn less than monolinguals not because acquisition of French creates a handicap, which it obviously does not, but because those lower in position within a given occupation and educational level are more likely to need a knowledge of French."[19] This interpretation tells us a great deal about the status of the French speakers in Montreal's work world in the 1950s.

Mutual Isolation

One of the most persistent themes in the study of Quebec in general and Montreal in particular is the remarkable degree of self-containment, in institutional terms, of the two major language groups. This situation was eloquently described in 1972 by a Quebec government commission trying, among other things, to determine why "a good portion of Quebec's population does not need to know French in the ordinary course of events."[20] The commission's report outlined this explanation for the apparently anomalous situation:

18. Ibid., p. 69.
19. Stanley Lieberson, *Language and Ethnic Relations in Canada* (London: John Wiley, 1970), p. 172.
20. Quebec, *The Position of the French Language in Quebec: Report of the Commission of Inquiry* (Quebec: Quebec Official Publisher, 1972), vol. 1, p. 134.

The answer lies in the social organization which serves as a framework for the everyday life of Quebecers. The Province has a double network of institutions and services. . . . Herein lies the explanation of this peculiar phenomenon of two communities living side by side without having to communicate with each other. . . . This double network of institutions and services is known fact. It is so well known and such an accepted part of Quebec life, that it escapes attention. . . . [I]t is seen at the legislative, judicial, educational and hospital levels; it is evident in the information media and entertainment fields (newspapers, magazines, radio, television and so forth); it applies in the area of culture and even at the . . . provincial administration level . . . ; and it exists in private organizations such as banks and even, to some extent, in commerce.[21]

Nowhere in the province has the English "network of services and institutions" been stronger than on the Island of Montreal.

Many of the most incisive descriptions of Montreal's dual nature can be found in the creative literature of both French and English Canada. The social isolation of the two linguistic groups has been a constant theme in novels that have Montreal as their main setting. Antoine Sirois studied 22 French and 12 English novelists whose work appeared between 1942 and 1965.[22] In virtually all cases the novelists implicitly or explicitly agreed with Hugh MacLennan's conception of English-French relations as consisting of "two solitudes,"[23] interacting with each other only to the extent required for English-speaking businessmen to control French-speaking politicians and workers. With respect to normal social, cultural, and religious relations, the two groups were consistently portrayed as totally aloof from each other.

The remainder of Part One shows how the organization of Montreal's municipal government, public education, and social services reflected and reinforced this pattern of aloofness and isolation. Until 1960 the French-Canadian political elite showed no serious commitment to changing the pattern of French-English relationships in Quebec that had persisted for about 200 years. After 1960, during the Quiet Revolution, there was a massive effort on the part of French-speaking political leaders to gain some measure of control over Quebec's burgeoning economy. Although some changes came quickly and the new

---

21. Ibid. For an analysis of the emergence of a "double system" of authority and institutions in colonized societies in general and Quebec in particular, see Denis Monière, *Ideologies in Quebec: The Historical Development*, trans. Richard Howard (Toronto: University of Toronto Press, 1981), pp. 9–21.

22. *Montréal dans le roman canadien* (Montreal: Marcel Didier, 1968).

23. *Two Solitudes* is the title of one of MacLennan's best-known novels (Toronto: Macmillan, 1957). It was first published in 1945.

Liberal government of Jean Lesage increased the powers and capabilities of the government of Quebec, the early years of the Quiet Revolution brought few major changes in the institutional isolation of Montreal's two major linguistic groups. Not until the late 1960s and the early 1970s did the inexorable pressures for modernization and majority rule finally begin to undermine the traditional French-Canadian policy of leaving the English of Montreal to govern themselves.

3

Municipal Government in Montreal

The period of French rule had virtually no impact on the structural development of Montreal's local government. For four years following the British conquest in 1760 Montreal was ruled by an English military governor, an office then replaced by a panel of 27 local magistrates, rotating two-by-two, empowered to make local ordinances. The magistrates were the effective administrators of Montreal until 1833.[1] In 1792 Montreal was officially given the status of a city and its boundaries were formally defined. At the same time the new city was divided into two wards, the boundary being Boulevard Saint-Laurent.[2] To this day, "the Main" (as it is known in English Montreal) is an official boundary between east and west for street-naming purposes and is also an unofficial boundary that divides the French and English sectors.

Incorporation

In 1831, when Montreal's population was 31,000, the legislature of Lower Canada passed an act incorporating the city for a limited period and giving it an elected council, but Montreal did not hold its first municipal election until 1833, the year the act was proclaimed. The 16 elected councillors chose Jacques Viger as the city's first mayor. In 1836, at the height of the political crisis that led to the Rebellion of 1837, the charter expired and was not renewed. Rule by magistrates was restored until 1840. In that year the governor-general granted Montreal a new charter, giving himself authority to appoint the new mayor and councillors. The appointment of Peter McGill as the second mayor of Montreal began the practice of alternating the office between English and French Canadians, a practice that lasted into the twentieth century. By 1843 councillors were once again electing the mayor, but in 1852 the procedure was changed to allow for

---

1. J. I. Cooper, *Montreal: A Brief History* (London: McGill-Queen's University Press, 1969), p. 25.
2. Raymond Tanghe, "L'administration de Montréal," *Le Canada français*, vol. 23–2 (October 1935): 125.

direct election by male property owners.[3] Male tenants (but not boarders or lodgers) received the vote in 1860.[4]

Guy Bourassa, the foremost student of Montreal politics, has divided the city's political history into three eras.[5] From 1843 to 1873 "wealth constituted the fundamental political resource: it conferred high social status and the right to lead."[6] During this period the council was usually about 60 percent English, reflecting their numerical strength and firm control of business and commerce. The second era, the 40 years between 1873 and 1914, was a period of transition during which the old elite's hegemony was finally broken. The process was aided in 1889 by introduction of the secret ballot. By the turn of the century French Canadians were constituting almost 70 percent of the council,[7] a change attributable to their increasing numbers and to the gradual withdrawal of the wealthy English from overt political activity. Bourassa's third era has lasted for the past 70 years. It is characterized above all by the electoral success of populist francophone mayors, three of whom have served in office for particularly long periods.

The transition from English to French dominance was not without its difficulties. In the late nineteenth century, politicians and journalists of both linguistic groups tended to guard jealously the prerogatives of their respective groups. French speakers attacked a "Scotchman" who was the autocratic superintendent of Mount Royal Park; English speakers were unhappy with the actions of the French-speaking police chief and the superintendent of water works. Both groups defended their own people. Debates about the installation of new city utilities were dominated by the issue of whether the French or the English benefited.[8] Such conflicts in the local council did not really disappear from public debate until it was finally clear that the French were in command. After they lost control of the city, the English were forced to turn to other, more subtle ways of protecting their interests.

3. Ibid., p. 27.

4. The assessed value of the rented dwelling had to be at least $300 or have an assessed yearly rental value of $30. See Province of Canada, *Statutes* (1860), Ch. 72, Section 2. Harold Kaplan is wrong in stating that tenants did not receive the vote until 1944. See his *Reform, Planning and City Politics: Montreal, Toronto, Winnipeg* (Toronto: University of Toronto Press, 1982), p. 338.

5. Guy Bourassa, "The Political Elite of Montreal: From Aristocracy to Democracy," in *Politics and Government of Urban Canada*, ed. Lionel D. Feldman and Michael D. Goldrick (London: Methuen, 1969), pp. 124–33.

6. Ibid., p. 125.

7. Ibid., pp. 126–28.

8. "A French Canadian" (pseud.), "Municipal Reform in Montreal" (first published in 1899), reprinted in *Saving the Canadian City: The First Phase 1880–1920*, ed. Paul Rutherford (Toronto: University of Toronto Press, 1974), pp. 320–21.

The English Retreat to the Suburbs

The withdrawal of the financial elite from local politics has been well documented in other cities, particularly in the United States. Robert Dahl's description of how the "entrepreneurs" gave way to the "ex-plebes" in the local politics of New Haven between 1842 and 1900[9] is a particularly apt parallel to the Montreal experience. E. Digby Baltzell's account of the withdrawal of the "Philadelphia gentlemen" from local politics[10] corresponds to the behavior of Montreal's English. Like their Philadelphia counterparts, Anglo-Saxon Protestants in Montreal channelled their public service away from government into private cultural and charitable institutions such as hospitals, libraries, art galleries, schools, and colleges. Most of the new local French-speaking politicians who replaced them were professionals and small businessmen who often combined local politics with a legislative position in Ottawa or Quebec City.

The English withdrawal was not only political. Like their American counterparts, thousands of wealthy English removed themselves physically from the central city. The movement to the suburbs began in the late nineteenth century. In 1881 Canadians of French ethnic origin were proportionately far less numerous in the City of Montreal than in the municipalities that were on the island, but outside the city. These municipalities were either rural parishes or working-class suburbs that had grown up around major industrial or transport installations outside the city.

Table 2 shows French Canadians comprising 79.9 percent of the population of these municipalities in 1881. At this time Canadians of British origin (including Irish) still lived largely within the city, although there were some working-class suburbs with large Irish populations. British Canadians constituted 41.2 percent of the population of the city. By 1921 the situation had changed substantially. Most of the previously independent French-Canadian working-class suburbs had been annexed by the City of Montreal, and many of the rural parishes in the western part of the island were populated by British-Canadian suburbanites. In 1921 French Canadians constituted only 47 percent of the island's municipalities outside the city, and British Canadians constituted only 24 percent of the city's population. This pattern of French dominance in the city and weakness in the suburbs has been the central feature of metropolitan politics in Montreal since the early 1920s, although the relative strength of British Canadians has also been declining in both sectors since that time.

9. *Who Governs?* (London: Yale University Press, 1961), p. 11.
10. *Philadelphia Gentlemen* (London: Collier-Macmillan, 1958), particularly p. 57.

Table 2– *Ethnic Origin of the Population of Montreal and Environs, 1881, 1921, and 1971*

	Island (%)	City (%)	Island Suburbs (%)
1881			
French	62.5	55.9	79.9
British	35.1	41.2	18.9
Others	2.4	2.9	1.2
	(N=193,171)[a]	(N=140,747)	(N=52,424)
1921			
French	60.7	63.1	47.0
British	27.3	24.0	46.5
Others	12.0	12.9	6.5
	(N=724,205)	(N=618,506)	(N=105,699)
1971			
French	59.0	64.2	50.5
British	17.0	10.9	26.9
Others	24.0	24.9	22.6
	(N=1,959,165)	(N=1,214,380)	(N=744,785)

Source: Data prepared from Canada, *Census of Canada, 1880–1881* (Ottawa: Maclean, Roger and Co., 1882), pp. i, 52, 56; Canada, *Sixth Census of Canada, 1921* (Ottawa: King's Printer, 1924), pp. i, 534, 542; and Canada, *1971 Census of Canada*, Bulletin 1.3–2.
[a] N is the total population evaluated.

Annexations

From 1883 until 1918 the City of Montreal annexed 23 suburban municipalities, many of these actions prompted by the impending bankruptcy of the suburb. Insolvency was often caused by extravagant land developers who, controlling the affairs of newly incorporated municipalities, used the municipality's credit to construct facilities such as parks, roads, sewers, and public buildings, thereby greatly enhancing the value of their land.[11] Moreover, industrial landholders were often given municipal tax exemptions as an incentive to locate in the new municipalities, the real losers being the unfortunate residential taxpayers. When eventually they were unable to bear the

11. Naturally enough, this pattern of events is not well documented. The best example of it is the City of Maisonneuve, which was annexed in 1918. However, given the huge debts of other annexed municipalities, it is only reasonable to conclude that many of these earlier annexations followed a similar pattern. For a careful reference to "apparently ill-advised real estate developments," see Quebec, Department of Municipal Affairs, *Study Commission of Intermunicipal Problems on the Island of Montreal* (Quebec: Queen's Printer, 1964), p. 7; also see Paul-André Linteau, *Maisonneuve ou comment des promoteurs fabriquent une ville* (Montreal: Editions Boréal Express, 1981).

burden, it was passed on, through annexation, to all the taxpayers in the City of Montreal.

The province often forced the City of Montreal to take over these totally unplanned and bankrupt municipalities. From 1881 to 1921 both the central city's territory and debt grew dramatically, and much of the city's financial trouble later in the twentieth century was caused by the debt burden inherited from the annexations. Similarly, the bizarre municipal boundaries that still exist on the Island of Montreal can largely be traced to this period. The city absorbed the bankrupt entities but was denied those few municipalities where expensive houses had been sold to people who could also finance their own services. Consequently, one still finds territorial anomalies such as Westmount, Outremont, Hampstead, and Montreal West (see Map 1, p. 6–7).

The first annexation—of Hochelaga in 1883—was probably the most important to the City of Montreal's linguistic balance between the French and the English. Hochelaga's population of about 4000 was 80 percent French-speaking.[12] One of the earliest and most comprehensive English-speaking historians of Montreal, W. H. Atherton, observed that this annexation tipped the city's delicate French-English balance decisively toward the French.[13] At the time, English-speaking municipal politicians in Montreal appeared capable of surviving if the city's boundaries remained static, but their days were clearly numbered if forced to contend with the new French-speaking suburban working class.

Sixteen annexations took place from 1901 to 1911, when the city's population increased by 75.7 percent (267,730 to 470,480). Slightly more than half the growth (54.1 percent) was attributable to annexations. Of the 109,705 people in the annexed municipalities, 69.6 percent were of French origin, 25.4 percent were British, and 4.9 percent were "others." Thus, the impact of annexation clearly increased French strength in the city, from 60.9 percent to 63.5 percent. During the same period, British strength declined from 33.7 percent to 25.8 percent, due partly to annexation and partly to a British exodus from the city. Between 1901 and 1921 such suburban anglophone municipalities as Baie-d'Urfé, Beaconsfield, Côte-Saint-Luc, Hampstead, Mount Royal, Pointe-Claire, and Roxboro were first incorporated.

Because the "others" constituted 5.4 percent of the city's population in 1901, at the time the annexations actually reduced their relative strength. But by 1911 the "others" made up 11.7 percent of the

12. Canada, *Census of Canada, 1880–81,* pp. 52, 56.

13. William Henry Atherton, *Montreal, 1536–1914* (Montreal: S. J. Clarke, 1914), vol. 2, p. 184. This point is also made by Robert Rumilly, *Histoire de Montréal,* tome 3 (Montreal: Fides, 1972), p. 144.

city's population,[14] an unprecedented increase caused by the arrival of large numbers of immigrants. These people were mainly Jews and Italians[15] who chose to settle in Montreal rather than joining the rush to Canada's western frontier.

The Montreal Metropolitan Commission

Metropolitan government for Montreal was first seriously advocated in a 1910 book by G. A. Nantel, a former provincial minister of public works and director of *La Presse*.[16] Nantel saw municipal federation for the whole Island of Montreal, rather than piecemeal annexations by the central city, as the best answer to Montreal's problems.[17] He urged that a general council of the City and Island of Montreal be formed under the aegis of the provincial government, comprising the city's mayor and council together with delegates from groups of other island municipalities. The council would be concerned with services for the whole island, particularly roads, and could be divided into commissions, following the procedure then used by the Montreal city council. Nantel was careful to emphasize that all towns, villages, and parishes would maintain their identities and most of their existing functions.[18] Although no action was taken on Nantel's scheme at the time, his proposals were remarkably similar to the main features of the metropolitan government finally implemented for Montreal 60 years later.

As might be expected, Montreal's first step toward metropolitan government grew out of practical political difficulties rather than from carefully considered, rational proposals. In 1920 four municipalities—Montreal North, Pointe-aux-Trembles, Saint-Michel, and Laval-de-Montréal—were approaching bankruptcy. Annexation appeared inevitable, but clearly the city would agree only if allowed to annex most of the rest of the island at the same time. It was also clear that the provincial government's solution was some form of metropolitan commission to force the wealthier suburbs to help pay the debts of the poorer ones. In January 1921 suburban mayors met to decide their strategy. Unlike their meetings in later years, this one was held at least partly in the presence of the press. Nine suburbs

14. Canada, *Fourth Census of Canada*, 1901, pp. i, 104–16; and Canada, *Fifth Census of Canada*, pp. ii, 104–12, 278–88.

15. Cooper, *Montreal*, p. 124.

16. Guy Bourassa, "La connaissance politique de Montréal: Bilan et perspectives," *Recherches sociographiques*, vol. 6 (1965): 161.

17. G. A. Nantel, *La métropole de demain: Avenir de Montréal* (Montreal: Adjutar Ménard, 1910), p. 123.

18. Ibid., pp. 128–29.

voted to accept the commission idea if annexation were the *only* alternative. Such wealthy "inner suburbs" as Westmount, Outremont, and Montreal West were part of this group. But 11 suburbs opposed the commission idea under any circumstances.[19] This group included suburbs such as Rivière-des-Prairies, Dorval, Sainte-Geneviève, and Pointe-Claire, which were far enough away from Montreal to consider themselves safe from all but the most wide-ranging annexations. Despite the suburban objections, the provincial government went ahead with the plans for a commission. At the legislative committee hearings on the resulting bill, Médéric Martin, mayor of Montreal, shocked his audience by injecting the linguistic factor into the debate. He claimed that the citizens of Westmount, Outremont, and Montreal West had avoided annexation only because "these gentlemen are English."[20]

When the debate was over, both the suburbs and the city had little choice but to accept the provincial government's compromise between their opposing interests. The compromise was embodied in the act that established the Island of Montreal Metropolitan Commission.[21] (In 1922 its name was changed to the Montreal Metropolitan Commission.)[22] The act called for a 15-member commission: seven councillors and the city comptroller from the City of Montreal; one representative each from Westmount, Outremont, Verdun, and Lachine; a single councillor to represent LaSalle, Saint-Pierre, Hampstead, Mount Royal, Saint-Laurent, and Montreal West; and a single councillor to represent Montreal North, Saint-Michel, Montreal East, Pointe-aux-Trembles, and Laval-de-Montréal. There was also a nonvoting commissioner appointed by the Department of Municipal Affairs. With some minor changes, this structure lasted until 1959.

The commission's original functions were purely financial. Except for the City of Montreal, no member municipality could issue bonds or contract loans, other than of a temporary nature, without the commission's approval. Any municipality failing to meet its obligations had all its financial affairs placed in the control of the commission. This provision was directed at the four bankrupt municipalities that had originally prompted the commission's creation. All member municipalities that were financially solvent were liable, in proportion to their share of the total property assessment in the commission's territory, for the interest on the debts of the bankrupt municipalities

19. *La Patrie,* January 11, 1921.
20. *Le Devoir,* March 10, 1921 (author's trans.). Outremont is now predominantly French.
21. Quebec, *Statutes* (1921), Ch. 140.
22. Ibid. (1922), Ch. 105.

and for the commission's operating expenses. Thus, the City of Montreal paid 85 percent of the total annual bill.[23]

Eventually, the defaulting municipalities were supposed to repay the others. In 1946 Pointe-aux-Trembles (which had annexed Laval-de-Montréal in 1925), Montreal North, and Saint-Michel collectively owed the other municipalities more than $22 million. As a result of a complete financial restructuring for the city and the commission, the creditor councils forgave this debt. The net effect was that, for the period 1921–46, the city subsidized the debtors by $17.9 million, whereas the others had paid out $4.2 million.[24] In general, the commission succeeded in its limited financial objective, but it did so largely at the expense of the City of Montreal.

Twentieth-Century Populist Mayors

Médéric Martin

Médéric Martin, the Montreal mayor who prompted the commission's establishment, is better known in Montreal history as the city's first successful working-class politican. His election as mayor in 1914 marks the beginning of the third and current era of Montreal local politics, characterized by powerful and popular mayors who, by mobilizing large masses of voters, were able to get themselves reelected frequently. Martin's rather dubious political practices made him a natural target for the English-dominated reform coalition of businessmen and progressives, which had long been fighting a losing battle in local elections against patronage-based political machines.[25] His popular appeal to French-speaking working people easily overcame the reformers' opposition. Moreover, Martin's election in 1914 against an English-speaking opponent violated the practice of alternating the mayoralty between French and English, a tradition that was never revived. In 1926 Mayor Martin campaigned successfully under the slogan "No more English mayors here."[26]

With one two-year interruption, Martin was mayor until 1928. During his tenure he presided over a thoroughly corrupt and virtually bankrupt city administration. In 1918 the Liberal-controlled provin-

23. Alfred John Pick, *The Administration of Paris and Montreal* (Montreal: Guy Drummond Publications, 1939), p. 129.

24. Quebec, *Intermunicipal Problems*, pp. 14–15.

25. For an account of this era that emphasizes that not all the reformers were English, see Michel Gauvin, "The Reformer and the Machine: Montreal Civic Politics from Raymond Préfontaine to Médéric Martin," *Journal of Canadian Studies*, vol. 13 (Summer 1978): 16–26. Also see Kaplan, *Reform*, pp. 325–32.

26. Quoted in Leslie Roberts, *Montreal: From Mission Colony to World City* (Toronto: Macmillan, 1969), p. 313.

cial government, whose members were themselves not free of questionable involvements in the Montreal property market, virtually took over the administration of the city. They replaced the board of control with a provincially appointed five-member administrative commission, leaving Martin as little more than a figurehead. In 1921 the provincial government restored some of Martin's powers and abolished the commission, in its place setting up an executive committee composed of and elected by councillors, which had substantial authority independent of both the mayor and the council. The executive committee still survives as a unique and important mechanism of Montreal's municipal government, and its chair sometimes even wields more political power than the mayor.

Camillien Houde

By the late 1920s Martin's political appeal was fading. He had clearly amassed considerable personal wealth during his period of alleged service to working people. He had also been unable to establish the same personal contact with the unskilled recent immigrants to Montreal that he had developed with the semiskilled longtime residents. In the election of 1928 Camillien Houde, a Conservative member of the provincial legislature since 1923, challenged Martin and defeated him by 22,000 votes.[27]

Houde's origins were even humbler than Martin's, and he gained great support from the people on whom Martin had once depended. Houde served as mayor from 1928 to 1932, 1934 to 1936, and 1938 to 1940, but did not have a firm grip on the City of Montreal, largely due to his heavy involvement in provincial politics. His political career was interrupted in 1940 when he was arrested after urging young men not to register under the National Resources Mobilization Act. He spent the next few years under military guard at Petawawa and Fredericton, thereby becoming a wartime hero in the eyes of many French Canadians.[28]

Prior to his arrest Houde had already lost most of his powers as mayor. In 1940, for the second time in his mayoralty, the provincial government had placed the city under trusteeship in an attempt to remedy its dangerous financial position.[29] Although the trusteeship was to last for four years, the provincial government acted quickly to

27. Cooper, *Montreal*, p. 163.

28. Robert Lévesque and Robert Migner, *Camillien et les années vingt suivi de Camillien au Goulag* (Montreal: Les Editions des Brûlés, 1978), pp. 151–76.

29. For an account of how the Great Depression caused a crisis in the city's financing, see Terry Copp, "Montreal's Municipal Government and the Crisis of the 1930s," in *The Usable Urban Past*, ed. A. F. J. Artibise and G. A. Stelter (Toronto: Macmillan, 1979), pp. 112–29.

give Montreal its twelfth form of city government since 1833.[30] The council's membership was increased to 99, one-third elected by the property owners in 11 new wards (Class A councillors), one-third by all householders voting in the same 11 wards (Class B councillors), and one-third by 13 designated public bodies such as universities, unions, and chambers of commerce (Class C councillors). The council elected a six-member executive committee, which in turn elected its chair and vice-chair. The mayor continued to be elected by all house-holders on a citywide basis.

With some modifications, the system lasted until 1962. Its main effect was to protect the interests of property owners and to bolster English representation on the council. The property-owning and English groups overlapped to a considerable extent, and both benefited from the creation of Class A and Class C councillors. But the English gained most from Class C, because they controlled six of the 13 designated organizations.[31] As with the tradition of having an English-speaking vice-chair of the executive committee, the existence of Class C councillors guaranteed the English a basic level of representation higher than the ordinary electoral process would be likely to produce.

The first mayor to be elected under the 1940 system was Adhémar Raynault, a political protégé of Maurice Duplessis. (Raynault, who was also mayor for a two-year period after 1936, was one of Houde's more durable political opponents.) The new electoral system, combined with close provincial supervision of the city's finances, eventually helped restore Montreal's financial reputation. Raynault, however, received little credit. Houde was released from internment in 1944 in time to stand as a candidate in the municipal elections that year, defeating Raynault by almost 15,000 votes.[32] For obvious reasons, Houde received virtually no English support. With a trace of bitterness, Raynault's memoirs suggest that, as usual, most English Montrealers simply did not vote—they used their political influence only on the national scene, where they had a greater chance of success.[33]

In 1947 Houde became the only mayor in this century to be elected by acclamation, and in 1950 he was elected yet again. During this period, Houde's Montreal was noted for its almost totally corrupt city government. The main feature of the corruption was the close relationship of the police force to criminal organization for gambling and prostitution. It was first exposed in 1949 and 1950 in articles in

30. Cooper, *Montreal*, p. 168.

31. Guy Bourassa, *Les relations ethniques dans la vie politique montréalaise*, Documents de la Commission royale d'enquête sur le bilinguisme et le biculturalisme, no. 10 (Ottawa: Information Canada, 1971), p. 148.

32. Adhémar Raynault, *Témoin d'une époque* (Montreal: Editions du jour, 1970), p. 174.

33. Ibid., pp. 178–79.

Le Devoir by Assistant Police Director Pacifique Plante.[34] Although Plante was dismissed from his position soon afterward, he continued his battle, supported by the almost exclusively French-speaking Civic Action League and its offshoot, the Committee for Public Morality. In 1950 the latter group succeeded in forcing a judicial inquiry into commercialized vice in Montreal.[35] The chairman of the inquiry was Judge François Caron. Its two investigating lawyers were Plante and Jean Drapeau,[36] a young lawyer with a strong nationalist political background. Judge Caron's report was made public in 1954. Although it implicated many prominent city politicians and police officers, Houde, who had refused to cooperate, was ignored and thus allowed to retire with a theoretically unblemished record.

Jean Drapeau was the Civic Action League's candidate to succeed Houde in the 1954 election. On the strength of his prominence during the Caron inquiry, Drapeau was the easy victor, although the league did not gain full control of the council. Once in office, however, Drapeau did little to solidify his political position. He was opposed in Quebec by Premier Duplessis, and his reputation among the English as a dangerous nationalist was confirmed when he replaced the queen's picture in the mayor's office with a crucifix.[37] In the 1957 election Drapeau was defeated by Sarto Fournier, a Liberal senator who was supported by virtually all of Drapeau's enemies. Although Fournier had a 4000-vote majority, his nebulous local party, the Greater Montreal Rally, won fewer council seats than the Civic Action League, and the period 1957–60 was one of political stalemate.[38]

Proposals for Metropolitan Reform

Although the Greater Montreal Rally claimed to be primarily concerned with establishing a more effective form of metropolitan government for Montreal, it was in reality little more than a Duplessis-sponsored, hastily assembled alliance of all those wanting to get rid of Jean Drapeau. Metropolitan government was a convenient issue because, although the Montreal Metropolitan Commission continued its

34. These articles were then published in a book entitled *Montréal sous la régime de la pègre* (Montreal: Editions de l'Action nationale, 1950).

35. J.-Z. Léon Patenaude, "Le Comité de moralité publique et l'enquête Caron," *Le Devoir* (Montreal), August 10, 1972.

36. For a recent fascinating biography of this crucially important person in modern Montreal politics, see Brian McKenna and Susan Purcell, *Drapeau* (Toronto: Clarke Irwin, 1980).

37. J. M. McIver, "The Administration of Montreal: Past, Present, and Future" (M. A. thesis, Carleton University, 1961), p. 158.

38. Roberts, *Montreal*, p. 340.

effective control of suburban municipal finances, it was unable to take other initiatives to deal with emerging metropolitan problems. It had little or no support from the rural-dominated provincial government in Quebec City, and suburban politicians in Montreal continued jealously to defend their turf against whatever reform proposals were advanced.

The Municipal Service Bureau and the Borough System

The first reform proposals dated back to 1928. In that year a private organization, the Municipal Service Bureau, published a most detailed and ambitious scheme for a renewed metropolitan government. The document suggested that the city be divided into 18 boroughs, each with a representative on the Montreal city commission. Other member municipalities of the existing Montreal Metropolitan Commission would be represented on the new commission in similar fashion to the old. The new commission would have jurisdiction over main drainage and roads, police and fire protection, public health, building bylaws, town planning and zoning, hospitals and public assistance, and general finance.[39] The realization that creating a viable and powerful metropolitan government would require drastic municipal boundary changes was—and still is—a major obstacle confronting serious reformers.

The Municipal Service Bureau was almost completely removed from active politics; hence, its proposals had no chance of being implemented. Its isolation from the French-speaking majority is shown by its defense of the borough system as "British in character and Canadian in spirit,"[40] a justification clearly not designed to rally popular French-Canadian support. Proposals similar to the borough plan were made in French by Raymond Tanghe, a geographer at the University of Montreal. He argued for a new level of metropolitan government to control public works, finance, police, public health, and construction standards. Whereas the Municipal Service Bureau tended to follow the British model, with no overt central presence in local government, Tanghe's proposals reflected the advantages he saw in the French prefectorial system. He believed that Montreal's metropolitan government would benefit from having a provincially appointed chair.[41]

After World War II the advocates of the borough system resurrected their proposals, perhaps hoping that political circumstances

39. Frederick Wright, ed., *A Symposium of Opinion on the Borough System of Government for Greater Montreal* (Montreal: Municipal Service Bureau, 1928), p. 11.
40. Ibid., back cover.
41. Raymond Tanghe, *La géographie humaine de Montréal* (Montreal: Arbour et Dupont, 1928), p. 279.

had changed in their favor. The new version[42] differed from the 1928 proposals only in that they placed much less emphasis on the desirability of splitting up the city. Practical politicians once again paid little or no attention to the scheme. One English-speaking local and provincial politician, George Marler, suggested that the suburbs recognize the city's preeminent position and rely on it to provide regional services at a fair, negotiated cost.[43] None of these post-war suggestions was accepted by the city or the provincial government. From this time on, little was heard from the predominantly English-speaking "good government" groups that had sparked most of the previous discussion of metropolitan reform. The borough plan was forgotten until it was resurrected in 1971 by the City of Westmount.[44]

The Paquette Report

Suburban Montreal's phenomenal growth immediately after World War II—and the great traffic problems caused by the new reliance on the automobile—forced politicians to reopen the issue of metropolitan government. In 1952 the provincial government authorized the City of Montreal to establish a commission to study Montreal's metropolitan problems. Later that year the city council established a 22-member body, including Mayor Houde, 14 city councillors, and six representatives from the other municipalities that were members of the Montreal Metropolitan Commission. The chairman was the chief judge of Montreal, Roland Paquette. The commission finally reported in early 1955, calling for creation of a new metropolitan organism to administer various intermunicipal services and to act as a general conciliator of all the island's municipal interests.[45] It was to have 14 members named by the city, 14 named by the island suburbs, and one by the provincial government. There would be a seven-member executive committee. The new body would be responsible for major sewer and water-supply systems, traffic control on main arteries, fire-prevention standards, public transport, and metropolitan planning. It would also administer the sales tax, coordinate property assessment for tax purposes, and regulate store closing hours and taxi permits.[46]

42. This can be found in Frederick Wright, ed., *The Borough System of Government for Greater Montreal* (Montreal: Municipal Service Bureau, 1947) and T. Taggart Smyth, "Metropolitan Re-organization in Montreal and District," *Municipal Review of Canada*, vol. 62–3 (March 1946): 4–6.

43. George C. Marler, "The Metropolitan Problem," *Metropole*, vol. 1–1 (April 1947): 11, 17.

44. Westmount's proposals are discussed in Ch. 7.

45. Montreal, *Rapport général et final de la Commission d'étude des problèmes métropolitains* (Montreal: 1955), pp. 3–9.

46. Ibid., pp. 71–75.

Four city councillors expressed reservations about the report, mainly because its recommendations placed many existing city functions under the control of a new government in which the city would lack a clear voting majority. One commission member, Councillor Donat Beauchamp of Lachine, was totally opposed,[47] arguing that the suburbs would lose too much power if the Paquette recommendations were accepted. He was convinced that most of the island's problems could be overcome without infringing on municipal autonomy.[48] Beauchamp's final point was that Premier Maurice Duplessis would never agree to these changes if the city urged them against the wishes of the suburbs. "I affirm that the municipalities can rest assured that for the present Premier, who has shown himself so able a defender against the encroachments of centralization, it will be impossible to acquiesce in such a demand on the part of the City of Montreal."[49] Although Beauchamp's analysis of metropolitan problems may have been rather unsophisticated, his knowledge of Duplessis ultimately proved quite accurate. But it was not the release of the Paquette report that tested Duplessis's intentions. The report was forgotten almost as soon as it appeared, mainly because the new Montreal mayor, Jean Drapeau, was uninterested in any form of metropolitan government.

It was Premier Duplessis who reopened the issue. In early 1957, faced with some difficult political decisions concerning the island's intermunicipal problems, he began to realize that some form of metropolitan government might absolve him of these embarrassing choices. He announced that within a year he intended to create a new metropolitan institution for the Island of Montreal.[50] Suburban response was not encouraging. Although most mayors phrased their objections in terms of local autonomy, one simply stated: "I don't know anything about metropolitan government; I don't want to know anything about it, and I'm against it."[51]

At a series of meetings arranged by the Montreal Board of Trade in 1957, various city and suburban representatives studied all the usual problems involved in metropolitan reorganization. They even tackled the question of how to respect the existence of separate French and English communities—but met with no success.[52] With characteristic extreme caution, Duplessis tried to make it appear that

47. Ibid., p. 76.
48. Donat Beauchamp, untitled typescript (Lachine: Metropolitan government file of Mayor R. J. P. Dawson, January 5, 1955), pp. 1–7.
49. Ibid., p. 9.
50. George E. Shortt, "Government of the Metropolitan Area of Montreal in the Light of Experience Elsewhere" (Typescript located at the Montreal Board of Trade, 1961).
51. Quoted in ibid., p. 84.
52. Ibid., p. 85.

he was not coercing anybody into metropolitan government. In August 1957, however, he implied that he would have to act without local cooperation if the island municipalities could not agree among themselves.[53]

The Suburbs Begin to Organize

The suburban response to Duplessis's initiative was led by Mayor Reginald Dawson of Mount Royal. In October 1957 he called a meeting of all the island's suburban mayors at Mount Royal's town hall. Fifteen municipalities sent representatives.[54] Some mayors supported the Paquette report because it gave the suburbs considerable control over the city. Mayor Playfair of Hampstead, a member of the Paquette commission, went so far as to suggest that if there were a city councillor from Notre-Dame-de-Grâce on the metropolitan institution, he could easily be swung to the suburban side.[55] As Notre-Dame-de-Grâce was the City of Montreal's most obviously English-speaking ward, Playfair was clearly implying that the interests of the suburbs and of English Canadians were very similar.

Other mayors, particularly those farther removed from the central part of the island, were much more suspicious of the Paquette recommendations. No one was sure exactly what the Quebec authorities intended, but everyone agreed the provincial government should be shown that the suburbs were currently paying their share of metropolitan costs through the sales and water tax and that the city's claims to the contrary were not true. Twenty municipalities were represented at a second meeting held one month later.[56] Mayor Dawson reported that he had recently met Paul Dozois, the minister of municipal affairs, and had been left with the impression that the government was not really ready to proceed. In fact, Dozois had suggested to Dawson that the suburbs ask the government to appoint a royal commission to study the matter.[57] With the sense of urgency removed, the mayors decided to do nothing further except establish a committee capable of reacting to future events.

The potential suburban strength that Dawson had attempted to mobilize was not needed on this occasion, due to Duplessis's lack of

53. Ibid., p. 88.
54. "Verbatim Report: Minutes of Meeting of Mayors of all Municipalities in the Montreal Area Re Metropolitan Government Held in the Elizabeth Salon, October 23, 1957, at 8:00 P.M." (Metropolitan government file of Mayor R. J. P. Dawson), p. 1.
55. Ibid., p. 5.
56. "Minutes of Meetings of Mayors of Municipalities in the Montreal Area Re Metropolitan Government Held in the Elizabeth Salon, Town Hall, November 20, 1957, at 8:00 P.M., Town of Mount Royal" (Metropolitan government file of Mayor R. J. P. Dawson), p. 1.
57. Ibid.

commitment to metropolitan government. But these two meetings are important in that they foreshadowed the various loose organizations later formed by the suburbs to protect their autonomy against city and provincial interference. It should be noted that the 1957 meetings were conducted in English by a chairman who was mayor of a wealthy English-speaking suburb. French-speaking suburbs were represented, but in a much less prominent role.

The Montreal Metropolitan Corporation

After the victory of the Greater Montreal Rally in Montreal's 1957 mayoralty election, the suburbs once again became concerned. In 1958 the new mayor, Sarto Fournier, acted on his party's electoral pledges to promote metropolitan government by appointing a 12-member committee to study the Paquette report and make recommendations for action. The chairman of the committee was Lucien Croteau, formerly associated with ex-mayor Camillien Houde and now Fournier's chief political organizer. Although the Croteau committee employed two outside consultants, its members were entirely drawn from the City of Montreal, and it was therefore viewed with considerable suspicion by the suburbs. Their suspicions were confirmed when the Croteau report was released in December 1958, calling for creation of Paquette's metropolitan body—but with far greater powers, including control over integrated police and fire departments.[58] The area to be covered by the proposed new "Corporation of Greater Montreal" included 45 municipalities: all of the Island of Montreal, all of Île-Jésus to the north, and eight municipalities on the mainland to the south (see Map 1, pp. 6–7). The corporation's 13-member council would consist of six directly elected representatives from the city and one each from six separate suburban electoral divisions. The chair would be appointed by the provincial government.[59] At a meeting in Mount Royal in January 1959, 34 suburban municipalities unanimously rejected the report.[60] The suburban position had hardened.

Premier Duplessis acted quickly to break a potential deadlock. Before the City of Montreal's council had a chance to commit itself to the Croteau report, he skillfully presented his own proposals for the establishment of a very weak Montreal Metropolitan Corporation. For a few days in February 1959 metropolitan government was publicly debated in the private bills committee of the Quebec legislative assem-

---

58. Montreal, *A Metropolitan Organism for Greater Montreal* (Montreal: 1955), pp. 69–71.

59. Ibid., p. 109.

60. Shortt, "Government of the Metropolitan Area," p. 95.

bly. The main municipal actors were Mayor Dawson, Mayor Fournier, and Croteau, all of whom appeared as witnesses. But Duplessis controlled the proceedings, overshadowing others. Finally, everybody agreed to his proposals. The new corporation would be made up of 14 members named by the city and one each from the same 14 municipalities that were part of the Montreal Metropolitan Commission. The chair would be appointed by the provincial government. The corporation was to take over the existing functions of the Montreal Metropolitan Commission and would also be empowered to provide norms for property assessment and to coordinate various intermunicipal services, to the extent that member municipalities agreed to such coordination.[61]

The agreement to establish such a weak corporation represented a great victory for the suburbs. They gained representation equal to that of the city—something they lacked on the commission—and lost none of their existing powers. Their satisfaction is demonstrated by this paragraph in the *Westmount Letter*, published by the city most associated with English power in Montreal: "The important point for all of us living in Westmount is that we are not to lose the standards of service we now enjoy. Westmount is in no way precluded from exercising *complete autonomy* in respect to what Council feels is best for the citizens and property owners."[62] [Emphasis in original]

On April 6, 1959, the Montreal Metropolitan Corporation came into existence. One year later the pro-metropolitan Greater Montreal Rally was annihilated at the polls, and Jean Drapeau was back in full control of the Montreal city council. Drapeau refused to cooperate with a metropolitan body over which the city did not have full control. The corporation remained as a legal entity until the end of 1969, but during its 10 years it accomplished nothing of significance. Its futile existence was proof that no metropolitan institution could be effective without the full political support of both the provincial government of Quebec and the City of Montreal. When the personnel of both these governments changed in 1960, the corporation was doomed.

The Politics of Caution

Premier Duplessis's response to the need for metropolitan reform on the Island of Montreal was typical of his style of government. He handled the problem personally, producing ad hoc compromises only when absolutely necessary. He sympathized with the desires of the

61. Quebec, *Statutes* (1959), Ch. 52, Div. 2.
62. Westmount, *Westmount Letter*, March 1959.

suburban mayors—some of whom were his own local political organizers—to remain in full control of their own municipalities. Just as
they saw a powerful metropolitan government as a threat to their local
influence, Duplessis saw it as a threat to his personal control over the
province. Because his political machine was based in rural Quebec, he
showed no understanding of the pressing urban problems constantly
confronted by the City of Montreal's French-speaking working class.

Moreover, despite the premier's reputation as a French-Canadian
nationalist, financial support from English-speaking companies was
vital to his government's survival. For this reason he was reluctant to
alienate the powerful residents of English-speaking suburbs by deny-
ing them full control over their own municipal services and institutions. Had Duplessis been in office after 1960 and faced Mayor Drapeau's powerful and united city administration he might have found
it politically impossible to ignore a strengthened Mayor Drapeau. But
political divisions within the city's government in the 1950s facilitated Duplessis's adoption of the suburban position.

This description of the evolution of municipal government in
Montreal prior to 1960 is not meant to suggest that the city-suburban cleavage ever became identical to the French-English cleavage.
Table 2 suggests that in the twentieth century about half of the
suburbanites on the Island of Montreal have been French Canadians
and that more non-French Canadians lived in the central city than
in the suburbs. Nevertheless, the French *were* comparatively under-
represented in the suburbs. Most French Canadians who did live in
suburbs lived in the poorer municipalities to the north, east, and
southwest of the city. The non-French, especially those of British
origin, were overrepresented in the suburbs, particularly those to
the west of the city.

Two important facts relating to French-English relations should
be emphasized about the municipal government system on the Island
of Montreal prior to the Quiet Revolution. First, the City of Montreal
was clearly controlled by French Canadians. Second, some suburban
municipalities—most notably Westmount, Montreal West, Hampstead, Mount Royal, Pointe-Claire, Beaconsfield, and Baie-d'Urfé—
were almost as English as any municipality in southern Ontario.

Lacking a powerful metropolitan government for the island as a
whole, or a strong provincial department of municipal affairs, these
English-speaking municipalities were remarkably autonomous. For legal purposes some of their documents and official papers had to appear
in French as well as English. But for all practical purposes they conducted their business in English. Because all were relatively wealthy,
they could afford a high level of municipal services, especially in fields
like policing, libraries, parks, and recreation. Undoubtedly, the existence of independent English-speaking municipalities on the western

half of the Island of Montreal was one of the most important institutional bulwarks of Montreal's English-speaking community.

In the 1960s and 1970s, when the status of these institutions became the subject of open political controversy, the existence of the English-speaking municipalities inevitably caused immense difficulties for the advocates of metropolitan reorganization. Any proposal to change municipal boundaries could also be interpreted as a proposal to change the local political strength of the French- and English-speaking citizens within the affected areas. In short, it is even more difficult politically to implement changes in linguistic relationships than it is to change the structures and functions of municipalities.

4

Schools and Social Services

New France's only recognizable social policy—to the extent that it had one—was that the church and the family were the crucial institutions for looking after the education and social welfare of the colony's inhabitants. The state intervened in these matters only by granting subsidies and giving official recognition to religious institutions.[1] The most serious government attempt to participate directly came in 1688, when the Supreme Council of New France issued a decree establishing a *bureau des pauvres* in each of the colony's towns and rural parishes. These *bureaux*, made up of the *curé*, a "director of the poor," and a secretary-treasurer, were concerned with ensuring that church alms, voluntary contributions, and revenues from selected fines were distributed only to those who genuinely deserved financial assistance. Although these *bureaux* have been called the forerunners of modern family social service in Quebec, they had little real influence and were certainly no threat to the paramount position of the church.[2]

The *bureaux* went out of existence at the time of the British conquest. British attempts to introduce an Elizabethan-style Poor Law were completely unsuccessful. The role of the church thus became even more important in the early years of British rule. Not until 1801 did the colonial government start granting subsidies to religious orders to help pay for looking after orphans and the mentally ill.[3] This began a long period of church-state partnership in the provision of social services, a partnership in which the church was clearly the dominant factor.

The same year saw the creation of the Royal Institution for the Advancement of Learning. It resulted from a profound dissatisfaction on the part of Montreal merchants and clergy with the chaotic state of public education in Lower Canada (Quebec).[4] The only schooling

1. Gonzave Poulin, *L'assistance sociale dans la province du Québec, 1608–1951*, Annexe 2 de la Rapport de la Commission royale d'enquête sur les problèmes constitutionels (Quebec: 1955), p. 29.

2. Ibid., p. 116.

3. Quebec, *Report of the Study Committee on Public Assistance* (Quebec: 1963), p. 30.

4. William Henry Atherton, *Montreal, 1535–1914* (Montreal: S. J. Clarke, 1914), vol. 2, p. 435.

available to French Catholics had been provided by a depleted group of priests and nuns, and the situation for Protestant children was scarcely better. Various church people and private entrepreneurs attempted to establish schools, but most were financially unsuccessful. The Royal Institution was supposed to establish a network of "royal schools" open to all children in Lower Canada. Because they were almost totally controlled by Protestants, however, the royal schools were boycotted by the French Roman Catholics. The Royal Institution failed in its original objective, but after inheriting land from the Scottish merchant James McGill in 1811, it established what is known today as McGill University.

School Boards

Local school boards in the United Province of Canada (now Ontario and Quebec) were first established by the Education Act of 1841, which provided for elected boards in all townships and parishes. They were given the responsibility of acquiring sites for schools, supervising their building and maintenance, appointing teachers, regulating courses of study, and selecting textbooks.[5] The act also contained provisions stating that the religious minority (Catholic or Protestant) in each township had the right to elect its own school trustees to administer its own schools.

These provisions were the origin of the right of religious dissent for school purposes, which still prevails in Quebec and Ontario. Concerning incorporated cities and towns (such as the City of Montreal), the 1841 act stated that the municipal council would be responsible for all public schools. But each municipality was also to establish a board of examiners consisting of an equal number of appointed Protestants and Catholics and presided over by the mayor. The board would administer the schools serving both religious groups and would divide into separate sections to administer those catering exclusively to one group or the other.[6] These provisions were not particularly satisfactory in Lower Canada and were drastically amended in 1845 and 1846.

The 1846 act "to make better provision for Elementary Instruction in Lower Canada"[7] reinforced the 1842 rule requiring school boards to levy land taxes on their inhabitants in order to benefit from any government subsidies for schools. Other provisions of the 1846

5. Quebec, *Report of the Royal Commission of Inquiry on Education in the Province of Quebec* (Quebec: 1963–66), vol. 1, p. 10.
6. Ibid., p. 11.
7. Province of Canada, *Statutes* (1846), Ch. 27.

act completely removed education from the jurisdiction of municipal councils. Cities and towns other than Quebec City and Montreal were required to adopt the system of local school boards outlined in the 1841 act. The act went on to state "that in Quebec and Montreal the municipal Corporation shall appoint twelve School Commissioners . . . six of whom shall be Roman Catholics and six Protestants; and such Commissioners shall form two separate and distinct Corporations, the one for the Roman Catholics and the one for the Protestants."[8] This provision was the origin of both the Montreal Catholic School Commission and the Protestant School Board of Greater Montreal, two public school systems that still exist.

School Boards and the Constitution

There were no major changes in the school law of Lower Canada before the creation of the Dominion of Canada in 1867. Section 93 of the British North America Act, now called the Constitution Act, places education squarely under the jurisdiction of the provinces. Yet because the architects of the federal union feared that a provincial legislature might one day attempt to abolish the existing rights of Catholics and Protestants, they included elaborate provisions in Section 93 aimed at restraining the power of provincial majorities from adversely affecting the school systems of the religious minorities.

There has been a good deal of debate among legal scholars concerning how Section 93 applies to Montreal.[9] There is general agreement, however, that the constitution at least protects the right of Catholics and Protestants to establish their own tax-levying school boards. The degree of constitutional protection afforded to other features of Montreal's educational arrangements is far from clear.

Until quite recently schools operated by Montreal's Protestant school boards have been almost exclusively English speaking. All non-Catholic immigrant groups have generally sent their children to Protestant schools, because these schools have been less religiously oriented than Catholic ones and have provided education more comparable to that found elsewhere in North America. Catholic school boards have provided almost all Montreal's French-language education, and they also became responsible for providing English-language schools for Catholic immigrant groups—first for the Irish and, more recently, for Italians and Portuguese.

8. Ibid., Ch. 27, Section 42.
9. The problem is analyzed in great detail in François Chevrette, Herbert Marx, and André Tremblay, *Les problèmes constitutionels posés par la restructuration scolaire de l'Ile de Montréal* (Quebec: l'Editeur officiel, 1971), Chs. 1–3. For a critique of this study, see Protestant School Board of Greater Montreal, *Report of the Legal Committee on Constitutional Rights in the Field of Education in Quebec*, 2d Supplement, n.d.

There is no constitutional provision in Canada for linguistic groups to control their own schools, and there is no protection for the religious interests of groups that are neither Catholic nor Protestant. In Montreal this situation has, at various times, caused difficulties for two groups: the Jews and the English-speaking Catholics.

Jews: Catholic or Protestant?

In 1870 Jews were first recognized in educational legislation for Montreal, when they were given the right to choose between having their school taxes allocated to the Catholic or the Protestant school board; their children were given the parallel right to attend the schools of whichever board was chosen.[10] Most Jewish groups found the Protestant system more hospitable, although some made special arrangements with the Catholic boards. In 1894 Montreal's Protestant school board agreed to subsidize the Baron de Hirsch school for Jewish immigrants, on the understanding that Jewish property owners in Montreal would choose to pay their taxes to the Protestant board. The upsurge of poor Jewish immigrants from eastern Europe immediately after this agreement was reached meant that the Protestants ended up losing a great deal of money.

Protestant resentment was clearly shown in 1902 when the Protestant board refused to award a scholarship that had been won by a Jewish boy whose father was not a taxpayer.[11] The provincial legislature entered the dispute in 1903, passing a statute for all Quebec stating that Jews were to be treated as Protestants for educational purposes, except that Jewish children would be excused from worship and would be allowed absences for Jewish holidays.[12] This arrangement worked moderately well until 1922, although Protestants in Montreal resisted all attempts to have a Jew named to the school board.[13]

Because of the post–World War I wave of Jewish immigration, the Protestants once again tried to get rid of their expensive obligation to educate Montreal's Jews. The result was sponsorship of litigation to clarify the legal status of the Jews of Montreal.[14] The case, known as *Hirsch v. Protestant School Commissioners of Montreal*, was finally ruled on in 1928 by the Judicial Committee of the Privy Council in London.[15] The judges found that the 1903 provincial act violated Sec-

10. Harold Ross, "The Jew in the Educational System of the Province of Quebec" (M.A. thesis, McGill University, 1947), p. 12.
11. Ibid., pp. 18–18a.
12. Quebec, *Statutes* (1903), Ch. 16.
13. Ross, "The Jew," p. 23.
14. Ibid., p. 54.
15. The Hirsch ruling is presented in Hyman Neatman, "The Place of the Jews in the Public School System of Montreal" (April 1940); and Annex B of Canadian Jewish Congress, "Brief to the Quebec Royal Commission of Inquiry on Education" (Mimeographed, 1962).

tion 93 of the British North America Act by granting Jewish children an absolute right to attend all Protestant schools and Jewish adults the right to be members of Protestant school boards. The judges maintained that to rule otherwise would be to diminish the established rights of Montreal Protestants to control their own schools.

The judges also held that the provincial legislature had the authority to establish separate school boards for Jews, wherever and however it wished. Many saw this as the only way out of the dilemma, and in 1930 the provincial legislature passed an act establishing a Jewish School Commission covering the entire Island of Montreal. The seven commissioners were appointed by the provincial government and had the power (in theory, at least) either to negotiate an agreement for Jewish education with another school board or to establish their own network of Jewish schools.[16]

Pressed by the Roman Catholic hierarchy and by anti-Semitic elements among French-Canadian nationalists, the government in turn exerted "irresistible pressure"[17] on the Jewish commissioners to negotiate with the Protestants rather than meet the demands of religiously conservative Jewish groups that a separate Jewish school system be established. In 1931 the commission reached the required agreements with both the Montreal and Outremont Protestant school boards. The agreements[18] were very similar to the 1903 act, and consequently there was little change from the perspective of the average Jewish family.

Once the agreements were signed, the government—still accused of being excessively pro-Jewish by some extreme Catholic groups—could retreat even farther from the principle of allowing Jews to determine their own educational arrangements. Stopping just short of abolishing the Jewish School Commission, the government sponsored new legislation removing all the commission's powers except to uphold or reject the original agreement.[19] All the commission members thereupon resigned in protest.[20] No members were ever again appointed, although the legislation providing for the Jewish School Commission remained on the books until 1972.

This bizarre series of events ended up clarifying the legal position of Montreal Jews, but it did little to change their actual relationship to the Montreal Protestant school boards. Between 1931 and 1972

16. Quebec, *Statutes* (1930), Ch. 61.
17. David Rome, *On the Jewish School Question in Montreal, 1903–1931* (Montreal: Canadian Jewish Congress, 1975), p. 127. See also Antonin Dupont, *Les relations entre l'Eglise et l'Etat sous Louis-Alexandre Taschereau* (Montreal: Guérin, 1972), pp. 253–73.
18. Rome, *Jewish School Question*, p. 130.
19. Quebec, *Statutes* (1930–31), Ch. 63.
20. Rome, *Jewish School Question*, p. 131.

Jewish children had the legal right to attend their schools because of the 1931 agreement. Although they continued to pay property taxes to the Protestant board, Jews could not be board members; in this way at least, they clearly lacked equal rights.

The 1931 agreement concerned only Jews living in the territories covered by the Montreal and Outremont boards. Most Jews living in other parts of Montreal had no *legal* right to go to Protestant schools, although most in fact did attend them. In some areas the highly complicated tax laws meant that Jews ended up paying higher school taxes than Protestants.

From any kind of liberal democratic perspective the situation was highly unsatisfactory.[21] Nevertheless, the general feeling on all sides seemed to be that nothing could be done lest any attempt to change or reinterpret Section 93 provoke political emotions that were best left undisturbed. The legal status of the Jews in Montreal remains unclear, as does that of other growing groups such as the Greek Orthodox and the Moslems. As a practical matter, however, virtually all non-Catholic groups have been absorbed within the Protestant system and have therefore been educated almost exclusively in English.

English-Speaking Catholics

The English-speaking Catholics are another rather anomalous group. Originally formed in the mid–nineteenth century by Irish immigrants, the group now comprises Catholics of many other ethnic backgrounds, particularly Italians, who have chosen to speak English rather than French. Constitutionally, the English-speaking Catholics are not entitled to separate educational structures, but the provincial educational authorities and Catholic school commissions throughout the province have traditionally recognized English-speaking Catholics and allowed them to have their own schools, wherever numbers permitted. The English-speaking Catholic system of education in Quebec has developed from a process of accommodation and compromise, whose success one English-Catholic educator (now the cardinal archbishop of Toronto) attributed to "the basic fairness of the French Canadian."[22] English-speaking Catholics have always been just as eager as Protestants to have English-language schools. The fact that they are officially within the same system as the French has made little or no difference to the linguistic practices of English-speaking Catholics.

The Montreal Catholic School Commission is the body with the greatest influence on the development of English-Catholic education,

21. See Canadian Jewish Congress, "Brief."
22. G. Emmett Carter, *The Catholic Public Schools of Quebec* (Toronto: W. J. Gage, 1957), p. 95.

because most of the province's English-speaking Catholics live in its territory. Between 1947 and 1973 the commission consisted of seven members, four appointed by the provincial government, and three by the archbishop of Montreal. By law, one appointee had to be English speaking.[23] Since 1928 the English-language school system has been virtually independent within the commission's administrative structures. In the 1940s the English-speaking gained almost complete control over curriculum and personnel policy and by 1960 had succeeded in establishing a dual linguistic structure in a school commission that was unified only at the very top.[24] Although some Montreal English-speaking Catholics still considered their educational facilities inadequate compared to those of the Protestants, Canon Carter was probably right when he wrote: "[T]he English catholics . . . have succeeded in moving forward in education more rapidly than perhaps any comparable group in the country. Beginning with practically nothing, they now have a completely organized system."[25]

Virtually no French Canadians argued that Irish Catholics should not have the right to manage their own schools, which no doubt explains how the Irish got so much freedom when they were finally in a position to claim it. But in recent years many have been arguing that the freedom granted Irish Catholics does not include the right to absorb Italian, Portuguese, and other European immigrants into the English-Catholic system, thereby assimilating them to the English-language group. The same issue arises, in a somewhat different context, when one looks at the way the Protestant system has been directing Greek Orthodox students toward the English language. (Chapter 8 treats this important aspect of the language issue in relation to recent attempts to rationalize and modernize the Island of Montreal's school system.)

Growing Demand for Educational Reform, 1925–1960

On the Protestant side, the most important structural change between 1846 and 1973 occurred in 1925, the year the Montreal Protestant Central School Board was created.[26] It represented a kind of federal union, involving the city board and 10 neighboring Protestant boards, and was brought about by the Verdun Protestant board's inability to pay its bills. Instead of providing direct economic assistance to Verdun, the provincial government thought the wealthier Protestant boards should collectively take responsibility for Verdun's debts.

23. Guy Houle, *Le cadre juridique de l'administration scolaire locale au Québec* (Quebec: 1966), p. 69.
24. Carter, *The Catholic Public Schools*, p. 95.
25. Ibid., p. 96.
26. Quebec, *Statutes* (1925), Ch. 45.

The creation of the central school board seems quite analogous to the creation in 1921 of the Montreal Metropolitan Commission. But the commission never went beyond its financial duties, whereas the central school board soon took over most of the administrative functions of its constituent boards. The suburban school boards had no reason to resist the leadership exercised by the city board, because all members of the central board were English-speaking Protestants and shared the same basic values and objectives.

By 1945, when the central board's name was changed to the Protestant School Board of Greater Montreal (PSBGM),[27] the local school boards had become little more than tax-collecting agencies. In the following years the PSBGM supervised a great expansion of the English educational system caused by the postwar "baby boom."

In 1965 the PSBGM and the City of Montreal's Protestant board both underwent one of their periodic changes in membership formula. A provincial act enlarged the city board to 10, five of whom were to be appointed by the province and five by the Protestant members of the Montreal city council. All were automatically also members of the PSBGM, now to have 25 members. The other 10 Protestant boards were entitled to one representative each. The most important change was the provision for the provincial government to appoint five Jews to the PSBGM. These appointments were to take place after consultation with "a highly representative institution of the Jewish community of Montreal."[28] One-fifth of the members of the PSBGM accurately reflected the Jewish community's strength among students in Protestant schools. Although the Hirsch judgment would support a good case that this entire provision was unconstitutional,[29] its makeup was never legally challenged while the PSBGM existed in this form, until 1973.

Placing Jews on the PSBGM was a kind of ad hoc measure to correct one of the antiquated Quebec educational system's most glaring anomalies. By the early 1960s, however, such measures were inadequate to cope with the growing demands for a completely new and possibly even secular system of educational structures. Most of Quebec's political, social, and economic leaders realized that their society could be modernized only if the educational system were modernized first.

The demands for modernization arose in part from the growing inappropriateness of the Catholic-Protestant cleavage as the school system's organizing factor. But by the early 1960s it was also commonly realized that Montreal's school system perpetuated some of the

27. Quebec, *Royal Commission on Education*, vol. 3 (1966), p. 188.
28. Quebec, *Statutes* (1965), Ch. 87, Section 3(c).
29. Neatman, "The Place of the Jews," p. 4.

most disagreeable features of the relationship between the French and English languages. English-speaking schools, especially Protestant schools, seemed almost totally incapable of turning out graduates who could speak French. This was undoubtedly related to the Protestant boards' general prohibition against hiring Catholics, even as French teachers. Although French-speaking youngsters often seemed to learn English more proficiently than English-speaking ones learned French, this was due more to factors outside the French-language schools than within them. In any event, the idea of creating public bilingual schools was heresy for both sides—to the French it meant assimilation, and to the English it meant lower standards.

The French Catholic school system seemed ill suited to preparing French Canadians for technical and managerial jobs in a modern economy. The Protestant system had American-style high schools that prepared students for both the job market and university, but the French-Catholic secondary school system was extremely weak, designed only for those less-gifted children who were unable to gain entrance to a church-run classical college. After eight years at college a student obtained a BA degree and the right to enter one of the traditional professional faculties in a university. Technical, scientific, or managerial education for French Canadians was almost nonexistent; consequently, it was hardly surprising that jobs in these fields were held largely by English Canadians. When Quebec's public educational system was reformed in the 1960s and 1970s, dramatic action was taken to correct this state of affairs. But despite numerous efforts, there was relatively little change in the organization of public education in Montreal. The system still relied on the Catholic and Protestant school boards as the principal units for local school administration.

Social Services: The Public Charities Act

The reader should understand that until well into the twentieth century, Quebec's social services were provided almost exclusively by the Roman Catholic and Protestant churches and by various ethnic-based organizations like the St. Patrick's Society. In 1882 provincial legislation entrusted municipalities with administering direct financial assistance to persons in need and with subsidizing charitable institutions. The function was discretionary rather than obligatory, however, and few municipalities exercised it.[30]

The first significant provincial intervention in social services took place in 1921, when the legislative assembly approved the Public

30. Quebec, *Report of the Study Committee on Public Assistance* (Quebec: 1963), p. 31.

Charities Act.[31] It was intended to provide financial assistance to any religious, charitable, or municipal institution that hospitalized or housed poor people unable to look after themselves. Under the act these institutions were to be recognized by a new provincial agency called the Bureau of Public Charities. Recognized institutions were to have one-third of the cost of looking after each person paid by the provincial government and one-third by the municipality in which the person lived. The institution itself continued its responsibility for the remaining third.[32] Although the act aroused considerable opposition from some Roman Catholics on the grounds that it would lead to a state takeover of the social services,[33] its later administration showed these fears to be totally unjustified.

In its original form the Public Charities Act did not apply to the work of social service organizations that assisted poor people living in their own homes, although the work and responsibilities of such agencies increased greatly during the first three decades of the twentieth century.[34] English-speaking agencies grouped themselves into three different federations to coordinate their activities and to raise and distribute charitable funds: (1) the Montreal Council of Social Agencies, which served Protestant charities; (2) the Federation of Catholic Charities, later known as the Federation of Catholic Community Services; and (3) the Federation of Jewish Philanthropies, later called Allied Jewish Community Services.[35]

These English-speaking federations were recognized as being methodical, efficient, and advanced,[36] but even they could not cope with the demands placed on them by the Great Depression of the 1930s. To give them additional help, the provincial government began subsidizing their financial assistance programs under the terms of the Public Charities Act, thereby treating them as "institutions without walls."[37] This was the beginning of a slow but growing process of government intervention in Montreal's social services for the English speaking.

31. Quebec, *Statutes* (1921), Ch. 79.

32. Esdras Minville, *Labour Legislation and Social Services, A Study Prepared for the Royal Commission on Dominion-Provincial Relations* (Ottawa: King's Printer, 1939), p. 55.

33. See Dupont, *Les relations*, pp. 73–108.

34. For a good account of these agencies see Terry Copp, *The Anatomy of Poverty: The Condition of the Working Class in Montreal, 1897–1929* (Toronto: McClelland and Stewart, 1974), Ch. 7. Also see Claude Larivière, *Crise economique et controle social: le cas de Montréal (1929–1937)* (Montreal: Editions Cooperatives Albert St. Martin, 1977), pp. 117–19, 213–22.

35. Quebec, *Report of the Commission of Inquiry on Health and Social Services* (Quebec: 1967–72), vol. 6, pp. 45–46.

36. Minville, *Labour Legislation and Social Services*, pp. 62–64.

37. Quebec, *Report on Public Assistance*, p. 33.

The influence of the religious orders retarded the development of lay social structures within Montreal's French-speaking community. The first lay agency, the *Bureau d'assistance aux familles* (later the *Société de service social aux familles*) was not founded until 1938. Prior to that the church had established various social service agencies in most of its dioceses to take advantage of government assistance to social service agencies. In Montreal these agencies were not federated until 1933, with the establishment of the *Féderation des oeuvres de charité canadienne-françaises*. Its activities were restricted to fundraising, and coordination was carried out by a parallel organization known as *Conseil des oeuvres de Montréal* (later the *Conseil de développement social du Montréal métropolitain*).[38]

At the outbreak of World War II Montreal had four separate federations of social service agencies. The English agencies of all faiths were now being coordinated by the Montreal Council of Social Agencies. Fundraising for Protestant and nonsectarian charities was carried out by a nominally separate group under the aegis of the Red Feather organization. Generally, each linguistic or religious group was allowed to go its own way. Because of their greater resources and lesser demand, the English-speaking agencies were able to provide an exceedingly high level of service. French-speaking agencies undoubtedly lagged behind, because their system of social service delivery was confused, splintered, and poorly coordinated.[39] Their church-dominated institutions seemed unable to cope with the complex social problems of the industrial age.

The Welfare State Comes to Quebec

Although a separate provincial Department of Social Welfare was first established in 1944, most aspects of social service remained under the jurisdiction of either the provincial secretary or the minister of health until 1957. In that year the department took responsibility for overseeing orphanages, nurseries, and social service agencies,[40] and the City of Montreal assumed a much more active role in social services. The city's welfare department was recognized as a public charitable institution with authority to grant financial assistance and to place children and sick and aged adults in residential institutions.

It now appeared that the Montreal municipal government was destined to replace the church in the field of social services. The trend was confirmed in 1959, when the city gained exclusive authority to administer financial assistance in its territory. It also took over the placement of all French-speaking residents requiring residential social

38. Quebec, *Report on Health and Social Services*, vol. 6, p. 46.
39. Minville, *Labour Legislation and Social Services*, pp. 62–64.
40. Quebec, *Report on Public Assistance*, p. 34.

assistance. Under the agreement, French social service agencies agreed to restrict themselves to prevention and rehabilitation. English agencies continued as before, except that they no longer granted any direct financial aid.[41]

This structurally shaky system came under great strain in the early 1960s. In 1959 Quebec signed a federal-provincial agreement providing for 50 percent federal funding of a general public assistance scheme for people without unemployment insurance who were unable to find work. "For the first time in the history of social security in the Province of Quebec, a social measure was adopted which, whatever may have been the legislator's intention, considered indigence, irrespective of the causes, as a factual situation justifying assistance by the State."[42] Previously there had been no uniform scheme of general assistance throughout the province, and social service agencies and municipal governments had chosen their recipients via a detailed and often humiliating series of means tests, which varied throughout the province.

Because the new scheme fell under the Public Charities Act, municipalities and social service agencies were each supposed to contribute. Costs grew dramatically due to high unemployment and the fact that the new scheme reduced the inhibitions of many who had previously been reluctant to apply for public assistance. Only the provincial government had adequate funds to pay its share. In May 1960, immediately before the provincial election, the requirement that social service agencies and municipalities contribute to the scheme was abolished.[43]

Faced with spiralling costs, the provincial Department of Social Welfare soon placed rigid financial controls on social service agencies and on those municipalities dispensing public assistance. This meant a further decline in the independence of the agencies. Moreover, the municipal social welfare departments became little more than funnels for federal and provincial funds. In fact, the provincial government soon established its own welfare offices throughout the province, except in Montreal. The provincial takeover also ended the unfortunate practices in some municipalities (including certain Montreal suburbs) of trying to reduce the number of resident indigents whom they might have to help support. Some municipalities actually even paid moving expenses of indigents whom they persuaded to relocate in another municipality.[44]

By the mid-1960s Quebec's social services were a tangled mess,

41. Ibid., p. 35.
42. Ibid., p. 55.
43. Ibid., p. 36.
44. Ibid., p. 154.

with hundreds of nominally private and independent institutions administering dozens of provincial programs under varying levels of central control. In Montreal the two linguistic groups had each developed their own completely self-contained systems for the delivery of personal services, and the religious groups within the English sector also still had considerable independence. Although rationalization and coordination throughout the province were obviously needed, it was not at all clear how this could be brought about, particularly in an area so diverse and heavily populated as metropolitan Montreal. By 1971 the Montreal Council of Social Agencies and the *Conseil de développement social du Montréal métropolitain* were beginning to pool their resources,[45] but from the viewpoint of the government, this was undoubtedly many years too late.

Local Institutions Perpetuate Differences

Prior to the 1960s there was no real political threat to the privileged social and economic position of English-speaking Montreal. There were no serious attempts to improve the position of the French language in business, and consequently English remained dominant. In the nineteenth century English representation in the governments of the Province of Quebec and the City of Montreal was quite substantial. Although this position eroded rapidly in the early twentieth century, the English seemed to have little cause for concern. Their unchallenged economic importance to both the province and the city gave English-Canadian businessmen many opportunities to influence French-Canadian government leaders concerned with jobs and economic growth. Successive provincial governments did nothing to prevent the emergence of an English network of suburban municipalities, schools, and social service agencies that in many ways provided services far superior to those received by French Canadians.

Chapter 3 described how large numbers of middle-class English-speaking people left the city for the independent suburbs from 1881 to 1921. Among other things, this migration allowed them to control land-use planning and policing within their own communities. This chapter shows how the structure of the educational and social service systems enabled members of the English-speaking economic and social elite (including those living in the city itself) to control the institutions that provided these important services to English-speaking citizens. This applies even to English-speaking Roman Catholics: although officially they were part of the predominately French Catholic

45. See *Report of the Activities of the Montreal Council of Social Agencies and Le Conseil de développement social du Montréal métropolitain* (Montreal: 1972).

school board, the English-language schools had substantial administrative independence. As far as social services were concerned, there was a distinct network of institutions for both English-speaking Catholics and Jews.

Because educational and social service institutions were established on the basis of religion, not language, and both French and English suburbs emerged, Montreal's local institutions reflected more than a single French-English cleavage. Nevertheless, the language division was crucial. Furthermore, it is highly significant that the structure of these institutions enabled a very large proportion of French and English Canadians to manage their local affairs with little reference to or contact with the other linguistic group.

The institutional cooperation and contact that occurred across religious barriers was mostly within the same linguistic group rather than between linguistic groups. Thus, English-speaking Catholics in the jurisdiction of the Montreal Catholic School Commission designed their system along the lines of the "high school" model used by English Protestants rather than copying the French system of vocational secondary schools and private classical colleges. Another example is the English-Catholic and Jewish social service agencies and their development of cooperative mechanisms with English secular institutions rather than with French-Catholic institutions.

No one wished to upset the traditional educational and social service arrangements prior to the late 1960s, but there were some serious attempts to alter municipal structures. Nevertheless, the creation of the Montreal Metropolitan Commission, and then the Montreal Metropolitan Corporation, had no effect on municipal boundaries. These bodies' limited functions related exclusively to what Oliver Williams has called "system maintenance" functions.[46] They were concerned above all with financial stability and in a limited way with promoting large-scale regional planning. Thus, for example, they imposed restrictions on capital borrowing and began the development of urban expressways. Both these activities encouraged rather than hindered the growth of independent suburbs.

Despite some western suburbs on the Island of Montreal being more than 90 percent English speaking and some eastern suburbs, more than 90 percent French speaking, the island has never had any formal governmental policy to encourage territorial linguistic segregation. The provincial government, in fact, has never attempted to subdivide any of its territory for linguistic purposes. Prior to 1974 the French and English effectively had the same legal status everywhere

---

46. Oliver P. Williams, "Life-Style Values and Political Decentralization in Metropolitan Areas," in *Community Politics: A Behavioural Approach*, ed. Terry N. Clark et al. (London: Collier-Macmillan, 1971), p. 59.

in Quebec, although there were remarkably few laws and regulations that governed language use. A large number of municipalities in the province were exempted from general requirements to issue official notices and bylaws in both languages,[47] but such minor occurrences of official unilingualism were scarcely noticeable to the average citizen and were never the subject of political controversy.

As an alternative to having a territorial language policy, prior to the 1960s provincial government policy encouraged the emergence of separate networks of important social institutions. Most notable in this regard was the school system. Despite the constitutional differentiation of the public school systems on a denominational basis, language (i.e., English and French) became the most significant cleavage line that determined how public education was organized. Social service institutions were also organized on a linguistic basis, but here addition of the separate Jewish sector to the English-Catholic and English-secular sectors emphasized the heterogeneity of Montreal's English-speaking population. Finally, the fact that many English- and French-speaking Montrealers lived in linguistically homogeneous municipalities, subject to relatively little outside control, reinforced the pattern of institutional segregation. This lasted until Quebec's Quiet Revolution, a series of events that severely strained the long-standing pattern of accommodation.

47. Quebec, *The Position of the French Language in Quebec: Report of the Commission of Inquiry* (Quebec: Quebec Official Publisher, 1972), vol. 1, pp. 238–39.

II

The Quiet Revolution

5

Quebec Politics and the Politicization of Language, 1960–1981

This chapter deals with Quebec's political environment in the 1960s and 1970s,[1] two decades of massive political and social change in Canada's only French-speaking province. At the beginning of the 1960s the vision of an independent French-speaking state on the shores of the St. Lawrence was the dream of only a handful of clerical nationalists. By the end of the 1970s Quebec's provincial government was controlled by a party dedicated to converting the province into a sovereign nation. In the early 1960s English-speaking people in western Montreal could live and work using only English almost as easily as English-speaking people in Toronto could. But in 1977 a provincial statute was passed that, among many other things, outlawed for most businesses the display of public signs written in English.

While these dramatic political changes were taking place, the provincial civil service in Quebec City was changing from a patronage-ridden collection of clerks, engineers, and lawyers to a modern government bureaucracy complete with economists, planners, and well-trained managers. In numbers alone, the civil service expanded from 21,000 to 66,000 between 1959 and 1979. In the same period the total provincial budget went up from $546 million to $13 billion.[2] This meant to people living in Montreal that the provincial government had acquired the ability to intervene in hundreds of matters previously controlled privately or by autonomous local institutions.

Changes in Montreal's municipal, educational, and social service systems cannot be studied without reference to political and governmental changes at the provincial level. Local government structures are profoundly influenced by social and political change, which is

1. For details concerning the complex evolution of political parties in Quebec, see the appendix.

2. Civil service figures for 1959 from J. E. Hodgetts and O. P. Dwivedi, *Provincial Governments as Employers* (Montreal: McGill-Queen's University Press, 1974), p. 188; 1979 figures come from Canada, Statistics Canada, *Provincial Government Employment* (January–March 1979), Cat. 72–007, p. 11. Expenditure figures are from Quebec, *Annuaire Statistique 1959*, p. 253, and Quebec, *Comptes publiques, année financière terminée le 31 mars 1979*, p. 17.

probably true in any society—even one like the United States, where features of local government are often entrenched in state constitutions. But it is especially true of a political system such as Quebec's, where a parliamentary majority in the provincial legislature is legally capable of changing the organization of local government as it sees fit.

As a result of Quebec's Quiet Revolution in the 1960s, many provincial politicians and bureaucrats committed themselves, consciously or unconsciously, to dismantling Montreal's dual French-English system of local institutions. But the depth and continuing importance of the linguistic cleavage proved these institutions much more resistant to change than the proponents of reform originally assumed.

The Quiet Revolution

The fundamental causes of the Quiet Revolution are rooted in the industrialization of Quebec in the late nineteenth and early twentieth centuries. This was a time of explosive growth in Canada as a whole, and Quebec, despite its apparent economic backwardness, was an equal participant. New investment in resource exploitation and manufacturing industries was accompanied by rapid urbanization. In 1870 only 19.5 percent of Quebec's population lived in incorporated municipalities with populations of more than 1000. By 1915 the figure was 49.6 percent.[3] Between 1871 and 1921 the population of the Island of Montreal increased from 144,000 to 724,000.[4]

Although French Canadians have always been less inclined to live in urban areas than other Quebec residents,[5] in this period of urbanization a great many French Canadians left their traditional rural homes. One principal reason was the very high rural birth rate and the lack of good new agricultural land. Migration of its surplus rural population to jobs in the United States posed a great threat to French-Canadian society. Between 1851 and 1931 about 700,000 French Canadians left their native province.[6] Despite their obvious preference for an agricultural economy, the leaders of Quebec's Roman Catholic church eventually realized that the church would be better off if French Canadians could find factory work in Quebec rather than in Massachusetts. Consequently, by the early twentieth century church leaders became reconciled to Quebec's industrial development.[7]

3. William F. Ryan, *The Clergy and Economic Growth in Quebec (1896–1914)* (Quebec: Les Presses de l'Université Laval, 1966), pp. 36–37.

4. See Table 1.

5. Kenneth McRoberts and Dale Posgate, *Quebec: Social Change and Political Crisis,* rev. ed. (Toronto: McClelland and Stewart, 1980), p. 34.

6. Ibid., p. 28.

7. This is the theme of Ryan's book *The Clergy and Economic Growth.*

If Quebec's greatest period of industrialization and urbanization was before World War I and these changes were the root cause of the Quiet Revolution of the 1960s, why was there a 50-year lag? The basic answer is that the church acted to avoid the usual effects of industrialization and urbanization. When Quebec's displaced agricultural population flocked to the factories and cities, the Roman Catholic church came with them. Catholic trade unions flourished, and externally controlled secular trade unions were kept out. The Catholic school system was perpetuated, despite its limited ability to prepare pupils for skilled work or management. Social services in the city remained strictly a matter for local priests and volunteer organizations. These distinct Catholic institutions perpetuated the separation and isolation of the two linguistic communities in Montreal and helped maintain the cultural barrier between French-speaking Quebec and North America as a whole.

The most commonly accepted interpretation of the Quiet Revolution's immediate causes is that the network of Catholic schools, social services, and trade unions grew too large and complex for the clergy to operate alone.[8] In the post-1945 period increasing numbers of well-educated lay people—many trained outside Quebec—were taking over important positions in Catholic institutions. Largely as a result of training in the social sciences, this growing new section of the French-Canadian middle class found the traditional roles of church and government in Quebec society unacceptable.

As long as the party in power respected the church's autonomy and provided subsidies for its schools and social services, the Catholic hierarchy ignored questions of political morality and raised few serious questions about foreign domination of Quebec's economy. In contrast, the emerging new French-Canadian middle class became concerned with both these issues. While generally remaining loyal Catholics, they looked to the provincial government of Quebec as the most appropriate institution to implement new policies to control and modernize Quebec's educational and social service systems and ultimately to gain control of its economy. Accordingly, they opposed the *Union nationale* government of Maurice Duplessis, seeing it as catering only to the patronage concerns of rural Quebec and to outdated emotions of traditional French-Canadian nationalism.

French-Canadian trade unionists, journalists, and intellectuals vigorously attacked the Duplessis government throughout the 1940s and 1950s,[9] with little success in electoral terms. Duplessis remained

8. This viewpoint has best been expressed by Herbert Guindon. See especially his "Social Unrest, Social Class, and Quebec's Bureaucratic Revolution," *Queen's Quarterly*, vol. 71 (1964): 150–62.

9. Most of their complaints can be found in Pierre Elliott Trudeau, ed., *The Asbestos Strike*, trans. James Boake (Toronto: James Lewis and Samuel, 1974). Also see Gérard Dion and Louis O'Neill, *Le Chrétien et les élections* (Montreal: Editions de l'Homme, 1960).

premier until he died in 1959. His *Union nationale* successor, Paul Sauvé, seemed intent on changing his party's traditional policies, but in early 1960 he also died suddenly. In the provincial election of June 1960 a badly shaken *Union nationale* was defeated by the provincial Liberal party led by Jean Lesage. Although much of the groundwork had been laid before he came to power, Lesage's election is usually considered the beginning of what came to be known as the Quiet Revolution.

The Quiet Revolution marked the rise to power of Quebec's new, modernizing middle class. Above all, this group was committed to reforming Quebec's political system so that it reflected their needs and aspirations rather than those of the clergy, small businessmen, farmers, and country lawyers. This was no revolution in a Marxist sense but rather a series of adjustments in the governmental super-structure, adapting it to the economic and social change that for the most part had already taken place.[10]

English Canada Responds

English-speaking Montrealers were among the most fervent pro-ponents of the new Lesage government. They supported its attempts to eliminate patronage and transform the provincial civil service into a more efficient and capable bureaucracy. In short, the Lesage govern-ment seemed to be transforming Quebec's political system so that it would actually be better suited to traditional Anglo-Saxon values and sensibilities. Paradoxically, this very tendency toward convergence in the two groups' values eventually posed the greatest threat to English-speaking economic dominance. French-speaking Quebeckers were now eager to participate in all aspects of Quebec society and no longer saw any legitimacy in their virtually systematic exclusion from top positions in the private sector. The stage was set for overt social con-flict based on language differences.

Initially at least, Canadians outside Quebec saw the Quiet Revo-lution as an encouraging sign. Many considered it an indication that Quebec's French-speaking majority finally had enough self-confidence to emerge from its defensive, clerical nationalism and to pursue poli-cies long since adopted elsewhere. Such policies included the nation-alization of Quebec's electricity suppliers in 1963 and the creation of a secular Department of Education in 1964.[11] Even the increasing de-mands for more provincial power were not necessarily seen as a threat

10. Denis Monière, *Ideologies in Quebec: The Historical Development*, trans. Richard Howard (Toronto: University of Toronto Press, 1981), p. 251.

11. For contemporary justification of these policies see Paul Sauriol, *The Nation-alization of Electric Power*, trans. Kina Buchanan (Montreal: Harvest House, 1962), and Paul Gérin-Lajoie, *Pourquoi le Bill 60* (Montreal: Editions du Jour, 1963).

but as further evidence that Quebec's French Canadians were finally sufficiently comfortable within Canadian federalism that they could take initiatives themselves rather than repeatedly reacting in a defensive way to proposals from English Canada. Some believed that this new French-Canadian self-confidence would ultimately lead to a more united Canada. But this line of thinking neglected the fact that Quebec is a well-defined territory with its own governmental apparatus. Instead of furthering integration into the larger Canadian community, demands for more provincial power eventually led to the demand for outright separation.

Revolutionary Nationalism

With the Liberals firmly in power and the Quiet Revolution clearly underway, a brand of nationalism emerged that saw little virtue in simply improving the position of Quebec's new middle class or in increasing the skills of Quebec's provincial bureaucracy. This new brand of nationalism was initially associated with a group of violent young extremists calling themselves the *Front de Libération du Québec* (FLQ). Their early activities, beginning in 1963, consisted of a series of bombings directed at various federal government and English institutions in Montreal. After a sporadic existence throughout the 1960s, the FLQ attained worldwide prominence in 1970 when some of its members kidnapped both the British trade commissioner in Montreal and a prominent provincial cabinet minister.[12] As a result of a massive army and police operation following the assassination of the minister, the FLQ was eliminated. Nevertheless, throughout the 1960s the terrorist threat was never far from the consciousness of most Montrealers, particularly the English speakers.

The strength of the FLQ, such as it was, lay in bombs—terrorism, not political theory. The theory was provided by a militantly socialist and nationalist periodical called *Parti Pris*. Contributors to *Parti Pris* saw Montreal as the bridgehead city for the English and American colonization of Quebec.[13] They saw Quebec as a North American Algeria and Montreal as its Algiers. This view was radically different from the conventional thesis of the Quiet Revolution, that is, that French Canadians had only themselves to blame for their political and eco-

12. The "October Crisis" has been extensively described and analyzed. The most useful book is Denis Smith, *Bleeding Hearts . . . Bleeding Country* (Edmonton: Hurtig, 1971).

13. The work of the *Parti Pris* writers is described in Malcolm Reid, *The Shouting Signpainters: A Literary and Political Account of Quebec Revolutionary Nationalism* (Toronto: McClelland and Stewart, 1972), and in Robert Major, *Parti Pris, idéologie et littérature* (Montreal: Hurtabise HMH, 1979).

nomic backwardness.[14] The *Parti Pris* group wrote a number of novels that strikingly portrayed the colonized status of the French-speaking Montrealer. One of their number, Pierre Maheu, wrote an article claiming that nobody can feel at home in Montreal: it is "the city of the others." French Canadians, though in the majority, do not own or control the city's most important economic institutions, he wrote, and English Canadians, on the other hand, are constantly aware that they belong to a privileged, threatened minority whose time is coming to an end.[15]

Provincial Politics in Turmoil, 1966–1970

By 1966 the possibility of a separate, independent Quebec had emerged as a legitimate political option. There were two separatist parties in the 1966 provincial election. The *Rassemblement pour l'indépendance nationale* (RIN) used the *Parti Pris* kind of analysis to advocate an independent, socialist Quebec, and another group, the *Ralliement national* (RN), argued for independence on more conservative grounds. Between them these two parties won 9 percent of the popular vote.

The Liberal Party and the *Union nationale* remained as the major contestants in provincial politics. The Liberals, still led by Jean Lesage, simply asked for a mandate to continue the Quiet Revolution and to consolidate its gains. The new leader of the *Union nationale* was Daniel Johnson, who, despite his name, was far more French than Irish. He had managed to resurrect the party of Duplessis by reflecting rural unease with the speed of social change in Quebec. While the separatist parties struggled on the extremes of the political spectrum and the Liberals confidently prepared for their next mandate, Johnson carefully organized his forces in those constituencies, mainly rural, that he thought he could win.

In the final analysis, Johnson did surprisingly well. In addition to dozens of rural successes, he also captured six east-end Montreal constituencies—just enough to give him a three-seat majority in the 108-member provincial legislature. Most *Union nationale* victories in Montreal were made possible by the fact that the separatist parties— particularly the left-wing RIN—drew enough votes from the Liberals to allow Johnson's candidates to win a small plurality. In this paradoxical way the left-wing separatists, who wanted even more change than had come about under the Liberals, facilitated the victory of a party committed to slowing the pace of the Quiet Revolution.

14. For the best-known expression of this viewpoint, see Pierre Elliott Trudeau, *Federalism and the French Canadians* (Toronto: Macmillan, 1968).

15. Pierre Maheu, "Montréal, la ville des autres," in *Parti Pris, Les Québécois Cahiers libres 99–100* (Paris: François Maspero, 1967), p. 151, (author's trans.).

Between 1966 and 1970 there were great changes in Quebec's political landscape. In 1968 Premier Johnson died and was replaced by Premier Jean-Jacques Bertrand. The Quebec branch of the Social Credit Party, which had made major breakthroughs in federal politics during the early 1960s as a reaction against rural and small-town economic stagnation, decided to enter provincial politics to capitalize on growing disillusionment with the *Union nationale*, a party that, especially under Bertrand, seemed capable of satisfying no one.

The most important political event in this period was the formation of the *Parti québécois* (PQ) in 1968. René Lévesque, one of Lesage's most important former ministers, left the Liberal party and created the new broadly based party, committed to Quebec's independence. The RIN and the RN disbanded, and their members were absorbed by the PQ, thus channelling virtually all elements of the growing independence movement into one political force.[16]

Montreal's Language Groups

Quebec's new nationalism of the 1960s had many effects, not the least being that it changed the way French-speaking residents of Quebec referred to themselves. Before the 1960s the term "French Canadian" was most commonly used. Those who believed fervently in the protection and advancement of the French language and culture were known as "French-Canadian nationalists." When the new brand of nationalist began to emphasize that their true homeland was the territory of Quebec, and not all of Canada, the term "Québécois" became increasingly popular. The label "French Canadian" came to be associated primarily with folkloric, submissive characteristics of the past.

The difficulty with the term "Québécois" is its inherent ambiguity. Does it mean a person of French ethnic origin whose family has lived in Quebec for many generations? Or does it refer to any resident of Quebec, even to those who speak no French? In reality, of course, being Québécois is a state of mind. Many French-speaking residents of Quebec who still believe in the federal connection use the term to show that they love Quebec as much as those who believe in Quebec's independence.[17] Many English-speaking people use the term to show that, as loyal citizens of Quebec, they are as committed to the pro-

16. John Saywell, *The Rise of the Parti Québécois* (Toronto: University of Toronto Press, 1977).

17. Hence the slogan "Mon non est Québécois," used by the federalist forces in the 1980 referendum campaign on Quebec's constitutional future. It means "My No is Québécois." The slogan is also a pun. The other meaning is "My name (nom) is Québécois."

vince as anybody else.[18] They dislike the term "English Canadian" because it suggests a lingering connection with England and does not signify any attachment to Quebec.[19]

One solution to the problem of terminology is the use of such terms as "English speaker" or "French speaker." But apart from their clumsiness, these terms denote little more than the ability to speak the language in question. Thus, a bilingual person is both a French speaker and an English speaker. Fortunately, there are two French words that, at least as used in Quebec, imply a large degree of mutual exclusiveness and are appropriate to describe members of Quebec's two major linguistic groups. These words are *francophone* and *anglophone*. They are now part of general English usage in Quebec and are slowly coming to be more commonly used in other parts of Canada. A francophone is a person who is most comfortable speaking French, and an anglophone is a person most comfortable speaking English.

In 1971 the Canadian decennial census collected data that for the first time came close to measuring the size of the francophone and anglophone groups, using answers to the question, "Which language do you speak most often in the home?"[20] Questions about ethnic origin and mother tongue were still asked, as in many previous censuses, but the responses to these questions are less useful in determining the numbers of people who are currently attached to one language group or the other.

Francophones: A Homogeneous Ethnic Group

It is still generally accurate to refer to Quebec's francophones as an ethnic group, because so few post-Conquest immigrants to Quebec have adopted the French language. In Quebec, there is virtually no difference in number between the people who are of French ethnic origin and those who use French regularly in the home (see Table 3). Census figures for 1971 confirmed that, both in metropolitan Montreal and in Quebec as a whole, over 90 percent of people who used French regularly in the home were also of French ethnic origin.[21]

Historically, this French group has been united by a common religion: the Roman Catholic church has played an inestimable role in preserving Quebec's French culture. Until recently at least, the

18. The term "Quebecker" is also used, in both English and French, to refer to an English-speaking resident of Quebec. To use this term in French implies that a Quebecker cannot be a real Québécois; to use it in English can imply a desire on the part of the user to assert the distinct identity of English speakers.
19. See Alain Médam, *Montréal Interdite* (Paris: Presses Universitaires de France, 1978), pp. 134–35.
20. Canada, Statistics Canada, *1971 Census of Canada.*
21. Ibid., Cat. 92–736.

Table 3– Population Characteristics in Selected Areas, 1971 and 1981

	Canada		Quebec		CMA[a] Montreal		Island of Montreal		City of Montreal	
	1971	1981	1971	1981	1971	1981	1971	1981	1971	1981
					(total population in thousands)					1019[f]
	21.568	24.343	6028	6438	2743	2828	1959	1760	1214	
					(percentage distribution)					
British/English										
ethnic origin[b]	44.6	43.5	10.6	7.8	16.0	11.8	17.0	13.8	10.9	9.0
mother tongue[c]	60.2	61.3	13.1	11.0	21.7	18.3	23.7	22.3	15.2	14.5
home language[d]	67.0	68.2	14.7	12.7	24.7	21.9	27.4	27.0	18.6	18.2
French										
ethnic origin	28.7	28.9	79.0	81.8	64.3	67.7	59.0	58.9	64.2	65.0
mother tongue	26.9	25.7	80.8	82.4	66.3	68.3	61.2	59.7	67.1	66.4
home language	25.7	24.6	80.9	82.5	66.3	68.6	61.2	60.0	67.5	67.2
Others[e]										
ethnic origin	26.7	27.6	10.4	10.4	20.7	20.5	24.0	27.3	24.9	26.0
mother tongue	12.9	13.0	6.1	6.6	12.0	13.3	15.1	18.0	17.7	19.1
home language	7.3	7.2	4.4	4.8	8.8	9.4	11.4	13.0	13.9	14.6

Source: Prepared from data found in Canada, 1971 Census, Cats. 92–723, 92–725, 92–725, 92–726 and Canada, 1981 Census, Cats. 95–942, 95–943 (vol. 3 —Profile Series B).

[a]Census metropolitan area, as defined by Statistics Canada.

[b]Ethnic origin was determined by responses to the following questions. 1971: "To what ethnic or cultural group did you or your ancestor (on the male side) belong on coming to this continent?" 1981: "To what ethnic or cultural group did your ancestors belong on first coming to this continent?" (1981 percentage excluded those reporting multiple ethnic origins.)

[c]Mother tongue refers to the language a person first learned in childhood and still understood. In the case of infants this term refers to the language most often spoken at home.

[d]Home language was determined by responses to the question, "Which language do you speak most often in the home?"

[e]In 1971 the largest of the "other" ethnic groups in CMA Montreal were Italians (160,605) and Jews (114,220). All other ethnic groups comprised fewer than 50,000 persons.

[f]Includes Pointe-aux-Trembles and Saint-Jean-de-Dieu, annexed by Montreal in 1980 and 1982, respectively.

influence of the church was so pervasive that it has been impossible to discuss French-Canadian society without also considering the church. In short, part of being a French Canadian involved being a Roman Catholic. Any attempt to isolate the influence of language, culture, religion, and nationality on the ethnic identity of Quebec francophones would be fruitless. All are inextricably intertwined.

A clear operational definition of "ethnic group" is not easy to devise. After a thorough study of sociological and anthropological approaches to ethnicity, Wsevolod W. Isajiw developed what he calls a "composite" definition, including both objective and subjective elements. For Isajiw, an ethnic group is "a group or category of persons who have common ancestral origin and the same cultural traits, who have a sense of peoplehood and the *Gemeinschaft* type of relations, who are of immigrant background and who have either minority or majority status within a larger society."[22] Under these criteria, Quebec's francophones have constituted one of the world's best examples of a clearly delineated ethnic group, but now the situation is changing. Recent government policies have encouraged immigration from French-speaking countries and have tried to ensure that non-French immigrants eventually become francophones. If successful, these policies could have a dramatic effect on the relationship between ethnicity and the use of French.

Anglophones: Only a Language Group

Quebec's anglophones are another matter altogether. Most of the early residents were Scottish, and many settled in rural areas south and west of Montreal. In the nineteenth and early twentieth centuries, however, the anglophone element became much more diversified ethnically and their presence in rural areas dwindled.[23] In fact, by 1971 nearly 75 percent of them were living in metropolitan Montreal. J. R. Mallory has pointed out some useful distinctions concerning anglophones living in Montreal.[24] He believes there is a substantial difference in outlook between those middle- and upper-class anglophones whose families are deeply rooted in Quebec and those who simply find themselves in the province for a few years as part of a business or professional career that requires constant mobility. Mallory suggested that many of the former group (which includes most of Montreal's

22. "Definitions of Ethnicity," *Ethnicity*, vol. 1 (1974): 118.
23. See Gary Caldwell, *A Demographic Profile of the English-speaking Population of Quebec, 1921–1971* (Quebec: International Centre for Research on Bilingualism, 1974).
24. See his "English Speaking Quebecers in a Separate Quebec," in *One Country or Two?* ed. R. M. Burns (Montreal: McGill-Queen's University Press, 1971), pp. 121–38.

Jews) have already become bilingual and would be likely to stay in Quebec even if francophone nationalist pressure increases. Members of the more mobile group, however, see no reason to become bilingual, are less tolerant of Quebec's idiosyncrasies, and are likely to be soon replaced by Quebec's emerging francophone middle class.

Mallory's third category includes migrants from the maritime provinces. Historically, Montreal has been the Canadian metropolitan center for the maritimes, but with the increasing importance of French in Montreal, these migrants now see Toronto as a more attractive magnet. Mallory's final category consists of recent immigrants, mainly Italians and other southern Europeans, who have come to Montreal since 1945 and who have been assimilated into the English group. The growing size of this group has been at the heart of the recent debate about language policy in Quebec.

Montreal's anglophones clearly do not constitute an ethnic group, at least not in the same sense that francophones do. For one thing, they are divided by religion. The separate English Catholic and Protestant networks of educational and social service institutions are ample testimony to this. Montreal's Jews have, of course, been largely educated in Protestant schools, but they have often been isolated from other anglophones in many important ways. In 1971, 4.2 percent of the population of metropolitan Montreal claimed "Jewish" as their ethnic origin.[25] Life in Montreal's Jewish areas has been so unique and distinctive that it has given birth to its own rich literature. The works of Mordecai Richler are the best-known examples.[26]

Prior to recent political attacks by Quebec nationalists, there had been little unity among Montreal anglophones. It would be clearly inaccurate to call anglophones an "ethnic group," although there is some evidence that a degree of political unity is now slowly developing. The extent to which anglophones have recently come to share common political interests as a self-conscious minority is considered throughout this book.

"Others": French or English?

Members of Montreal's "other" ethnic groups have been more carefully studied than those whose origins are in the British Isles, particularly the Italians. In 1971, 5.6 percent of metropolitan Montreal's residents were of Italian ethnic origin.[27] After the French and British they were the largest group. The Italians are also notable as the group that was most likely to send their children to French schools

25. Canada, *1971 Census*, Cat. 92–723.
26. See especially Richler's *The Apprenticeship of Duddy Kravitz* (Toronto: McClelland and Stewart, 1969). The novel was first published in 1959.
27. Canada, *1971 Census*, Cat. 92–723.

voluntarily. This phenomenon was more pronounced some 40 years ago, when there were far fewer pupils in the school system and just under half were going to French schools. By 1962–63, according to a study done for the federal Royal Commission on Bilingualism and Biculturalism, 25 percent of Italian-Canadian parents were sending their children to French-language schools.

The most common reason Italian parents gave for preferring French schools was that they were closer than English schools. The most common reasons Italian parents gave for preferring English schools were that English education would facilitate moving to other parts of Canada and would make it easier for their children to get jobs. In general, Italians considered English to be more useful for advancement at the place of work.[28]

The most important feature of the Italian community, however, is that most of its members have simply not had time to be assimilated into either major language group. In 1961, for example, 62 percent of the people of Italian origin in metropolitan Montreal were born outside Canada.[29] Moreover, census figures for 1971 show that almost 70 percent of people of Italian origin were still using Italian more than any other language in their homes.[30] Thus, in many respects the linguistic future of the Italian population is still uncertain.

In the early 1970s Paul Cappon conducted an exhaustive study[31] of personal relationships between immigrants and francophones in Montreal by observing patterns of interaction in small, controlled discussion groups. He concluded that conflict between francophones and immigrants was of the type Lewis Coser would call "non-real."[32] It was non-real because francophones often used immigrants as scapegoats for the anglophones, who, because of their economic dominance, were the real object of francophone hostility.[33] Immigrants were more likely to be targets for this hostility because they usually live and work in much closer proximity to francophones than anglophones do. In these circumstances it is hardly surprising that many immigrants tended to identify with anglophones.

Table 3 presents the various types of available ethnic and lin-

28. Jeremy Boissevain, *The Italians of Montreal*, Study No. 7 of the Royal Commission on Bilingualism and Biculturalism (Ottawa: Information Canada, 1970), pp. 37–39.

29. Ibid., p. 2.

30. Calculated from Canada, *1971 Census*, Cats. 92–723, 92–726.

31. *Conflit entre les néo-canadiens et les francophones* (Quebec: Les Presses de l'Université Laval, 1974).

32. Lewis Coser, *The Function of Social Conflict* (Glencoe, Ill.: Free Press, 1957), p. 49.

33. Cappon, *Conflit*, pp. 127–29.

guistic data for Canada, Quebec, and three different geographical versions of Montreal. It shows that, for Canada as a whole, many more people use the English language on a regular basis than there are people of British ethnic origin. In contrast, slightly fewer use French than there are people of French ethnic origin. This reflects the weak position of the French language outside Quebec.

Within Quebec the number of people who speak French is slightly greater than the number who are French by ethnic origin. What is notable about the figures for Quebec, however, is that even in this province, the English language has more drawing power than the French. This is particularly evident in metropolitan Montreal. For example, the 1981 figures showed that 67.7 percent of the people in metropolitan Montreal are of French ethnic origin, and 68.6 percent use the French language most often in the home. The comparable figures for British ethnic origin and use of the English language in the home are 11.8 percent and 21.9 percent, respectively. This clearly suggests that a much higher proportion of people with "other" ethnic origins have adopted English as their usual language than would be expected if the "others" were to split according to the prevailing French-English proportions.

These figures further suggest that if the "others" group continues to grow, as it has constantly since 1871, there could be a substantial decline in the proportions using the French language in metropolitan Montreal. This assumption has caused a good deal of debate among Quebec demographers and is one of the main motivations behind the introduction of controversial legislation to protect and encourage the use of the French language in Quebec.[34] The implications of the legislation are discussed later in this chapter.

Montreal: Bilingual City?

Table 4 shows the extent to which Canadians, Quebeckers, and Montrealers were capable in 1971 of speaking the country's two official languages. The most notable feature of these data is the relatively high degree of bilingualism found in Montreal. More than one-third of Montreal's population could converse in both official languages. It should be noted, however, that those who used French in the home (and did not have English as a mother tongue) were more likely to be

34. See Jacques Henripin, "Quebec and the Demographic Dilemma of French-Canadian Society," in *Quebec: Society and Politics,* ed. Dale C. Thomson (Toronto: McClelland and Stewart, 1973), pp. 155–66; H. Charbonneau, J. Henripin, and J. Legaré, "L'avenir demographique des francophones au Quebec et a Montréal en l'absence de politiques adéquates," *Revue de géographie de Montréal,* vol. 24 (1970): 199–202; and Quebec, *The Position of the French Language in Quebec: Report of the Commission of Inquiry* (Quebec: Quebec Official Publisher, 1972), vol. 3, pp. 168–84.

Table 4– *Ability to Speak Official Languages in Selected Areas by Home Language, 1971*

Home Language	Ability to Speak Official Language				
	ENGLISH ONLY (%)	FRENCH ONLY (%)	ENGLISH AND FRENCH (%)	NEITHER (%)	NUMBER[a] (000s)
Canada					
English	94.9	—	5.1	—	14,099
French	—	70.0	30.0	—	5,477
Others	68.4	2.7	7.3	21.6	1,482
TOTAL	67.1	18.0	13.4	1.5	21,568[a]
Quebec					
English	66.4	—	33.6	—	814
French	—	75.3	24.7	—	4,821
Others	33.5	14.9	26.9	25.0	254
TOTAL	10.5	60.9	27.6	1.1	6,028[a]
CMA Montreal					
English	66.7	—	33.3	—	637
French	—	63.1	36.9	—	1,793
Others	33.9	13.6	28.6	23.9	226
TOTAL	18.5	42.4	37.1	2.0	2,743[a]

Source: 1971 Census, Cats. 92–726, 92–776.

[a] French and English home-language figures do *not* include those whose mother tongue is the other official language. "Others" home-language figures do not include those who have French or English as a mother tongue. Inclusion of these groups would artificially inflate the levels of bilingualism within the "English," "French," and "others" home-language categories. If a person who uses English most often in the home has French as a mother tongue (language first learned and still understood), it would be highly misleading to count him or her as a bilingual anglophone. Such a person is more accurately described as a francophone who might well be in the process of becoming an anglophone. Figures in the total include everybody and therefore accurately reflect the overall level of bilingualism in each territory.

bilingual (36.9 percent) than those who used English in the home and did not have French as a mother tongue (33.3 percent).[35] The language of the minority is once again shown to have greater drawing power.

Although tables 3 and 4 clearly show a French-speaking majority in Montreal, the same data also demonstrate that the French language is weaker in Montreal than in Quebec as a whole and that English seems more attractive to immigrants than French. The data also suggest that as a linguistic minority, anglophones have been remarkably negligent about learning the language of the majority.

35. There were 46,095 anglophones (i.e., people who use English most at home) whose mother tongue was French and only 25,855 francophones whose mother tongue was English. Consequently, the disparity in bilingualism is even greater than the table suggests. If these people had been included in the table, the disparity would have appeared to have been significantly less, because almost 20 percent of the bilingual anglophones would have been people who learned French before they learned English.

In a metropolitan area in which two-thirds of the population use French in the home, one would normally expect the burden of becoming bilingual to be on the anglophones. It has not been so in Montreal, and this is one of French-speaking Quebec's great historical grievances. The relative strength of the two major linguistic groups in Montreal has become a highly sensitive political issue that in a number of ways has figured in political debates over local government institutions and boundaries.

Language: The Territorial Dimension

The political implications of Montreal's linguistic cleavage are aggravated by the continued concentration of anglophones in the western part of the island. Map 2 shows the pattern of residential segregation on the Island of Montreal in 1971. Unshaded areas cover census tracts where more than 50 percent of the inhabitants claim English as the language used most often in their homes.[36] In heavily shaded areas more than 50 percent use French, and lightly shaded areas have no linguistic majority.

In 1971 the proportions for home language use on the Island of Montreal were: French, 61.2 percent; English, 27.4 percent; and others, 11.4 percent. (See Table 3.) If the francophone populations were distributed evenly throughout the island, every census tract would have a French majority. That 88 of the 414 inhabited census tracts are classified as anglophone indicates the extent of Montreal's linguistic residential segregation.[37] All of the 88 anglophone tracts are in the western part of the island. In 1970, 70 of them had an annual family income higher than the median for the census metropolitan

36. Census tracts are areas within cities whose boundaries are defined by Statistics Canada. The population of each tract is usually between 2500 and 8000. See Canada, *1971 Census*, CT–4A, Introduction.

37. For more sophisticated analyses of residential segregation using 1951 and 1961 census data, see Norbert Lacoste, *Les caractéristiques sociales de la population du grand Montréal* (Montreal: Les Presses de l'Université de Montréal, 1958); "Les traits nouveaux de la population du 'grand Montréal,' " *Recherches sociographiques*, vol. 6 (1965), pp. 265–82; Pierre George, "Essai d'interprétation géographique des statistiques de population de l'agglomération de Montréal," *Revue de géographie de Montréal*, vol. 21 (1967): 361–74; Stanley Lieberson, "Linguistic and Ethnic Segregation in Montreal" (Unpublished study for the Royal Commission on Bilingualism and Biculturalism, McGill University, Department of Geography); " 'Montreal' Population: A Study in Four Volumes," prepared for the Royal Commission on Bilingualism and Biculturalism; Bryn Greer-Wooton, "The Urban Model," in *Montreal Field Guide*, ed. Ludger Beauregard (Montreal: Les Presses de l'Université de Montréal, 1972), pp. 9–31; Jean-Pierre Thouez, "La structure spatiale des caractéristiques socio-economiques de Montréal," *Recherches sociographiques*, vol. 14 (1973): 81–116.

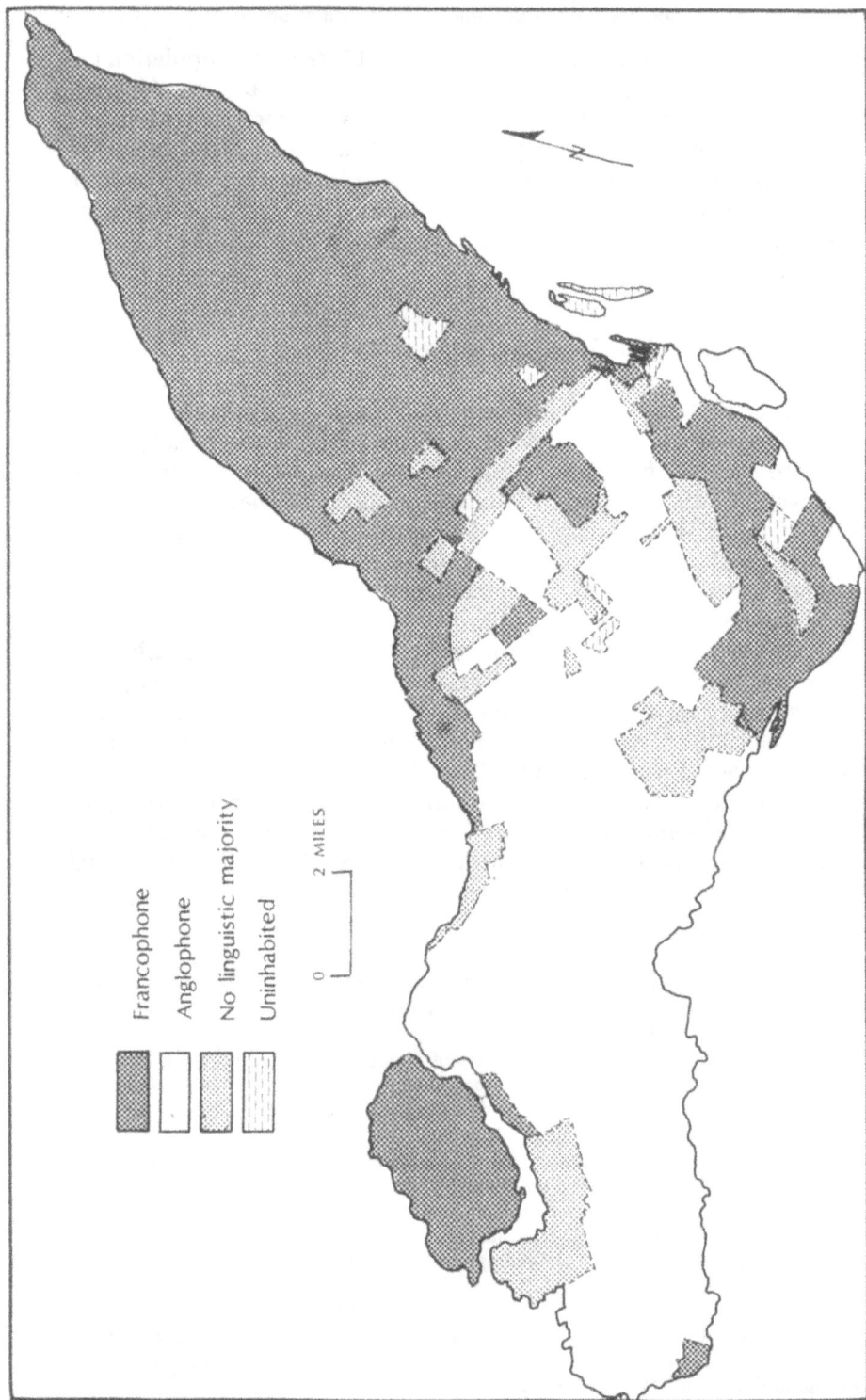

Map 2

Language Use on the Island of Montreal

Francophone

Anglophone

No linguistic majority

Uninhabited

0   2 MILES

area.[38] In short, the data confirm the common perception that western Montreal Island is a kind of gilded ghetto for middle- and upper-class anglophones.

Until quite recently there has been little doubt that Montreal's central business district was also anglophone territory. Most anglophones did not live there, of course, but each morning they streamed in from the west in trains, buses, and cars to take command of the offices and the major department stores. Francophones were left with a collection of neighborhood commercial areas where smaller stores and business enterprises catered to an exclusively French-speaking clientele.[39]

The decline of the English presence in the central business district is one recent manifestation of efforts by francophones to become the managers of their own economy. Francophones have pursued this goal in two principal ways: (1) through provincial legislation that not only governs language use in the workplace but also controls the language used on external signs and advertising and (2) by fostering the expansion of the central business district toward the east so that new large-scale office and commercial development takes place in areas where French has traditionally been dominant. This land-use policy is of special interest to students of urban politics.

Prior to about 1970 there was no evidence of any government policy to direct new development to French-speaking areas. In 1961 private developers located Canada's first modern skyscraper, *Place Ville Marie*, in an area that was even more English dominated than the older business district.[40] The building of *Place Ville Marie*, and other office buildings that followed, seemed to reinforce the link between the business world and Montreal anglophones.

In the 1970s, however, governments began to intervene to redress the balance. The City of Montreal expropriated land to the east of the major department stores, allowing *Les Caisses populaires Desjardins* (French Quebec's major network of credit unions) to build a huge office, hotel, and shopping complex across the street from the municipally owned concert hall. Similarly, the provincial government has

38. Income data from Canada, *1971 Census*, CT–4B; 1981 census tract data produce similar results. Of 447 inhabited census tracts, 92 had anglophone majorities; of these 67 had annual family incomes higher than the average for the census metropolitan area. Not surprisingly, the territorial distribution is also similar to that portrayed in Map 2. 1981 figures calculated from Canada, Statistics Canada, 1981 *Census of Canada*, Fiche Documentation CTY8–1B23 and CTC8–1B11.

39. Jean Laponce, "The City Centre as Conflictual Space in the Bilingual City: The Case of Montreal," in *Centre and Periphery: Spatial Variation in Politics*, ed. Jean Gottman (Beverly Hills, Calif.: Sage, 1980), pp. 149–62.

40. For details, see William Zeckendorf, *Zeckendorf* (New York: Holt, Rinehart and Winston, 1970), Ch. 15.

recently built a convention center and the federal government, a major office complex, both in the immediate vicinity. In short, *Place Ville Marie*, built in the early 1960s, and *La Complexe Desjardins*, built in the 1970s, are centers for notably different economic units, the former for the English-dominated, Canadian-oriented private sector and the latter for the French-dominated public sector and for businesses operating primarily in Quebec.

In addition, several factors, including language legislation, have made English far less dominant even in the kinds of companies that have headquarters in the *Place Ville Marie* area. The core of the world's third-largest French-speaking city is finally becoming French.[41] Thus, the anglophone who is unwilling or unable to speak French is finding the center of Montreal an increasingly alien environment. If they are to feel comfortable using their language in Quebec at all, anglophones will have to rely increasingly on their own residential areas for a "hospitable" linguistic environment.

Bills 63 and 22: Language in the Political Arena

Demands for an explicit Quebec government language policy emerged only in the late 1960s; they reflected vital changes in the cultural identity of Quebec francophones. The Roman Catholic church no longer had sufficient strength to nurture and protect the French identity in North America. The stereotype of the sturdy farmer working his land with the help of a dozen children was no longer an appropriate symbol of French Quebec's economic aspirations. Quebec francophones had largely been urbanized and secularized and were much more open to the anglicizing influences of mass-consumption society.

In short, French Quebeckers had only their language to protect them from total assimilation to the North American way of life. Under these circumstances, it is not surprising that they began defining themselves primarily in terms of language and taking legislative steps to protect the language. Nor is it surprising, given the strength of anglophones, that the situation in Montreal was the primary target of the language legislation.

The Saint-Léonard School Crisis

The immediate need for a language policy grew out of a decision by the Catholic school commission in Saint-Léonard, a municipality in the eastern part of the Island of Montreal with a large Italian minor-

41. Paris and Kinshasa, Zaire, are larger.

ity. On November 20, 1967, the commission voted to abolish the special bilingual (French and English) classes, mainly attended by Italian immigrants, and to replace them by unilingual French classes.[42] The decision immediately caused extreme bitterness and controversy both in Saint-Léonard and throughout the province. Two opposing pressure groups—the Association of Parents of Saint-Léonard and the *Mouvement pour l'intégration scolaire* (MIS)—fought for political support.[43]

In school board elections held June 9, 1968, the MIS gained complete control and announced its intention to implement its unilingual policy fully.[44] As the crisis grew, the *Union nationale* government of Premier Jean-Jacques Bertrand was finally forced to take a position. This proved extremely difficult, because throughout its period in office from 1966 to 1970 the UN, still based primarily in rural Quebec, was desperately trying to straddle the fence between the conflicting forces of French unilingualism and Quebec nationalism on the one hand and bilingualism and Canadian federalism on the other.

On December 9, 1968, the government introduced an ambiguous plan that reflected the UN's dilemma. The proposed legislation compelled school boards to provide both French and English education "to all children domiciled in the territory under their jurisdiction if they are deemed capable of following such courses and if their parents are desirous of enrolling them therein."[45] This rather ambiguous legislation satisfied neither side in the Saint-Léonard dispute but seemed to enrage French unilingualists more than anglophones. When Premier Bertrand announced this legislation, he also formed a commission, headed by Professor Jean-Denis Gendron, to conduct "an inquiry into the position of the French language in Quebec and measures to be taken to insure its full expansion, and to inquire into the linguistic rights of Quebec citizens."[46]

While the legislation was being debated, and as the Gendron commission launched its study, Quebec politics was largely dominated by the question of whether immigrant parents should have the right to send their children to English schools. On September 10, 1969, tensions in Saint-Léonard reached a climax when about one thousand French unilingualists took to the streets, causing massive property damage and considerable violence.[47] By this time the rioters

42. Richard Issenman, *St. Léonard Put in Perspective—Background to a Crisis* (Montreal: Montreal Star, 1970), p. 5.
43. For details of their activities, see John E. Parisella, "Pressure Group Politics: Case Study of the St. Léonard Crisis" (M.A. thesis, McGill University, 1971).
44. Issenman, *St. Léonard*, p. 9.
45. Quebec, Assemblée nationale, *Bill 85* (1968).
46. Quebec, *The Position of the French Language in Quebec: Report of the Commission of Inquiry* (Quebec: Quebec Official Publisher, 1972), vol. 1, p. iv.
47. Issenman, *St. Léonard*, p. 13.

were far more concerned with the larger provincial scene, because within Saint-Léonard itself they seemed to have virtually won their case.

After the riot it became clear to Premier Bertrand that the provincial government must regain the initiative, and on October 23, 1969, he introduced Bill 63, a slightly modified version of his earlier proposal for a legislative solution to the problem. After making the general statement that "all school commissions must teach courses in French to all children within their territory who are deemed capable and desirous of enrolling for them," Bill 63 went on to make this vital additional statement: "They shall be given in the English language to any child for whom his parents or the persons acting in their stead so request at his enrollment."[48] Regardless of what anglophones and immigrants thought of the rest of the bill, they all welcomed this provision, but it further outraged the unilingualists.[49] The debate on Bill 63 was relatively short; it was opposed only by René Lévesque of the *Parti québécois*, one dissident Liberal, two dissident members of the UN, and an independent.[50] After numerous demonstrations outside the National Assembly and turbulent debates within, the bill became law on November 28. This brought the immediate crisis in Saint-Léonard to an end. Italian parents could once again, if they wished, send their children to English-speaking schools. But the unilingualists had not given up, and the larger issues were far from resolved.

Robert Bourassa and Bill 22

After many delays, the Gendron commission finally reported in December 1972, recommending a comprehensive plan to achieve "the general goal of making French the common language of Quebecers."[51] Special emphasis was placed on making French the main language of work in all the province's industrial, commercial, and public service establishments. But the report did not recommend explicit legal sanctions that the Quebec government might use to enforce such a policy. In the field of education the report specifically recommended against any legally coercive measures "at this time."[52] Instead, the commissioners called for the implementation of a set of noncoercive measures to encourage immigrant children to attend French schools. In general, the

48. Quebec, *Statutes* (1969), Ch. 9, Section 4.
49. See Robert J. Macdonald, "In Search of a Language Policy: Francophone Reactions to Bills 85 and 63," in *Quebec's Language Policies: Background and Response*, ed. John R. Mallea (Quebec: Les Presses de l'Université Laval, 1977), pp. 219–42.
50. Quebec, *Débats* 8 (1969): 3549.
51. Quebec, *The Position of the French Language*, vol. 1, p. 291.
52. Ibid., vol. 3, p. 273.

commissioners took what seemed a logical position that the problem of directing immigrant children toward the French educational system would tend to solve itself, once it was apparent that French was becoming the essential language of work within the entire province.

The Gendron report was received by a Liberal government led by Robert Bourassa, a young economist first elected to the legislature in 1966. Bourassa had replaced Lesage, following the latter's retirement as Liberal leader in early 1970. Bourassa then went on to soundly defeat both the *Union nationale* and the *Parti québécois* in the provincial election of April 1970. Bourassa's main political objective was to use Quebec's role within the Canadian federation to promote economic development in the province while also insisting that Quebec be given increased control over social and cultural policies. Although he won another election in 1973, he was eventually defeated in 1976 by René Lévesque's *Parti québécois*, the party that believes in Quebec's political independence combined with an economic association with the rest of Canada.

Although clearly a federalist, Bourassa also believed in improving the position of the French language and in furthering the economic interests within Quebec of its French-speaking citizens. The problem for Bourassa was to take firm action to advance these objectives, while continuing to promote outside investment in Quebec. If he appeared too harshly anti-English, he would discourage such investment; if he appeared too accommodating to English-speaking interests, Quebec nationalists could portray him as a mere agent of foreign economic and cultural interests. Like his predecessor, Premier Bertrand, Bourassa tried to steer a middle course. In mid-1974, following his massive election victory the previous year, he finally unveiled Quebec's Official Language Act, commonly known as Bill 22.[53] After extensive public hearings it became law on July 31, 1974.

Bill 22 tended to go slightly beyond the main Gendron recommendations concerning the legislative promotion of French but still did not meet the demands of the most fervent Quebec nationalists. The law declared French "the official language of the province of Quebec" but stated that official "texts and documents" may be accompanied by an English version.[54] Bilingual "texts and documents" were made compulsory for all municipalities and public educational institutions whose clientele was more than 10 percent anglophone.[55] French was made the language of internal communication for all public and educational authorities, except those whose clienteles were

53. Quebec, *Statutes* (1974), Ch. 6.
54. Ibid., Sections 1–2.
55. Ibid., Section 9.

more than 50 percent anglophone, in which case both languages were to be used.[56]

In the private sector all business firms were expected to apply for "certificates . . . attesting that they have adopted and are applying a francization program"[57]; details of what constituted "francization" were to be established by regulation. Firms without the necessary certificate would not "be entitled to receive the premiums, subsidies, concessions, or benefits from the public administration . . . or to make with the government . . . contracts of purchase, service, lease or public works."[58] Other sections of the law stated that various forms, contracts, and receipts must be in French unless specifically requested by clients in another language. Furthermore, by 1979 there could no longer be any outside advertising that did not include the use of French.[59]

As far as education was concerned, Bill 22 stated that although "the language of instruction shall be French . . . the school boards, regional school boards and corporations of trustees shall continue to provide instruction in English."[60] In addition, however, the law also stated that "an existing or future school board . . . cannot validly decide to commence, cease, increase, or reduce instruction in English unless it has received prior authorization from the Minister of Education, who shall not give it unless he considered that the number of pupils whose mother tongue is English and who are under the jurisdiction of such body warrants it."[61]

Students were to be educated in English only if they could prove sufficient knowledge of the language. Similarly, anglophone children could go to French schools only if they could prove sufficient knowledge of French. Students lacking sufficient knowledge of either language were to be educated in French. It was left up to the minister of education to establish the necessary testing procedures to implement the above rules.

This part of Bill 22 was the most controversial. It removed the existing right of Quebec parents to choose the language of education of their children.[62] Bill 22 was attacked by the *Parti québécois* and other nationalist groups for giving too many concessions to the use of English; by English-speaking groups for removing their established

56. Ibid., Sections 12–13.
57. Ibid., Section 26.
58. Ibid., Section 28.
59. Ibid., Sections 33–37.
60. Ibid., Section 40.
61. Ibid.
62. Ibid., Sections 41–43.

rights;[63] by some French Canadians for limiting their children's opportunity to learn English; and by everybody for being too vague and imprecise.

In any event, it ultimately proved a monumental failure, contributing to the defeat of the Bourassa government by the *Parti québécois* in 1976. Bill 22 stayed on the statute books only three years, when it was replaced in 1977 by a new, much tougher law. Nevertheless, the passage of Bill 22 in 1974 was a decisive event for English-speaking Montrealers, who were shown to be incapable of defending their traditional language rights. The old pattern of behind-the-scenes negotiation and compromise between English-speaking business interests and provincial politicians had broken down.

The Impact of the *Parti Québécois*

The Quebec provincial election of November 1976 brought the *Parti québécois* (PQ) to power. This led to dramatic changes in Quebec's language legislation and in 1980 to a provincewide referendum on Quebec's constitutional future. These two developments preoccupied Montrealers in both linguistic groups, increasing tensions between them. An analysis of the 1976 election results makes it quite obvious how wide the political differences between Montreal's anglophones and francophones had already become. Not since the federal conscription referendum in 1944 had the two groups split so clearly in voting for conflicting political alternatives.

Until 1976 voting behavior differences between French and English in Montreal had not been obvious. At the federal level both groups had voted overwhelmingly Liberal ever since 1896. Moreover, for the previous five federal general elections Liberals won every seat on the Island of Montreal, in some cases capturing over 80 percent of the popular vote. The Liberal Party's identification with the province of Quebec and with the principle of bilingualism in Canada as a whole had a natural appeal for both francophones and anglophones. In recent years, however, French-speaking constituencies have had lower voting turnouts than the English-speaking, and there has been a noticeable trend for French-speaking areas to have a higher percentage

---

63. Michael Stein, "Bill 22 and the Non-Francophone Population in Quebec: A Case Study of Minority Group Attitudes on Language Legislation," in *Quebec's Language Policies*, ed. Mallea, pp. 243–65; and Gary Caldwell, "English-speaking Quebec in Light of its Reaction to Bill 22," *American Review of Canadian Studies*, vol. 6 (1976): 42–56.

of rejected ballots.[64] These differences undoubtedly reflect either a reduced degree of attachment to federal politics on the part of many francophones or outright alienation. But the federal level is not where francophone nationalist feelings have been most evident.

Quebec's independence movement has operated almost exclusively within the confines of the provincial political system. In the general elections of 1970 and 1973, the first two contested by the *Parti québécois*, it won only seven and six constituencies, respectively, out of 108 and 110. Ten of these 13 victories were in the east end of the Island of Montreal. In constituencies in the English-speaking western part of the island the party did very poorly, in some cases winning less than 10 percent of the popular vote.[65] In these areas anglophones voted overwhelmingly Liberal, a pattern that had started in the 1930s after Maurice Duplessis took over the provincial Conservative Party and converted it into the *Union nationale*. From that time, Montreal anglophones viewed the provincial Liberals as the strongest advocates of the federal connection to the rest of Canada and have voted accordingly. Until 1976 they had always been joined by large numbers of francophones, thereby preventing an obvious voting split along linguistic lines.

In 1976 the *Parti québécois* won 17 of the 39 constituencies on the Island of Montreal and 38.2 percent of the popular vote. In the province as a whole it did even better, winning 71 of 110 constituencies and 41.4 percent of the popular vote.[66] The apparent relative weakness of the PQ on the Island of Montreal is explained by its inability to win support from anglophones. The PQ's domination of francophone Montreal is clearly shown in Map 3, where the shaded area represents seats won by the PQ in 1976. The shaded area corresponds almost exactly to the areas of francophone residential concentration shown in Map 2, p. 74.

René Lévesque and Bill 101

Unlike the Liberal government of Robert Bourassa, the PQ government of René Lévesque came to office in 1976 with no support from English-speaking Montreal and with a clearly defined language program. The Lévesque government published its language policy on

64. These observations derive from a study of the official reports of the federal chief electoral officer for the federal general elections of 1968, 1972, 1974, 1979, and 1980.

65. See the official reports of Quebec's chief returning officer for the provincial general elections of 1970 and 1973.

66. Quebec, Chief Returning Officer, *Elections 1976* (Quebec: Quebec Official Publisher, 1977).

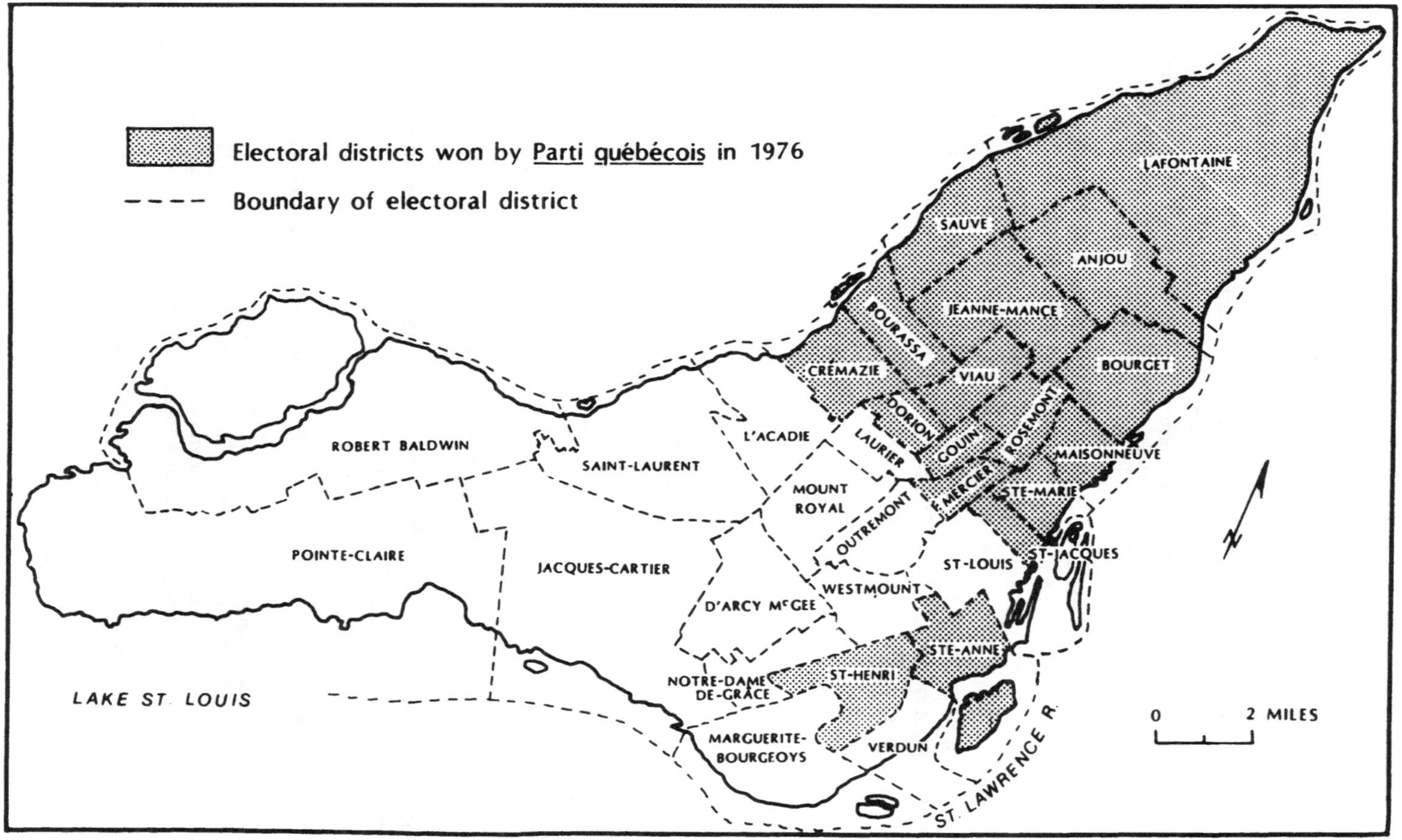

Legend:
Electoral districts won by Parti québécois in 1976
Boundary of electoral district

LAFONTAINE
ANJOU
BOURGET
MAISONNEUVE
SAUVÉ
JEANNE-MANCE
ROSEMONT
VIAU
STE-MARIE
ST-JACQUES
ST-LOUIS
BOURASSA
CRÉMAZIE
DORION
GOUIN
LAURIER
ST-ANNE
ST-HENRI
VERDUN
L'ACADIE
MONT-ROYAL
OUTREMONT
D'ARCY McGEE
WESTMOUNT
NOTRE-DAME-DE-GRÂCE
MARGUERITE-BOURGEOYS
SAINT-LAURENT
JACQUES-CARTIER
ROBERT BALDWIN
POINTE-CLAIRE
MOUNT ROYAL

LAWRENCE R
ST. LAWRENCE
LAKE ST. LOUIS

2 MILES
0

Map 3
Provincial Election Results on the Island of Montreal, 1976

April 1, 1977, in the form of a White Paper[67] outlining its interpretation of the history of the French language in Canada and its proposals as to how French should be protected and nourished in Quebec. The White Paper generated a great deal of debate and much concern among anglophones. Draft legislation was tabled by the end of April, and on August 26, 1977, after a summer of continuing controversy, the Charter of the French Language (known commonly as Bill 101) became law.[68] The final version differed only in detail from the government's original White Paper proposals.

Like Bill 22, which it repealed, Bill 101 declared French to be the official language of Quebec.[69] Unlike Bill 22, it implemented the principle by stating that only the French versions of Quebec statutes, regulations, and court judgments would be official.[70] Although this part of the law had far less practical impact than other sections, it was nevertheless of great symbolic importance because it appeared to violate Quebec anglophones' only constitutionally protected linguistic rights.

Section 133 of the British North America Act specifically states that both French and English have certain guaranteed legal protections within the Quebec legislature and courts. To no one's surprise, this part of Bill 101 was quickly challenged in the courts, and on December 13, 1979, the Supreme Court of Canada ruled these provisions of Bill 101 invalid because they went beyond the constitutional authority of the Quebec legislature.[71] The *Parti québécois* tried to turn the judgment to its political advantage, claiming it as yet another example of the way Canadian federalism has restricted the free development of French-speaking Quebec.

The other parts of Bill 101 had a greater impact on the ordinary life of Quebec residents, especially those living in the linguistically divided area of Montreal. French was declared to be the language of "the civil administration," which includes all municipalities, school boards, and health and social service facilities. The municipalities in which the majority of residents speak a language

67. Quebec, *Quebec's Policy on the French Language* (Quebec: Quebec Official Publisher, 1977).

68. Quebec, *Statutes* (1977), Ch. 5.

69. For a detailed comparison of the two bills and their different ideological foundations, see William D. Coleman, "From Bill 22 to Bill 101: The Politics of Language under the Parti Québécois," *Canadian Journal of Political Science*, vol. 14 (1981): 459–85.

70. Quebec, *Statutes* (1977), Ch. 5, Sections 7–13.

71. The text of the judgment is printed in *The Globe and Mail* (Toronto), December 14, 1979. But see *The Globe and Mail*, April 7, 1981, for a further ruling saying that the provisions of Section 133 do not apply to municipalities and school boards.

other than French were given until the end of 1983 to adapt to these provisions.[72]

School boards and health and social service facilities were, however, allowed to continue using English if, and as long as, the majority of their clientele was English speaking.[73] The bill also made it difficult for employers to insist on the ability to speak English as a condition of employment[74] and for anybody doing any kind of business in Quebec to issue any printed material not containing French.[75] Except in clearly defined circumstances, all signs and posters were to be solely in French.[76]

The most controversial part of the bill related to access to English-language schools. Only children whose mother or father received his or her elementary education in Quebec were allowed to attend English schools.[77] Other transitional provisions made various exceptions for parents already living in Quebec who received education in English elsewhere and for families who already had older children attending English schools. Exceptions were also made for children with serious learning disabilities and for children whose parents were staying in Quebec temporarily.[78] Limiting access to English schools to those children having one parent educated in English in Quebec prevents the English school system in Quebec from augmenting the number of its students by enrolling children of people newly arrived in the province. Given the relatively transient nature of much of Montreal's anglophone population, a substantial decline in the relative size of Montreal's English school system seems inevitable.[79]

Bill 101 has been much more popular among Quebec francophones than Bill 22 ever was. Mayor Jean Drapeau of Montreal is reported to have explained this by saying: "Bill 101 was an exercise in revenge against the English while Bill 22 tried to be reasonable."[80] Despite this, even anglophones seemed less bitter about Bill 101 than

72. Quebec, *Statutes* (1977), Ch. 5, Section 25. In late 1983 this provision was amended so that such municipalities will not have to use French as their sole language of internal communication. They now must be capable only of providing services to the public in French. See *Le Devoir*, December 19, 1983.

73. Quebec, *Statutes* (1977), Ch. 5, Section 26.

74. Ibid., Section 46.

75. Ibid., Section 51.

76. Ibid., Section 58.

77. Ibid., Section 73. This provision now appears to violate the provisions of Canada's Constitution Act of 1982. See Ch. 10.

78. Ibid., Sections 81, 85.

79. For projections of the island's French and English school population through the 1980s, see Conseil scolaire de l'Ile de Montréal, *Prévisions des populations scolaires francophones et anglophones de l'Ile de Montréal* (Montreal: 1980), pp. 46–47.

80. Quoted in François Cloutier, *L'Enjeu: Memoires politiques, 1970–76* (Montreal: Stanké, 1978), p. 93 (author's trans.).

they were about Bill 22,[81] probably because they anticipated the worst from the *Parti québécois,* whereas they had expected better from the Liberals, whom they had consistently supported. Bill 101's other advantage was that it really did appear to represent a long-term resolution of the language issue. In contrast, Bill 22 appeared inherently unworkable and subject to change at any time, partly because of the intense opposition from both anglophones and francophones.

French: The New Language of Work

Like Bill 22, Bill 101 had provisions designed to increase the use of French in the management of Quebec businesses. Both bills provided for "francization" certificates, which companies could obtain after a government agency either approved a program leading to the increased use of French or agreed that French was already the firm's major language. Under Bill 22 lack of a francization certificate meant that a company would be unable to do business with the government, whereas under Bill 101 any firm employing more than 50 people had to obtain such a certificate or face possible fines of up to $2000 a day.[82]

One irony of Bill 101 is that shortly after its passage, evidence was collected showing that the long-standing economic disparities between anglophones and francophones had already dramatically decreased. In a document prepared for the Economic Council of Canada, Jac-André Boulet compared data from the 1961 and 1971 federal censuses and from a special survey conducted in early 1978 of almost 1000 male workers in metropolitan Montreal, carried out for Quebec's *Office de la langue française.* He found that in 1961 there was a 51 percent divergence between the average earnings of francophones and anglophones. By 1970 the divergence was reduced to 32 percent, and by 1977 it was only 15 percent.[83]

Boulet's identification of the top 15 percent of workers by earnings revealed that in 1961 the proportion of francophones in this group was 44 percent, in 1970 it was 57 percent, and in 1977 it was 70 percent. The study also showed that the proportion of unilingual anglophones in the workforce had decreased from 13 percent in 1961 to 5 percent in 1977, whereas the proportion of bilingual anglophones

81. For reactions in the English press, see Nadia Brédimas-Assimopoulos and Michel Lafferière, *Legislation et perceptions ethniques: Une étude du contenu de la presse anglaise au vote de la Loi 101* (Quebec: Editeur officiel, 1980).

82. Quebec, *Statutes* (1977), Ch. 5, Sections 136, 206.

83. Jac-André Boulet, *L'evolution des disparités linguistiques de revenues de travail dans la zone métropolitaine de Montréal de 1961 à 1977,* Document 127 du Conseil economique du Canada (Ottawa: 1979), p. i. For more data and analysis, see Boulet, *Language and Earnings in Montreal, A Study Prepared for the Economic Council of Canada* (Ottawa: Minister of Supply and Services Canada, 1980).

increased from 10 percent to 13 percent in the same period.[84] The average annual earnings of unilingual anglophones increased by 70 percent, those of bilinguals increased by 102 percent, and those of francophone unilinguals and bilinguals increased 125 percent and 119 percent, respectively.[85]

Despite the apparent trend toward equality in earnings, some hard facts remained. In 1977 the difference in annual income between francophones and anglophones was still $2185. The difference between unilingual anglophones and unilingual francophones was even greater—$2451.[86] Such figures are just cause for indignation among many Quebec francophones. Paul Bernard and Jean Renaud have countered Boulet's analysis by claiming that because the 1980s will see less social change and economic growth than the 1960s and 1970s, future progress toward equality is not as likely as a simple extrapolation of Boulet's figures would suggest. High-paying jobs in Montreal still held by anglophones will pass to francophones only if some kind of linguistic quota system is established. Bernard and Renaud also point out that if Boulet's analysis is extended throughout Quebec and includes workers of both sexes, the economic disparities between francophones and anglophones will be substantially greater than when the comparison is restricted to male workers in metropolitan Montreal.[87]

Nevertheless, evidence suggests that francophones in Montreal, even unilingual ones, had already been making a great deal of economic progress even before the passage of Bill 101. Viewed in this light, perhaps the francization provisions of Bills 22 and 101 were not completely justified. On the other hand, it can also be argued that it was precisely the fear of such legislation that led anglophone managers in Montreal to anticipate the new laws and bring the French language and francophones into their businesses more rapidly than would otherwise have been the case.

Regardless of the causes of the recent improvements in francophones' economic position, it can no longer be argued that Quebec's French Canadians constitute an "ethnic class"[88] permanently rele-

84. Boulet, *L'evolution des disparités linguistiques*, pp. ii–iii.
85. Ibid., p. 15.
86. Ibid.
87. *Le Devoir*, March 9, 1979. Bernard and Renaud collected the data for the *Office de la langue française*, which was used by Boulet. Their analysis is contained in Paul Bernard et al., *L'evolution de la situation socio-economique des francophones et des non-francophones au Québec (1971–1978)*, Collections Langues et Sociétés, Office de la Langue française (Quebec: Editeur officiel, 1979).
88. Jacques Dofny and Marcel Rioux, "Social Class in French Canada," in *French-Canadian Society*, vol. 1, ed. Marcel Rioux and Yves Martin (Toronto: McClelland and Stewart, 1964), p. 312.

gated to low-income positions. Neither can it still be argued that the nonfrancophone group in Montreal is overwhelmingly middle class. Unskilled immigrants from southern Europe have replaced older and more skilled immigrants previously originating in Britain and northern Europe. In short, the class composition of both francophone and anglophone groups in Montreal is becoming more alike, because both are becoming much more diverse. This means that anglophones, francophones, and immigrants are now more frequently competing for the same jobs at all levels in the occupational hierarchy. These circumstances would lead one to expect an increase in the political salience of language differences.

The 1980 Referendum and the 1981 Provincial Election

Even if the *Parti québécois* cannot take all the credit for improving the economic position of Montreal's francophones, it did force the province to confront the question of its future in relation to the rest of Canada. The PQ won the 1976 election by attacking the mistakes of the Bourassa government and by promising not to bring about Quebec's independence without a mandate from the people, to be obtained through a referendum held during its first term in office. After much delay, the referendum took place in May 1980. Even using a question that asked for a mandate to *negotiate*, but not to *implement*, a sovereignty-association agreement with the rest of Canada, the PQ won only 40.4 percent of the provincial vote. On the Island of Montreal the independence referendum got a majority in only three of the 31 constituencies. Nevertheless, there was still a noticeable difference in the voting behavior of francophone and anglophone areas. The no vote rarely went above 60 percent in francophone areas, but it topped 90 percent in the anglophone constituencies of D'Arcy McGee and Pointe Claire.[89] The 1980 referendum debate climaxed a long period of apprehension on the part of Montreal anglophones, and the result was about the best they could have hoped for. Not only did the federalist forces win but it also seemed quite evident that a majority of the francophones voted to give the federal connection at least one more chance.

The results of the 1980 referendum caused most observers to expect that the PQ would have great difficulty in being reelected as the provincial government. To the chagrin of most anglophones, this was not the case. In the provincial general election of 1981 the PQ increased its share of the popular vote to 49 percent and won 80 of the 122 constituencies in the enlarged provincial legislature.

89. Quebec, Le Directeur général des élections, *Rapport des résultats officiel du scrutin, Référendum du 20 mai 1980* (Quebec: 1980).

On the Island of Montreal, however, the PQ won fewer seats in 1981 than it had in 1976. This was because in 1976 many nonfranco-phones voted *Union nationale* as a protest against Bill 22, thereby allowing the PQ to win a few seats with only a minority of the popular vote. In 1981 it was a straight two-party election, with virtually all nonfrancophones backing the Liberals. In these circumstances, the PQ won only 13 of the 33 new constituencies.[90] Most commentators on the 1981 election did not interpret it as a reversal of the referendum result but rather as a desire on the part of Quebec voters to support a party that, in general, had provided five years of honest, capable, and progressive government.

After the election of 1981 it was clearer than ever that the refer-endum of 1980 had clarified nothing concerning the future role of anglophones in Quebec. Although the *Parti québécois* government ap-peared increasingly flexible on many of the details of its language policy, its overall effect continued to make it difficult for headquarters of Canadian and multinational companies to remain in Montreal. Con-sequently, there is small comfort for Montreal anglophones in the knowledge that Quebec remains in the Canadian federation. In fact, rather than resolving the issue of the anglophone minority's fate within Quebec, the referendum debate actually diverted attention away from the issue.[91] But it can hardly be ignored, at least by the anglophones.

Anglophones and Language Legislation

The events described in the next four chapters—the creation and operation of a metropolitan government, establishment of a unified police force for the Island of Montreal, attempts to restructure the school system, and reorganization of the social services—took place mainly before the passage of major language legislation and the coming to power of the PQ. In this period anglophones still hoped that the emphasis on promoting French would prove to be a passing fancy. Many francophones were still reluctant to use their numerical strength in Quebec provincial politics to upset generations of English domi-nance. In these circumstances caution was the watchword concerning issues affecting the linguistic balance of power in metropolitan Mon-treal. For Quebec francophones, the introduction and passage of Bill

90. *The Globe and Mail,* April 15, 1981.

91. Two works are exceptions to this general statement: Sheila McLeod Arno-poulos and Dominique Clift, *The English Fact in Quebec* (Montreal: McGill-Queen's University Press, 1980), and Reed Scowen, "Reflections on the Future of the English Language in Quebec" (Mimeographed, 1979).

22, and especially Bill 101, marked the end of this period of careful accommodation.

Through Bill 101, Quebec's French-speaking majority decided which language was to be used within various local institutions, and under what circumstances. This was a major accomplishment, notwithstanding the fact that most anglophones still reject the bill's main thrust. But what Bill 101 has not done (and cannot do) is define the relative autonomy, in political terms, of the French- and English-speaking groups on the Island of Montreal. Their relative autonomy depends not so much on the designation of the appropriate language for any particular situation but on the extent to which the structure of local institutions reflects the existence of the two distinct groups.

The passage of the language legislation alerted anglophones to their political weakness. They are now even more likely to cling to their cherished local institutions than they were in the 1960s and early 1970s. Plans for local boundary changes and regionalization of various services—even if advanced strictly on the grounds of organizational rationality—are now much more likely to meet fervent opposition.

Reorganizing Montreal's Local Government

6

Creating the Montreal Urban Community

When the government of Jean Lesage took office in June of 1960, Sarto Fournier was still the mayor of Montreal and the Montreal Metropolitan Corporation was only one year old. But within a few months Fournier was defeated and the corporation was doomed. This chapter treats the ensuing political battles over alternatives to the corporation and the sudden emergence of the Montreal Urban Community in 1969.

The 1960s was a decade of bitterness in intermunicipal relations on the Island of Montreal. With the Quiet Revolution underway, there was intense pressure for institutional reform in all aspects of government, even at the local level. Moreover, the Municipality of Metropolitan Toronto and the Corporation of Greater Winnipeg had emerged as viable metropolitan governments to an extent never even approached by either the Montreal Metropolitan Commission or the Montreal Metropolitan Corporation.[1] Although everyone wanted the governmental structures of the Island of Montreal to be reformed, there was little consensus as to how it should be done. Unlike Toronto and Winnipeg, the question of structural reform in Montreal was complicated and retarded by the presence of the two linguistic groups, whose relations were being dramatically changed by the Quiet Revolution.

"One Island, One City"

When Jean Drapeau was out of office between 1957 and 1960 he made a national reputation for himself by speaking publicly about a wide variety of federal and provincial issues.[2] For a time it appeared

1. See Albert Rose, *Governing Metropolitan Toronto* (Berkeley: University of California Press, 1972); George Rich, "Metropolitan Winnipeg: The First Ten Years" in *Urban Problems: A Canadian Reader*, ed. Ralph R. Krueger and R. Charles Bryfogle (Toronto: Holt, Rinehart and Winston, 1971), pp. 358–70; and Harold Kaplan, *Reform, Planning and City Politics: Montreal, Winnipeg, Toronto* (Toronto: University of Toronto Press, 1982), Chs. 11, 14.

2. These speeches were published as *Jean Drapeau vous parle* (Montreal: Editions de la cité, 1959).

that his political future might lie outside Montreal, but Drapeau decided instead to reenter municipal elections, this time as the undisputed leader of his own highly disciplined local party. As a result of some rather treacherous maneuvering in 1960, Drapeau disassociated himself from the Civic Action League, taking most of its city councillors with him to form the new Civic Party.[3] Drapeau's action, just before the 1960 election, came too late for the league to react effectively.

Easily defeating Fournier, Drapeau and his Civic Party followers won 46 of the 66 Class A and B seats.[4] In a simultaneous referendum, 74.7 percent of the electors followed Drapeau's advice by voting to abolish the Class C councillors (those appointed by various designated organizations). Voters in English areas of the city were understandably less willing than the French to part with this special form of representation.[5] Moreover, they did not appear to trust Drapeau any more than before.

In any event, the 1960 election marked the destruction of the Civic Action League, a scrupulously democratic movement for honest local government, and its replacement by an authoritarian political party devoted only to maintaining Jean Drapeau in office. Apart from Drapeau himself, the party's main asset was Lucien Saulnier, an experienced councillor who was to serve as chair of the executive committee for 10 years.

Drapeau's first objective was to restructure Montreal's system of government, and his new system came into effect in 1962. The mayor retained substantial authority, although most of the city's normal administration remained in the hands of the executive committee, comprising the mayor plus six members elected by the council on the nomination of the mayor. The committee then chose its own chair and vice-chair.[6] The city council included 45 members, three each from 15 electoral districts. Starting in 1962, municipal elections were to be held every four years. In subsequent elections the size of the council was slowly expanded. In 1978 the number of councillors was set at 54, all to be elected from single-member districts.[7]

The early 1960s were Mayor Drapeau's years of greatest accom-

3. This is described in full from an anti-Drapeau perspective in J.-Z. Léon Patenaude, *Le vrai visage de Jean Drapeau* (Montreal: Editions du jour, 1962). See also Brian McKenna and Susan Purcell, *Drapeau* (Toronto: Clarke Irwin, 1980), pp. 123–29.

4. John Irwin Cooper, *Montreal: A Brief History* (Montreal: McGill-Queen's University Press, 1969), p. 192.

5. Guy Bourassa, *Les relations ethniques dans la vie politique montréalaise*, Document 10 of the Royal Commission on Bilingualism and Biculturalism (Ottawa: Information Canada, 1971), p. 42.

6. Marcel Adam, *La démocratie à Montréal* (Montreal: Editions du jour, 1972), p. 30.

7. For the final version of the boundaries of these districts, see *Le Devoir*, August 26, 1978.

plishment. He launched the building of Montreal's luxurious subway system, presided over a real-estate and construction boom that made Montreal the envy of other growth-oriented Canadian cities, and began preparation for the highly imaginative site of Expo '67. Drapeau's successes in these years seemed to establish him as a central figure in the Quiet Revolution. By 1962 he had not only consolidated his support in French-speaking Montreal but he also managed to win, for the first time, the wholehearted support of English-speaking voters. They no longer perceived him as primarily a Quebec nationalist but rather as a visionary promoter and manager, concerned above all with the economic well-being of the City of Montreal.

Contemporary observers were much more likely to see the apparently modernizing and innovative features of Drapeau's policies rather than the more secretive and authoritarian aspects of the process by which these grand schemes were carried out. The popularity of Drapeau's early accomplishments explains much of his continuing success, but the way he brought them about eventually alienated the more democratically minded leaders of the Quiet Revolution.

Drapeau's Metropolitan Strategies

Jean Drapeau's objective respecting metropolitan affairs was quite simple: he wanted complete control over the island's essential services. His strategy involved three main lines of attack. First, he wanted a voting majority for the city on the Montreal Metropolitan Corporation. As we saw in Chapter 3, the corporation was originally established in 1959 when Maurice Duplessis was premier of Quebec and Sarto Fournier was mayor of Montreal. In order to offend neither the English-speaking suburbs nor his political allies in the French-speaking suburbs, Duplessis had established equality of representation between the corporation's central city and suburban members. When Mayor Drapeau inherited this arrangement in 1960 he found it intolerable. In making the city's case for increased representation, Drapeau's main political lieutenant, Lucien Saulnier, explained why: "The Montreal Metropolitan Corporation—and all other systems of metropolitan government—are unthinkable and out of the question because they imply a decrease in the influence of the French language group."[8] Because the suburbs had more metropolitan representation than their population entitled them to, Saulnier's remark was undoubtedly accurate. In any event, although the city failed to get the representation formula changed, the refusal of Drapeau and Saulnier to cooperate with the corporation completely undermined any usefulness it might have had.

8. Quoted in Roger-J. Bédard, *La bataille des annexions* (Montreal: Editions du jour, 1965), p. 28 (author's trans.).

The second part of the city's strategy was to gain control of essential metropolitan functions such as public transit and regional planning. The city took the initiative in public transit by starting to build Montreal's subway system in 1961 without financial assistance from either the province or the suburbs. Before the project was completed in 1966, however, the provincial government had forced the suburbs served by the public transit network to contribute,[9] but by this time Drapeau was clearly in control.

In the field of regional planning, Drapeau instructed city employees to draw up a plan for metropolitan expansion to the year 2000. The end product was an impressive audio-visual display presented during Expo '67.[10] Although "Horizon 2000" had little practical effect, it demonstrated that the City of Montreal was the only government with the ability to engage in metropolitan planning.

The third element in the city's strategy was the most important one: Drapeau and Saulnier wished to annex all the island's municipalities. This would fulfill Saulnier's prophecy that "history, geography and economics will insure that eventually there will only be one city on all the territory of the Island of Montreal."[11] Wishing to woo both the francophone and anglophone suburbanites, Drapeau and Saulnier did not couch their annexation appeal in terms of French domination. In fact, Drapeau (more than Saulnier) saw the City of Montreal as a great cosmopolitan world metropolis in which English Montrealers should be proud to share, even if it meant higher taxes. Drapeau never seemed to understand that many suburban citizens, both francophone and anglophone, were not affected by appeals to civic prestige and that anglophones living in small municipalities had strong linguistic motivations for clinging to their apparently insignificant and parochial institutions.

In 1961 the city proposed that its executive committee be empowered to annex a municipality simply by having the necessary resolution approved first by the Montreal city council and then by the Quebec Municipal Commission.[12] This would have replaced the existing system, which required the approval of both councils and of the electorate in the municipality to be annexed.[13] The Lesage government refused Drapeau's demands.

9. Quebec, *Statutes* (1965), Ch. 86, Section 4.
10. For descriptions of "Horizon 2000," see Marcelo Barcelo, "La métropole en l'an 2000," *Maintenant*, no. 78 (juin-juillet 1968): 172–74; Ludger Beauregard, "Montreal, The Year 2000," in *Montreal Field Guide*, ed. Ludger Beauregard (Montreal: Les Presses de l'Université de Montréal, 1972), pp. 193–97; and Jean-Claude Marsan, *Montreal in Evolution*, trans. Arnaud de Varent (Montreal: McGill-Queen's University Press, 1981), pp. 331–37.
11. Quoted in Bédard, *La bataille*, pp. 14–15 (author's trans.).
12. Ibid., p. 16.
13. Quebec, *Statutes* (1959–60), Ch. 102, Sections 13–30.

The city made another attempt to obtain "easy annexation" powers in 1963. This time the province made some changes. Under the new system, a city proposal for annexation would go to the council of the affected municipality. If accepted, the annexation would proceed, although citizens had a right to force a binding referendum. If the local council rejected the proposal, the City of Montreal could apply to the Quebec Municipal Commission to hold a binding referendum in the affected municipality.[14] This system, still in force today, enabled Montreal to get around an intransigent suburban council, but annexation was still impossible if a majority of residents opposed.

Shortly after passage of these new rules Montreal annexed the bankrupt municipality of Rivière-des-Prairies—the first major annexation in 45 years. Although Montreal and Rivière-des-Prairies were not contiguous (see Map 1, pp. 6–7), the new area provided the city with both a strong territorial base in the east of the island and much-needed undeveloped land for future growth. In early 1964 Montreal also annexed the tiny northern municipality of Saraguay. Neither annexation caused much controversy, but they did demonstrate to suburban mayors the seriousness of the city's intentions to expand.

Establishing the Blier Commission

In February 1964 the minister of municipal affairs, Pierre Laporte, named a three-member commission to study: (1) intermunicipal problems on the Island of Montreal; (2) regrouping of municipalities on the island, or reorganization of the political structures; and (3) other municipal or intermunicipal problems concerning the island's municipalities and citizens.[15] The commission's appointment temporarily released the government from the need to make its own policy decisions. It is difficult to know what the government's other objectives may have been, particularly as Montreal had already been extensively studied. Laporte appointed as chair Camille Blier, an assistant deputy minister in the department of municipal affairs, and let the main protagonists name the other two members. Drapeau chose Lucien Saulnier, and the suburbs responded with Reginald Dawson, the mayor of Mount Royal.

Immediately after the Blier commission was created, the island's suburbs formally joined in an organization called the Intermunicipal Co-ordinating Committee (ICC). It grew out of the informal meetings that had continued ever since Mayor Dawson had called his colleagues together in 1957 to discuss Duplessis's plans for metropolitan government. Since that time, suburban representatives had gone to

14. Ibid. (1963), Ch. 70, Sections 1–11.
15. Quebec, *Report of the Study Commission on Intermunicipal Problems on the Island of Montreal* (Quebec: 1964), p. viii.

Quebec City once or twice a year to fight various expansionist proposals in private bills that Montreal presented to the legislature. In the face of the renewed annexation initiative, the suburbs recognized the need for a more sophisticated organization able to obtain expert legal and public relations advice. For appearances' sake, it was perhaps no accident that the ICC's first president, vice-president, and secretary were all francophones.[16] Prior to the formal creation of the ICC, the suburbs had fought disorganized, ad hoc battles against Montreal under a leadership that often seemed to be dominated by wealthy anglophones. This did not project an image that was helpful for a politically active group at the height of Quebec's Quiet Revolution. By mid-1964, however, the ICC was firmly established as a francophone-led bilingual group devoted to protecting the vital interests of suburban Montreal. Rather than attempting to mobilize mass opinion, it concentrated on presenting the provincial government a united front of suburban mayors prepared to counter the centralizing policies of Mayor Drapeau.

The ICC presented a brief to the Blier commission, and 16 suburban municipalities also made their own submissions. The suburbs generally called for either some form of regional government covering an area larger than the Island of Montreal or a provincially appointed, semijudicial body to adjudicate intermunicipal disputes involving such functions as roads, sewers, and planning. The main thrust of these briefs was that no municipality should be forced out of existence against the will of its citizens. Seventeen briefs were presented by private citizens and organizations (other than the ICC). Most of these supported the suburban position, but one, by a group of property owners in Saint-Michel,[17] recommended their municipality's annexation by Montreal. The Montreal Policemen's Brotherhood urged unification of all the island's police forces. The City of Montreal did not present a brief, claiming that its arguments were sufficiently well known and that Saulnier was quite capable of expressing them when the need arose.[18]

Annexation Battles

Before the ICC presented its brief, the commission's work was brought virtually to a complete halt. In mid-July 1964 Saulnier an-

16. Bédard, *La bataille*, p. 63.

17. Saint-Michel does not appear on the map because it is now part of the City of Montreal. It was located immediately west of the existing municipality of Saint-Léonard.

18. A list of all the briefs presented can be found on p. 75 of Quebec, *Intermunicipal Problems*. Most of them are available in the library of the Department of Municipal Affairs, Quebec City. They are systematically discussed in Bédard, *La bataille*, Ch. 3.

nounced that Montreal would continue its annexation attempts, regardless of the activities of the commission on which he sat. On the same day that the ICC was supposed to present its brief to the commission, Montreal's city council approved annexation resolutions for Roxboro, Saint-Michel, and Pointe-aux-Trembles. The ICC refused to present its brief under these circumstances, urging Laporte, the minister of municipal affairs, to halt all annexation proceedings. Laporte pointed out that he had no legal power to do this. The ICC thereupon took the initiative in mid-August, announcing that it would provide all possible aid to the three municipalities threatened by annexation. Each planned to hold its annexation referendum on September 3, to demonstrate the extent of citizen opposition to the city's plans.

At the same time, the ICC finally presented its brief to the commission, calling for a grand scheme involving the creation of two new levels of government.[19] The first would group municipalities into boroughs, which would deal with such functions as roads, water supply, and sewer systems. The second would comprise all the boroughs in metropolitan Montreal, grouped together to provide for such functions as public transit and regional planning. Not surprisingly, this complex system would also require an intermunicipal relations board to adjudicate disputes among the municipalities, the boroughs, and the regional authority.[20] This scheme was so complex and far reaching that it could hardly be taken seriously. The very unlikelihood of its being adopted was actually a virtue of sorts, as all the suburbs could thus agree to it. It also served the valuable public-relations purpose of appearing positive, outward looking, and imaginative. The suburbs had not previously been noted for progressive positions.

By the time its brief was presented the ICC was obviously more concerned with the annexation battle than with the Blier commission. It considered the September 3 referenda extremely important. Perhaps sensing that the ICC now held the initiative, Saulnier announced in advance that Montreal would urge the province's municipal commission to hold its own referenda, regardless of the September vote.

When the votes were counted, two suburbs had rejected annexation decisively and the third approved annexation by a modest majority, with a comparatively low turnout.[21]

19. Bédard, *La bataille,* pp. 67–70.

20. Intermunicipal Co-ordinating Council, *Memoire présenté à la commission d'étude sur les problèmes intermunicipaux dans l'Ile de Montréal* (Montreal: 1964).

21. Bédard, *La bataille,* p. 51.

	For Annexation	Against Annexation	% Voting
Saint-Michel	1035	2068	51
Pointe-aux-Trembles	871	676	39
Roxboro	481	788	73
TOTAL	2387	3532	

Despite Saulnier's resounding defeat in Saint-Michel and Roxboro, he continued the proceedings to annex Pointe-aux-Trembles. The suburbs in turn, of course, claimed overall victory against Saulnier's annexation policy. Moreover, at the regular suburban municipal elections on November 2, anti-annexation candidates were decisively elected in all three municipalities. In Pointe-aux-Trembles the Quebec Municipal Commission conducted a final, official annexation referendum. This time it was defeated by 1141 to 1065 votes.[22] The city's most ambitious annexation crusade had failed.

The annexation debate in Saint-Michel and Pointe-aux-Trembles was principally over the two municipalities' financial difficulties. The issues involved local personalities and the question of whether the property tax would be higher in or out of the City of Montreal. The debate had no linguistic dimension, both suburbs being in the east end of the island and both overwhelmingly francophone.

Roxboro, a predominately anglophone suburb in the west part of the island, was a different matter. The mayor, René Labelle, came from an old French-Canadian family that had been in Roxboro long before the anglophone suburbanites, although the latter's representatives were by then dominating the town council. Labelle realized that he and his followers would lose control if the town stayed independent but that perhaps they could retain power as Jean Drapeau's agents in a future Roxboro ward of the City of Montreal. He was eager to respond to Saulnier's annexation initiatives but was blocked by the council's anglophone majority. In the subsequent referendum campaign, Saulnier promised many improved amenities for the town after annexation, with no increase in taxes. Because Roxboro had been totally built up, he claimed the town itself would be unable to provide these improvements without raising its taxes above Montreal's rate. In the elections of November 2, 1964, W. G. Boll, the leader of the anglophone councillors, became mayor by decisively defeating Labelle's main annexationist ally. This episode demonstrated that the anglophone suburbanites had gained full political control of the town, thus

22. Ibid., p. 74. Pointe-aux-Trembles was eventually annexed by the city in 1982 (see Ch. 7). It was located immediately to the east of Montreal East.

ensuring that Roxboro would never again be an obvious target for annexation.[23]

Searching for a Solution

At the height of the annexation controversy the Blier commission was beginning to draft its report, without the aid of research staff. From the beginning the chairman's main objective clearly was to find a compromise between the positions of Dawson and Saulnier acceptable to both of them and to the minister of municipal affairs. Blier's first proposal was that the island suburbs elect members to the Montreal city council so that they might participate in governing and financing various regional concerns such as an integrated island police force.[24] Mayor Dawson rejected this idea as impractical. He felt that the ICC brief deserved serious attention. Blier responded by claiming that the brief was drafted "in the sole interest of the suburbs and not with a view to the common interest. To avoid at any given time that the City of Montreal would have too much power, they want to create another level of government or finally a board, something which to me seems inconceivable."[25] Word soon leaked out to the other suburban mayors that Blier was not looking on their viewpoint with much sympathy. In mid-September they asked Mayor Dawson to resign from the commission in protest against Blier's antisuburban position. Dawson rejected this request so that he would be able to continue presenting the suburban case.[26]

Blier's next proposal was that the island be divided into two cities, one based on the City of Montreal, the other on Pointe-Claire. All municipalities east of Pierrefonds, Dollard-des-Ormeaux, and Dorval would be annexed to Montreal, and Pointe-Claire would become the nucleus of a powerful new anglophone municipality covering the area of metropolitan Montreal commonly known as the West Island.[27] Given Dawson's position as mayor of the inner suburb of Mount Royal, it is not surprising that he also rejected this proposal. There is no evidence that West Island politicians were even informed of this proposal, which they might well have accepted as a substantial guarantee that they would be free of the city for a good many years to come.

23. These events are described in the *North Shore News* (Pierrefonds, Quebec), June 25–November 5, 1964.
24. Quebec, Department of Municipal Affairs, *Procès-Verbaux: Commission d'étude des problèmes intermunicipaux de l'Ile de Montréal* (Quebec: 1964), vol. 2, 8th meeting, August 18, 1964.
25. Ibid., 9th meeting, August 28, 1964 (author's trans.).
26. *The Gazette*, September 16, 1964.
27. Quebec, *Procès-Verbaux*, vol. 2, meetings of December 8–13, 1964.

Blier's Final Compromise

Because Laporte had insisted that the report be unanimous, Blier was forced to make yet another attempt at compromise. This time he returned to the main theme of his original proposal, suggesting establishment of a "Montreal General Council" of 70 members, 46 to be the members of the Montreal city council and the other members coming from the suburbs, according to their respective populations. An executive committee would be made up of the seven members of the City of Montreal executive committee, who would be joined by three suburban representatives. The council would have jurisdiction over various "regional services," including social welfare, property valuation, fire protection, police, health, and public transit. Blier originally proposed a two-thirds majority be required for any major council decisions, but Dawson objected, as this would allow a united city vote to push through projects against a united suburban vote.[28] The ensuing compromise was a masterpiece of ambiguous phraseology. It appeared in the report as follows: "The rules of procedure shall be so drafted as to provide for the possibility that the representation of Montreal may form a block and render the representation of the suburban municipalities inoperative. Therefore the majorities required for decisions of the General Council must be such as not to prevent the representatives of the suburbs from exercising their prerogatives."[29]

The report was not favorably received when released in January 1965. Everyone recognized it as a patchwork compromise between two diametrically opposed positions. Mayor Drapeau claimed that the report gave him "three-quarters of a loaf," which was better than none, and said that annexation attempts would resume if the report were not fully implemented.[30] The chair of the ICC labeled the report as a "dishonest, subterfuge formula."[31] Mayor Dawson drew considerable suburban criticism for failing to take a tougher position. In light of Dawson's steadfast opposition to the favored proposals of both the city and the provincial government, it is hard to understand why his accomplishments were not given more recognition by his like-minded colleagues.

Guy Bourassa has attempted to analyze the role of the ethnic (i.e., linguistic) factor in the Blier deliberations. First, he made the important point that the debate involved very few organizations other than municipal governments, some property-owners' associations, and specialized professional groups. It did not become a popular issue

28. Ibid., meetings of December 15–23, 1964.
29. Quebec, *Intermunicipal Problems*, p. 67.
30. *The Gazette*, February 1, 1965.
31. Ibid., February 8, 1965.

involving political parties, trade unions, and employers.[32] Except in an area such as Roxboro, where the anglophone population felt genuinely threatened, the whole issue seemed rather technical and removed from everyday concerns. Nevertheless, the arguments got a good deal of attention in the media of both language groups, although only the local weeklies became passionately concerned.[33] Bourassa's analysis of the briefs presented to the commission and of interviews conducted with the participants suggests that suburban anglophone leaders expressed more concern with the virtues of small, democratic, responsive local governments. Suburban francophone leaders, on the other hand, objected to the city's financial and political practices.[34] In some interviews, participants openly acknowledged that although the ethnic factor was not publicly mentioned, it was at the heart of much of the debate.[35] Bourassa clearly agrees with this viewpoint but is quick to admit that it is difficult to prove.

Between 1964 and 1981 Montreal made one further annexation. In 1968 Saint-Michel was placed under the control of the Quebec Municipal Commission because of alleged corruption in the city administration. The Saint-Michel council then held another referendum on annexation, which this time was approved by 5043 to 2947 (i.e., 63 percent in favor.)[36] Because of suspected illegalities, a special provincial law was passed to validate the annexation proceeding.[37] Saint-Michel became part of the City of Montreal on October 24, 1968. The Quebec Municipal Commission then investigated Saint-Michel's city administration and in 1970 published a report documenting the corrupt practices of Mayor Bergeron and some of his colleagues.[38] Concurrently, the same commission reported on the unethical practices of Anjou's Mayor Crépault.[39] Both men, prominent officials of the ICC, were discredited by these investigations. Perhaps understandably, the ICC was no longer an important factor when the suburbs were next engaged in major negotiations about the government of metropolitan Montreal.

32. Bourassa, *Les relations ethniques*, p. 109.
33. Ibid., pp. 113–15.
34. Ibid., pp. 119–21.
35. Ibid., pp. 115–17.
36. *Le Devoir*, October 21, 1968.
37. Quebec, *Statutes* (1968), Ch. 94.
38. Quebec, Quebec Municipal Commission, *Rapport sur l'administration de la Cité de Saint-Michel* (Quebec: 1970).
39. Quebec, Quebec Municipal Commission, *Rapport de la commission d'enquête sur l'administration de Ville d'Anjou* (Quebec: 1970). There was a similar report in 1969 about patronage and administrative irregularities in Pointe-aux-Trembles. The reports of the Quebec Municipal Commission make fascinating reading for anyone who wishes to understand the nature of municipal corruption in east-end suburban Montreal in the 1960s.

The Lack of Provincial Action

After the Blier report was released in early 1965 a special provincial cabinet committee was established to study it and suggest legislative action. The ICC urged the cabinet to reject the report on the grounds that "for the most part its presentation is confused and confusing, its statements unjustifiable and unrealistic."[40] When the City of Westmount urged the provincial government to "go slow" on the Blier recommendations, Laporte responded that there would be enough time for everyone to have his or her opinion heard. Having accepted the Blier report only as the expression of his minimum objectives, Saulnier was not satisfied with Laporte's apparent vulnerability to suburban appeals.[41]

Meanwhile, however, Laporte's main immediate reason for not responding to the Blier report was his preoccupation with his bill for the voluntary amalgamation of municipalities (Bill 13), which became law in April 1965.[42] Its chief objective was to reduce the number of Quebec municipalities from 1600 to 900. Most of the opposition came from the rural areas to which it was primarily directed. Mayor Art Séguin of Pointe-Claire, however, speaking for the ICC, objected on the grounds that under the bill's provisions, municipal councils could abolish their municipalities without consulting the electors.[43]

During its period of operation (1965 to 1971), Bill 13 did not succeed in reducing the number of municipalities in Quebec. It was never used on the Island of Montreal and was used only to a limited extent in the rest of the province.[44] In the short run the debate about the bill diverted attention from the Blier report, but in the longer run it helped promote the resurgence of the *Union nationale* in rural Quebec, leading to the change of government in 1966. The Liberal government was therefore put out of office without having done anything about the problem of governing the Island of Montreal.

On the other hand, the Liberals had taken drastic action in another part of metropolitan Montreal. Legislation passed in 1965 formed the City of Laval out of the 14 municipalities on Île-Jésus and the tiny islands surrounding it.[45] For our purposes, the Laval amalgamation was important because it proved the provincial government

40. Quoted in *Montreal Star*, February 19, 1965.
41. Ibid., March 9 and 11, 1965.
42. Quebec, *Statutes* (1965), Ch. 56.
43. *Montreal Star*, February 22, 1965.
44. For a description of some of the Bill 13 amalgamations, see Jean Meynaud and Jacques Leveillée, *Quelques expériences de fusion municipale au Québec* (Montreal: Editions nouvelle frontière, 1972).
45. Quebec, *Statutes* (1965), Ch. 89.

was willing and able to make significant municipal changes in the Montreal area.

That Île-Jésus was an island and overwhelmingly French of course made the process easier than it otherwise might have been. The government also tried to encourage amalgamation in the south-shore area, but due to difficulties in defining the appropriate territorial extent of a unified south shore and to the fact that a few municipalities in the area, particularly Saint-Lambert, were composed of wealthy anglophones, no comprehensive policy was ever adopted. Furthermore, Laporte himself represented a south-shore constituency and would therefore have had to suffer personally the political consequences of unpopular government action. In later years a few important amalgamations did take place, but the south shore remains an area plagued by intermunicipal disputes and problems.

When the *Union nationale* took over the provincial government in 1966, Premier Daniel Johnson appointed Paul Dozois as minister of finance and municipal affairs, the latter post being the portfolio Dozois had held under Duplessis. Dozois inherited the unsolved problems of local government on the Island of Montreal. While he was in opposition in 1964, Dozois had advocated the "two cities" solution, with Montreal annexing the entire central and eastern parts of the island, leaving a new anglophone city to be established in the west. At the time, Dozois admitted that this could never be accomplished voluntarily but argued that the province was obliged to use its authority to force this type of change for the protection of the common good against a collection of particular interests.[46] In 1966, however, when he was once again facing political realities as a minister in the government, Dozois flatly contradicted this policy, stating that he would not force any municipal amalgamation not approved by the local taxpayers.[47]

The Montreal Urban Community: First Version

In 1968 Premier Johnson appointed Dr. Robert Lussier as minister of municipal affairs, leaving Dozois as minister of finance. Lussier took over a department whose civil servants had been impressed by recent local government innovations in France. On January 1, 1968, "*communautés urbaines*" were established for the French urban areas of Lille-Roubaix-Turcoing, Bordeaux, and Strasbourg. Local municipal councils sent delegates to a council for the urban community, and the latter had jurisdiction over such matters as planning, roads, sanitation, water supply, public transport, secondary schools, housing, industrial

46. *Le Devoir*, February 19, 1964.
47. *The Gazette*, September 3, 1966.

estates, hospitals, and recreation facilities.[48] Ministry officials soon convinced Lussier that this French model could be adopted in some parts of Quebec where intermunicipal problems were most serious.

On June 11, 1969, Lussier introduced a plan in the Quebec National Assembly calling for creation of a Montreal Urban Community. In the next two days he tabled similar plans for the Quebec City and Hull areas. The Montreal plan called for a 10-member executive committee, five to be chosen by the city council from among its members and four by suburban municipalities from among their municipal councils. There would also be a chair, initially appointed by the provincial government but later directly elected by all island residents. Members of the executive committee would serve four-year terms, during which they could not hold any other municipal office. In addition to the executive, there would also be a large council consisting of all Montreal's councillors plus the mayors of the other 28 municipalities. The main functions of the new Montreal Urban Community would relate to policing, air- and water-pollution control, and regional planning.[49]

Reaction to Lussier's proposals was unfavorable. Lucien Saulnier called them "contradictory and ridiculous."[50] He also stated that they could not stand serious analysis and were an insult to the Montreal administration.[51] Saulnier's main objection related to the composition of the executive committee. Politicians such as he could not serve at both levels, and the City of Montreal's appointees would be unable to overcome a provincial-suburban alliance. In general terms, the city opposed the plan because its provisions for the executive committee departed from the Blier recommendations—and in the suburbs' favor.

As the Blier recommendations had represented Saulnier's "limits" in accepting a separate level of metropolitan government, it is not surprising that he objected strenuously to Lussier's plan. On the other hand, the suburbs were suspicious because Lussier's plan implied the same threat to them that they had seen in the Blier report: the eventual takeover of intermunicipal services by the City of Montreal. Although many participants in the latest debate did not wish to revert to the bitterness of the Blier commission debate, the same divisive issues were still present. Lussier's plan attempted a compromise but satisfied no one.

48. Samuel Humes and Eileen Martin, *The Structure of Local Government* (The Hague: International Union of Local Authorities, 1969), p. 535.

49. *The Gazette*, June 12, 1969.

50. Quoted in *Montreal Star*, June 12, 1969.

51. Ibid., June 18, 1969.

Another Retreat

The experience of the Montreal Metropolitan Corporation had demonstrated that metropolitan institutions could not function without the City of Montreal's active cooperation. Lussier must have realized this, because on September 24 he announced that implementation of his plan would be postponed for one year.[52] His rapid retreat suggests that he may never have been personally convinced of the immediate need for his own plan. Because Lussier had obviously not mobilized any support for the plan in advance, it can be presumed that its presentation was simply a gesture to show that although not fully committed to dealing with the problem, the government was concerned with it.

This latest retreat was just another in a long series. From 1960 until September 1969 governments formed by both the Liberal and *Union nationale* parties had proven reluctant to tamper with the island's complex municipal structure. There were many reasons, not the least of which was that other pressing demands associated with the Quiet Revolution kept municipal reform at a relatively low level of priority. In comparison with education, for example, Quebec's municipal system was in less obvious need of reform. Another factor inhibiting metropolitan reform was the Quiet Revolution's fundamental concern with enhancing the capability and influence of the provincial government based in Quebec City. Thus, it is understandable that this government's ministers were unwilling to give control of the province's largest metropolitan center to a new level of government having jurisdiction over more than a third of the province's total population.

Variations of the factors just noted were also relevant in other Canadian provinces, including Ontario and Manitoba. But the situations of these provinces were different from that of Montreal, where changes in municipal boundaries and functions would also upset delicate patterns of French-English accommodation, of which municipal arrangements were an important part. The Liberals were especially conscious of the need to avoid alienating their strong base of support in anglophone suburbia. Although they implemented many reforms that centralized political power within the Quebec government, they never threatened the existence or viability of any local institutions dominated by anglophones.

The *Union nationale* government, in office from 1966 to 1970, faced different restraints. It had no pressing need to conciliate anglophone suburban interests, but it lacked urban strength and thus did not have adequate political resources to contest the powerful adminis-

52. Ibid., September 25, 1969.

tration that controlled the City of Montreal. Because Drapeau and
Saulnier objected to any reformed metropolitan arrangement they
could not control, the first *Union nationale* plan for a Montreal Urban
Community was foiled.

The Police Strike of October 1969

Throughout 1969 police officers in the City of Montreal tried to
negotiate a pay claim giving them the same salaries as the police
officers in metropolitan Toronto. Their basic objective was to increase
the salary of a beginning constable from $7300 to $9200 a year.[53] They
based their case largely on the grounds that their jobs were demonstra-
bly more difficult than those of Toronto police officers. Between June
1968 and October 1969 two officers on duty in Montreal had been
killed and more than 250 injured.[54] Most of the violence against the
police resulted from linguistically based demonstrations and bombings, matters with which the Toronto police rarely had to contend.

The period of serious demonstrations in Montreal started on
Saint-Jean-Baptiste Day (June 24), immediately preceding the 1968
federal election.[55] This was followed in rapid succession by occupations and demonstrations by thousands of francophone "CEGEP" (ju-
nior college) students objecting to the shortage of university places;
militant action by taxi drivers protesting the Murray Hill Company's
ground transport monopoly at Dorval airport; the demonstration in
March 1969 aimed at converting McGill into a French-language university; and the various street confrontations over immigrants' access
to English-language schools.[56] By October 1969 large demonstrations
with accompanying violence had become a regular feature of Montreal
life, a development that affected Montreal's police officers more than
anybody else.

In the first week of October 1969 word was leaked to the Montreal police that the arbitration commission set up to study the pay
claim had awarded them a basic raise of only $1180 a year, leaving
them far below Toronto's pay scale.[57] The response of the police officers' brotherhood (their union) was to call a "study session" at the

53. *The Gazette*, October 3, 1969.
54. Ibid., October 8, 1969.
55. Because of Prime Minister Trudeau's televised defiance of the rioters, this
event has been considered a vital factor in the decisive electoral victory that he achieved
on the next day.
56. These matters are discussed in Robert Chodos and Nick Auf der Maur,
Quebec: A Chronicle, 1968–1972 (Toronto: James Lewis and Samuel, 1972), pp. 13–15,
28–29.
57. *The Gazette*, October 8, 1969.

Paul Sauvé arena in east-end Montreal. Such sessions had been held before by off-duty police officers, but the unique feature of this one was that all the officers were expected to convene at the same time, thus leaving the entire city without protection. The police took this action without any apparent warning, and on October 7, 1969, Montreal's police were effectively on strike for a period of 16 hours. The police remained in the Paul Sauvé arena throughout this period, at one point shouting down Lucien Saulnier before he had a chance to address them.

As soon as the police left the streets, central Montreal slipped into a state of near anarchy. The provincial government reacted to the crisis by placing all Montreal-region police forces under the temporary control of the Quebec Provincial Police and by sending its officers, who usually operate in rural Quebec, into the city. At the request of the province, the federal government provided 600 troops to guard important buildings and thoroughfares.

Before order was reestablished there were 9 armed bank robberies, 30 other armed robberies, and 494 complaints involving $853,882 worth of reported damage.[58] Most of the violence took place at the headquarters of the Murray Hill Company, where taxi drivers, Murray Hill employees, and provincial police officers shot at each other. One provincial policeman was killed.[59] Because suburban police forces remained on duty, there was no trouble outside the boundaries of Montreal. Never were suburban citizens more appreciative of their independent police forces.

On the evening of October 7, the provincial government presented a bill to the National Assembly to force the police to go back to work. With all-party support, it became law a few hours later. The police chose to obey the new law, and early on October 8 they reported for duty once again.[60]

Saulnier's Solution

While the strike was in progress Mayor Drapeau was on an economic promotion visit to St. Louis. Accordingly, Lucien Saulnier, the chairman of Montreal's executive committee, was the politician most involved with the police during the strike and in its immediate aftermath. At the provincial level, ministers had no alternative but to leave Saulnier in control. The *Gazette* commented that it was Saulnier who "presented Montreal's case to the Quebec Government, who informed, advised, and guided the government in the prompt action it took to

58. Ibid., October 24, 1969.
59. Chodos and Auf der Maur, *Quebec*, pp. 30–31.
60. *The Gazette*, October 8, 1969.

bring the police walk-off to an end."[61] One of the most important political results of the strike was to force the *Union nationale* government and Saulnier into a working relationship, with Saulnier clearly the dominant partner.

Although Saulnier had made predictable statements about police irresponsibility during the strike, he was fully aware that he could not afford to criticize their illegal action continually. The police were needed as much as ever to control political demonstrations, particularly one scheduled for the end of October over language rights in schools. Saulnier's objective was to settle with the police at virtually any cost. On October 23 he announced that the city would give the police a raise of $1450, thus giving them a salary 54.2 percent above the average industrial wage in Montreal. (The salary level of Toronto police officers was at that time 54.2 percent above the average industrial wage in Toronto.) The Montreal police were quite satisfied with this method of calculating parity, particularly as they also won victories on virtually all other clauses affecting grievance procedures and working conditions.

When announcing the settlement, Saulnier pointed out that Toronto's metropolitan police force had a per capita annual cost of $19.47, whereas Montreal's was $27.92. He went on to say:

> Montreal's police department is effectively the shield which protects all of the Island of Montreal. Justice would almost be restored if the cost of all police services of Montreal Island were shared by all citizens of the island. If the police services in Montreal were unified as in Toronto they would have some 4,845 policemen with a total annual cost of $39,679,121 for a population of 1,931,793 persons—and if equally divided the cost would be $20.54 per capita.[62]

Saulnier's strategy was to have the suburbs pay for much of the city's increased police costs. The next day Lussier announced provincial support for this strategy. He summoned the suburban mayors to his Montreal office to tell them that the police strike had convinced him of the urgency of taking action to share police costs and of establishing some form of metropolitan government. This action effectively reversed his September decision to postpone consideration of the metropolitan government issue for one more year.

Weakness on All Fronts

During the police strike the provincial government, the suburbs and the City of Montreal all demonstrated crucial weaknesses. The

61. Ibid.
62. Ibid., October 24, 1969.

government lacked urban support and feared the impact of further mass demonstrations, which it had counted on the Montreal police to contain. The strike showed that the police could not again be considered reliable unless they were paid considerably more money. Only by forcing the suburbs to contribute could the government ensure that Lucien Saulnier would be able to maintain law and order in the province's most important city.

The suburbs were weak because they had virtually no influence within the *Union nationale*. They were not well organized, possibly because their official leader, Mayor Crépault, president of the ICC, was being investigated for corruption. In some ways the City of Montreal's position was weakest of all. The strike had shown the fragile nature of the city's authority over its own police officers. It had also demonstrated that the city was in an extremely precarious financial position, largely due to overexpenditures related to Expo '67. Montreal simply could not afford to pay competitive salaries, even to its most important employees.

But the city did have Lucien Saulnier, a man with far more political skill than could be found among the other participating groups. Saulnier realized that he could exploit everybody's weaknesses, finally bringing the island's suburbs under the effective control of the City of Montreal. In late October and November 1969 he spent a great deal of time consulting with the provincial government. On November 28 Robert Lussier presented a new plan for a Montreal Urban Community to the Quebec National Assembly,[63] a plan containing nothing with which Lucien Saulnier did not agree. In less than four weeks it became law.

The single most important fact about the Montreal Urban Community (MUC) is its creation in a moment of crisis. From the provincial government's point of view, the only significant objective was to establish a mechanism whereby the suburbs would be forced to share police costs. All else was peripheral. The intensity of the crisis was much greater and more obvious than the service crises that had sparked the creation of metropolitan institutions in Toronto and Winnipeg. The government wanted action so badly that the predictable suburban objections were virtually ignored.

An important point must be emphasized before commenting further on the politics of the MUC. The explosiveness of the city's political, social, and economic situation made policing unusually crucial in Montreal in the late 1960s. This explosiveness was constantly reflected in street demonstrations and marches and in the terrorist activities of the FLQ and other extremist groups. When such incidents occurred, the city's police were on the front line. Their work was clearly much more difficult and dangerous than that of any other police force in Canada. This was in large part due to their having to

63. Quebec, l'Assemblée nationale, *Débats*, 28e Legislature, 4e Session, 8: 4365.

deal with serious threats caused by people who were acting on their perceptions of the unjust relationship between francophones and anglophones.

Consequently, it can be argued not only that the introduction of metropolitan government for the Island of Montreal was delayed because of the linguistic cleavage but also that the hurried adoption of a metropolitan solution in late 1969 was precipitated by the political situation caused by the cleavage. Although this seems paradoxical, it appears to be an accurate interpretation of the complicated political developments.

The Creation of the MUC

Lussier's proposals for a Montreal Urban Community reflected the urgent desire of both the province and Montreal to ensure that the island's suburbs contributed to the city's increased police costs. The MUC was to be established on January 1, 1970, and as of that date all island police costs were to be consolidated. Each municipality would then contribute to the total bill in proportion to its share of the total assessed value of the island's property. The MUC itself, on the recommendation of a Public Security Council (PSC), was to decide the extent to which the existing police forces were eventually to be unified.

The other important difference between the new proposals and the original ones concerned the structure of the MUC's executive committee. Lussier now called for a 12-member committee, seven to be the members of the City of Montreal's executive committee and the other five members to be suburban mayors. There would be no provincial representatives and no provision for the future direct election of the chair. These changes reflected Saulnier's insistence that city politicians have full control of any new metropolitan institution. Most of the *Union nationale*'s elected members were rural in origin and the MUC proposals were of limited interest to government backbenchers. They were content to let Lussier give Saulnier whatever was necessary to restore stability in Montreal.

In contrast, the Liberals, with their strength in suburban Montreal, were deeply concerned about the issue of metropolitan government. They had a general commitment to institutional reform in Quebec and claimed to support the overall objectives of the new plan. Jean Lesage, who had announced his intention to retire from the Liberal leadership, was the party's main spokesman on the issue. As a member of the provincial legislature for a Quebec City constituency, Lesage had a special interest in the government's plan to create similar metropolitan institutions in Quebec City and Hull. Lesage's eventual support of the MUC bill's prompt passage was probably due to the government's pledge that it would act simultaneously in solving municipal problems of the provincial capital. Although the bills creating the Quebec Urban Community and the regional community around Hull received even less publicity than the MUC bill, they were presented and approved at about the same time.[64]

Largely because of his imminent retirement, Lesage was unable to convince his followers in suburban Montreal to adhere to the official Liberal position. Georges E. Tremblay, a Liberal member whose constituency included Montreal North, summed up their thoughts when he said, "This is a hypocritical bill, this is a hypocritical way of approving annexation."[65] Individual Liberals opposed to the bill were not powerless. Their main weapon was time. If Lussier wanted the MUC to be operating on January 1, he could not afford to provoke the Liberals into debating it for more than a few days. Lussier was therefore prepared to make concessions, but only if they did not upset his new arrangement with Lucien Saulnier. His first concession to the Liberals and the suburbs was to allow the MUC bill (Bill 75) to be referred to the municipal affairs committee of the National Assembly, where interested municipalities and unions could make representations before the bill received second reading. It was here that the plan underwent its closest public examination.

Bill 75 and the Legislative Process

The committee held its hearings on December 10 and 11, 1969.[66] The discussion had little or no pattern, each witness taking up various aspects of the bill in no apparent order. In all, six areas of major concern were expressed.

1. *Haste vs. delay.* Suburban spokesmen claimed that the bill needed far more study than it could possibly be given in the three-week period before it was intended to become effective. Drapeau and Saulnier, pointing to the numerous study commissions of the past, were the most eloquent advocates of the need for immediate legislation.

2. *Financial provisions.* The main problem regarding finance related to the sharing of police costs. Lussier calculated that the total island police costs would make up $53,300,000 of the initial budget of $72,709,000. Most of the other $19,409,000 in

64. The institutions of the Quebec City and Hull communities are described in Louise Quesnel-Ouellet, "Canada: Quebec," in *International Handbook on Local Government Reorganization*, ed. Donald C. Rowat (Westport, Conn.: Greenwood Press, 1980) pp. 20–32.

65. Quebec, *Débats* 8: 4743 (author's trans.).

66. The transcript of these hearings can be found in Quebec, *Débats*, Commission permanente des affaires municipales, 8: 4007–4154.

expenses were attributable to services then being provided by individual municipalities. This led him to claim that because the government would grant a subsidy of $8,939,000 to the MUC during its first year, the total costs for all the municipalities would be reduced by that amount.[67] The suburbs hastened to point out that most suburban municipalities would in fact pay much more money to the MUC than they would for their own police. Thus, only Montreal and a very few poor suburbs would benefit from the provincial subsidy and sharing of police costs.

3. *Police unification.* Although the two issues were often confused, the question of police unification is different in principle from the sharing of police costs. The bill called for the establishment of a three-member Public Security Council (PSC) consisting of a provincial judge and the chiefs of the Quebec and Montreal police forces. The PSC could recommend to the MUC council various steps to coordinate, and possibly to unify, the island's police forces. The suburbs objected to the composition of the PSC and offered various arguments against unification. The government refused to respond, contending that the desirability of police unification should be decided by the PSC and the MUC after their establishment. Lussier did, however, eventually yield to some of the suburban pressure, enlarging the PSC to four members and adding one suburban police chief.

4. *City of Montreal dominance.* The suburbs objected strenuously to the city's proposed dominance of the executive committee, but they made little headway.[68] They were more successful in attempting to gain additional power within the council, which was to consist of the 52 city councillors and the mayor of Montreal plus one representative from each of the 28 other municipalities. This gave the city a clear majority that—given the cohesiveness and dominance of Drapeau's Civic Party—could easily be swung against the suburbs should the need arise. As a concession to the suburbs, the bill originally stated that in order for a motion to be approved, it had to receive support from at least one-third of the suburban representatives and one-third of the Montreal councillors. This meant that the suburbs were given a form of veto. If at least two-thirds of the suburban mayors were opposed, a motion was not successful, regardless of the total

67. Ibid., p. 4040.
68. Not until 1982 did the provincial government increase suburban influence. For details, see Ch. 7.

vote in the entire council. During a rather confused debate, when proposals were put forth to further protect the suburbs, Saulnier made this statement: "Concerning the right of veto, we say that it is operative if one third of the suburban municipalities oppose a measure or one half—I am no longer objecting to a half—but of the members present."[69] Saulnier appeared confused at this point and, in his confusion, made an important concession to the suburbs. The bill did not provide for a one-third suburban veto as Saulnier implied. Saulnier's words were understandably taken to mean that he was willing to allow one-half of the suburbs to exercise a veto instead of two-thirds. Although Saulnier's concession on this point was apparently unintentional, the government made the change. For proper approval, a motion in the MUC council was to require the support of the majority of votes cast and the support of at least one-half of the Montreal councillors present and one-half of the suburban mayors present.

5. *Weighted votes in the MUC council.* The government originally proposed that each council member have one vote, although the suburban mayors represented populations that varied widely in size. Lesage suggested a system of weighting votes according to the size of the population represented. Understandably, the larger suburbs voiced strong support. Lussier eventually announced that each suburban mayor would cast one vote for every 1000 residents in his municipality and that each of the 53 Montreal representatives would have as many votes as the city's population divided by 53,000. The weighted vote system would not affect the veto provisions; thus, successful measures would still need the approval of half the suburbs and half the city representatives.[70]

6. *Territory of the MUC.* A number of suburban representatives suggested that the MUC would be more effective if it included Île-Jésus and the south shore as well as the Island of Montreal, a change that would also have conveniently diluted the influence of the City of Montreal. The government refused to consider such a radical change.

Much time was spent discussing whether Île-Bizard should be included. This small island, squeezed between the western parts of Île-Jésus and the Island of Montreal (see Map 1, pp. 6–7) was attractive for MUC purposes because

69. Ibid., p. 4112 (author's trans.).
70. Quebec, *Statutes* (1969), Ch. 84, Sections 52–53.

it contained valuable undeveloped land that could in the future be useful for both recreation and housing. Despite protests from the mayor of Île-Bizard,[71] the government refused to change its position, and the island municipality remained within the boundaries of the MUC.

When the National Assembly finally voted on the second reading of Bill 75, the few Liberals present (mostly from suburban Montreal) voted against it. Lesage claimed that they still supported the bill in principle but objected to the minister's refusal to answer Liberal arguments against specific provisions.[72] In reality, however, it appeared that Lesage simply could not control the suburban Liberals, who by then had recognized the full financial implications of the MUC for their municipalities. As debate dragged on in the Committee of the Whole, Premier Jean-Jacques Bertrand finally intervened, criticizing those suburban mayors and Liberal members who claimed to be in favor of the principle of the bill: "I think that, in the final analysis, those who say they are for are really against. And to avoid showing that they are against, they say: Change it. If the government changed it, they would come back again and say: We are for, you know, but we are against such-and-such an aspect of the bill. A government has to live up to its responsibilities."[73] Although he was making a partisan political point, Bertrand also seemed to be summing up the situation quite accurately. On December 18 the bill finally received its third reading. There was no recorded vote, but two West Island Liberals said they would have broken party ranks and voted against the principle of the bill. Lesage was no doubt being totally candid in saying he was neither surprised nor upset by the open split in his party.[74] He had achieved his main objective of preventing a suburban filibuster. Two weeks later, on January 1, 1970, Montreal and Quebec urban communities came into being, and in fiscal terms, the two central cities were the main beneficiaries.

Functions of the MUC

When created, the MUC was little more than a legal shell. Except for inheriting office furnishings, a few employees, and some financial responsibility from the dormant Montreal Metropolitan Corporation,[75] the MUC came into being with no planning or administrative apparatus whatsoever. Its wide-ranging legislated functions notwithstanding, the MUC's immediate purpose was to serve as a conduit for funds and

71. Quebec, *Débats*, affaires municipales, 8: 4009.
72. Quebec, *Débats*, 8: 4930.
73. Ibid., p. 5111 (author's trans.).
74. Ibid., p. 5285.
75. Quebec, *Statutes* (1969), Ch. 84, Sections 362–64.

not as an important force in the management of Montreal's urban development.

In political terms, the stated rationale for the MUC was that it could provide much-needed metropolitan services benefiting all Island of Montreal residents. Although there was no immediate transfer of existing municipal services to the new institution, it came into being with an impressive list of potential functions: the assessment of property, the establishment of a development plan, the centralized processing of municipal data, the elimination of air pollution, traffic control on main thoroughfares, the supply of drinking water, sewage and garbage disposal, construction standards, the coordination of police and fire services, and (if deemed necessary) the unification of municipal police departments. Until the MUC acted concerning any of these functions, the member municipalities were to retain their existing jurisdiction. Once the MUC was involved, however, it could take complete control if it wished. The MUC council was also given the authority, with the approval of the provincial cabinet, to take over jurisdiction in recreation and regional parks, public housing, integration of fire services, and libraries.[76] So far, the MUC has added only the administration of regional parks to its original list of potential functions.

The Montreal Urban Community Transit Commission

The creation of the MUC also affected the administrative arrangements concerning public transit. The Montreal Transit Commission, a special-purpose body that had been serving the central and eastern portions of the Island of Montreal and the south-shore municipality of Longueuil, became linked to the MUC instead of to the City of Montreal. Hence its new name: the Montreal Urban Community Transit Commission (MUCTC).[77] There was in fact very little change in the nature of public transit services. The new transit commission carried on in much the same way as the old. It had three members—a chair appointed by the provincial government, one member appointed by the City of Montreal, and one by the suburbs.[78] The operating deficits of the MUCTC are shared by the participating municipalities in proportion to their share of total property assessment.[79] Because arrangements to extend the MUCTC service to the West Island were not made until 1979, municipalities in that area were not involved in commission affairs, financial and otherwise, before that year.

The MUCTC has the authority "to organize, possess, develop, and administer, within its territory, a general network for public trans-

76. Ibid., Sections 112–14.
77. Ibid., Section 268.
78. Ibid., Section 274. For 1982 changes, see Ch. 7.
79. Ibid., Section 304.

portation above or beneath the surface of the ground."[80] It should be noted that it lacks authority for actual construction of facilities such as subways, these being reserved for the MUC itself. But the municipalities served by the MUCTC share the costs of such construction in the same way that they share the MUCTC operating deficits. When construction is completed, the operation of the new facilities is turned over to the commission.[81]

A Noncontroversial Reform

Passage of the MUC Act caused little public controversy, probably for four principal reasons. First, controversial bills concerning language rights (Bill 63) and the reorganization of Montreal's educational system were being debated at the same time.[82] The emotions raised by these bills ensured that the media, also preoccupied with the Liberal leadership race, gave little attention to the MUC debate. Second, because of Lesage's cooperation, the government was successful in rushing the legislation through. Moreover, the short debate took place immediately before Christmas, which made it more difficult to organize the opposition. In any event, the MUC Act was approved before the suburbs had an opportunity to mobilize public opinion against it.

Third, the bill appeared to deal primarily with technical matters of interest only to municipal politicians and administrators. The bill's immediate financial implications for most suburban taxpayers were not made clear. Although the question of police unification was potentially explosive, the government skillfully maintained that the issue would be decided later. Finally, many informed observers were reluctant to oppose important details when the bill's apparent objective—to provide the Island of Montreal with a government able to control such vital matters as regional planning, public transit, and water and air pollution—was so obviously desirable. All these factors helped ensure that when the MUC actually began to operate, most citizens had no idea how and why it had come into being.

Implications of Change

The MUC Act did not mention language. It was passed in 1969, five years before enactment of Quebec's first general language legislation, Bill 22. Consequently it was simply assumed that French would be the chief working language of the Montreal Urban Community. It was quite clear that within the new institution, anglophones would be

80. Ibid., Section 269.
81. Ibid., Section 318.
82. The latter bill is discussed in Chapter 8.

treated in the same way as anglophones within the City of Montreal or as francophones within a predominantly anglophone suburb. Many official documents were to appear in both languages, but complete institutional bilingualism was not guaranteed. English could be used at meetings of the MUC council and its executive committee, but at the risk of not being fully understood. Given the political reality of the time, residents of anglophone suburbs were willing to resign themselves to these arrangements.[83]

The anglophone suburbs were less willing to accept the eventuality that they might find their municipalities losing jurisdiction over any important urban services. While these services were still controlled at the local level, there would be no problem ensuring that a citizen's use of English would not be to his or her disadvantage. But if a service were transferred to the MUC, there would not be the same certainty.

Despite these considerations, language use did not figure prominently in the debate about the MUC, the overriding issues being the financing of the police and the distribution of power within the Island of Montreal between Montreal and the suburbs. The creation of the MUC increased the resources and power of the City of Montreal and decreased the resources and power of the independent suburbs. This in turn, however, had an influence on language. Because of the territorial distribution of the two main linguistic groups, the MUC's creation could only mean that anglophones would tend to lose, and francophones would tend to gain.

The creation of the MUC in late 1969 meant that after a tortuous passage beginning early in the decade, Mayor Drapeau had gained much of what he originally sought. Although "One Island, One City" remained a distant dream, the MUC had the potential of being an acceptable substitute. It was a form of metropolitan government in which City of Montreal executive committee members and councillors would clearly dominate. Without Drapeau's approval, nothing could change. Moreover, the city's financial problems were greatly eased, as mandatory suburban subsidies for the city's police force would soon be flowing in.

What Drapeau perhaps did not foresee was that suburban representatives on the MUC, by using their veto, could effectively prevent the MUC from being used as another institution to promote his grandiose ambitions. Drapeau also seemed unaware that by giving up financial responsibility for the city's police, he would inevitably lose political responsibility and, ultimately, political power.

---

83. Because of Bill 101, however, the MUC after 1977 could no longer issue bilingual official communications. This prompted objections from some English-speaking mayors. See *Le Conférencier* (Bulletin d'information de la Conférence des maires de la Banlieue de Montréal), vol. 1, no. 11 (December 1980), p. 6.

7

The Montreal Urban Community
in Operation

Like its predecessors, the MUC received enough potential jurisdiction from the provincial government to become an extremely important governmental institution. Although it has clearly had more
impact on the public than either the Montreal Metropolitan Commission or the corporation, so far it has definitely not developed into as
strong a government as observers of metropolitan bodies in Toronto or
Winnipeg might have expected.

A recent study argues that after their initial opposition, suburban
municipalities finally came to accept the MUC, realizing its usefulness in providing certain common services and in protecting their
common islandwide interests against the growing problems caused by
increasing urbanization beyond the Island of Montreal.[1] While this is
undoubtedly true, it overlooks the fact that within the Island of Montreal, the MUC has failed to emerge as an institution able to make
authoritative decisions on various local political conflicts. In short, it
has not been able to act as a true government. This chapter considers
the reasons that the MUC has not lived up to its apparent potential.

Leadership

Although suburban politicians realized that the MUC would
largely be dominated by the City of Montreal, they basically saw it as
politically and legally separate from the city. Drapeau, on the other
hand, considered the MUC as an extension of Montreal, established to
deal with certain problems that could be solved only on an islandwide basis. Although he acknowledged the need for limited suburban
participation, he saw no reason that Montreal should radically change
its ways to accommodate suburban desires. An example of the different viewpoints concerned the choice of a meeting place for the MUC

---

1. Gérard Divay and Jean-Pierre Collin, *La Communauté urbaine de Montréal: de
la ville centrale a l'île centrale*, Rapport de recherche no. 4, Institut national de la
recherche scientifique—Urbanisation (Montreal: 1977).

council. Drapeau felt it should meet in the chambers of the city council, that being the most convenient place for most members. The suburbs opposed this, arguing that the meetings should be held on "neutral ground." Although the first meeting was held at the University of Montreal, Drapeau eventually won out, and subsequent meetings were held at the Montreal city hall. Drapeau also felt that the MUC could be staffed largely by City of Montreal employees working under contract with the community, whereas the suburbs felt that the MUC needed its own separate and independent civil service.

Saulnier as MUC Chair

Mayor Drapeau also believed that the political leadership of the MUC should virtually be the same as that of the City of Montreal. He thought Lucien Saulnier should preside over the executive committee of the MUC, just as he did over the executive committee of the City of Montreal. Drapeau envisioned himself as symbolic head of the MUC, presiding over the public meetings of its council the way he presided at the meetings of the Montreal city council. At the first meeting of the MUC council on February 9, 1970, Saulnier and Drapeau were acclaimed to these respective positions,[2] the suburbs being at this early stage too disorganized and unsure of themselves to use their veto. Although they could have blocked the choice of Saulnier and Drapeau, they lacked the power to elect their own candidates. They had in fact no real alternative except to accept the takeover of the MUC by the Drapeau-Saulnier team.

Saulnier quickly established his complete control over the MUC executive committee. At first the suburban members caused him little more concern than his faithful majority from the city. Saulnier's greatest procedural victory was to impose the same conventions of secrecy and cabinet solidarity at the MUC level that already prevailed within the City of Montreal. Saulnier himself was the only public source of information about executive committee activities. Other members were expected not to talk to the press about their positions on forthcoming issues, certainly not if they opposed the majority position.

Although public opposition and various unofficial leaks occurred later, the surprising feature of early MUC development was Saulnier's success in controlling the suburban representatives. His accomplishment was made possible by the general reluctance of suburban politicians to appear to be obstructing the work of a man who was obviously getting things done and by the rather passive, unquestioning habits of the Montreal press.[3] City hall reporters, who reluc-

---

2. Montreal Urban Community, *1970 Annual Report* (Montreal: 1971), pp. 3–4.
3. See Marcel Adam, *La démocratie à Montréal* (Montreal: Editions du jour, 1972), Ch. 7.

tantly accepted the Drapeau-Saulnier policy of news management at city hall, seemed to consider it quite natural when these policies were extended to the MUC. Nor were suburban politicians well placed to object to Saulnier's tactics, as many suburban councils tended to conduct their internal arguments in private. Thus, suburban mayors could hardly object when Saulnier insisted on the same policy at the metropolitan level.

As the City of Montreal's October 1970 election approached, Saulnier announced his wish to retire from city politics. But he also said he would accept a special appointment from the provincial government to continue his position with the MUC,[4] which would require special legislation to change the procedure for choosing the MUC executive committee chair. A bill was duly presented to the National Assembly by Maurice Tessier, the new Liberal minister of municipal affairs. The only dissent came from the *Parti québécois*, which wanted the chair to be elected by the executive committee rather than appointed by the government.[5] The new act provided for the chair to be appointed by the provincial government for a nonrenewable, four-year term. When that appointee eventually left the position, succeeding chairs would be elected according to the original provisions of the 1969 MUC Act.[6]

This episode clearly demonstrated how essential Saulnier was to the MUC. Everyone involved was willing to change the rules in a special way to accommodate his personal requirements. From October 1970 until his resignation from the MUC in February 1972 Saulnier served as the provincially appointed leader of the MUC. For a man who had previously insisted that Montreal's metropolitan government not be led by a provincial appointee, his acceptance of this position seemed hypocritical. For all practical purposes, however, the only change was that Saulnier could now devote his full attention to MUC affairs.

The last 12 months of Saulnier's tenure were difficult. The Liberal government finally made it clear that they would not allow the city to wholly dominate metropolitan politics. During the same period, the suburbs overcame their reluctance to oppose Saulnier's policies and began using their veto in the MUC council with increasing effectiveness. Finally, in January 1972 *Le Devoir* published a series of damaging articles accusing Saulnier's brother, Jean-Jacques, of corrupt behavior while pursuing his career as a high-ranking city police officer.[7]

4. *The Montreal Star*, July 18, 1970.
5. Quebec, *Débats*, 29e Legislature, 1e Session, 10: 1205–14.
6. Quebec, *Statutes* (1969), Ch. 84, Section 13.
7. See *Le Devoir*, January 12 and 13, 1972.

When Saulnier resigned he claimed he had accomplished his main mission: "to put in place the structures and mechanisms essential to the life of MUC."[8] Leaving aside the complex subject of police unification, it is worthwhile to review Saulnier's administrative achievements. Apart from overseeing the growth of the secretariat and the creation of a separate treasury department, he also supervised the creation of six separate functional departments, each with its own director. By the end of 1971 the MUC employed more than 1500 people, not counting police officers.[9] Most of these employees were transferred from the civil service of the City of Montreal. Although Saulnier had many enemies when he retired, virtually everyone acknowledged that he was probably the only person who could in such a short time have transformed the MUC from a legal shell into a functioning government.

Hanigan and DesMarais

Mayor Drapeau insisted on replacing Saulnier with another member of the city's executive committee, but the suburbs felt they now had a right to place one of their own people in the top position. When the MUC council met in special session on February 16, 1972, to elect Saulnier's successor, Mayor Drapeau nominated Lawrence Hanigan, a Civic Party councillor since 1960 and a member of the executive committee since 1970.[10] The suburbs proposed Yves Ryan, the mayor of Montreal North. After three ballots failed to produce the necessary dual majority from the city councillors and the suburban mayors, the latter group finally gave way and supported Montreal's nominee.

Hanigan served as chair of the MUC executive committee from 1972 to 1978. While he was in office, the provincial government was constantly reassessing the future of the MUC, consistently refusing to give it either the funds or the authority it needed to expand its activities further. Hanigan was able to do little more than continue the programs Saulnier had begun. His main virtue was his style of leadership. He was far more cautious and less abrasive than Saulnier, and this enabled him to gain at least some suburban support.

Hanigan's successor was from the suburbs: Pierre DesMarais II, the mayor of Outremont. Given Mayor Drapeau's original desire to maintain clear control of the MUC, it seems surprising indeed that DesMarais was chosen. Yet he was elected on the first ballot, and the only opposition came from the Montreal Citizens Movement, a left-wing party that had unexpectedly won 18 council seats in the 1974

8. Ibid., February 11, 1972.
9. MUC, *Annual Report 1971*, p. 14.
10. *Le Devoir*, March 27, 1972.

Montreal elections.[11] In the 1978 municipal elections, which came a few months after DesMarais took control of the MUC, the Montreal Citizens Movement saw its delegation to the Montreal council reduced to only one. Montreal municipal politics were back to normal, with Mayor Drapeau ruling almost completely unchallenged.

Why did Drapeau consent to the election of a suburban mayor like DesMarais? Despite the temporary strength of the Montreal Citizens Movement, Drapeau could have used his majority in the city council to veto any suburban nominee. An explanation offered in the press was that by approving DesMarais, well known as a Liberal Party supporter, Drapeau insured himself against the federal Liberal organization being turned against him in the November 1978 municipal elections.[12] And in fact, although a young and often rebellious Liberal MP, Serge Joyal, challenged the mayor in 1978, he did so without support from the established Liberal organization, winning only 25.5 percent of the popular vote (against 60.9 percent for Drapeau and 12.5 percent for the MCM candidate).[13]

A more likely explanation is that by 1978 Drapeau had enough experience to realize that as far as the City of Montreal was concerned the MUC had already delivered all the benefits it was designed to provide. Because he could use the city veto power to stop any changes in these established policies, there was nothing to lose by letting the suburbs have the top position. Drapeau also protected his position by making it quite clear that he had still not accepted the principle that the position of executive committee chair should consistently alternate between Montreal and suburban representatives.[14]

As chair, DesMarais has been a staunch defender of the MUC rather than some kind of suburban saboteur. Writing on the tenth anniversary of its creation, DesMarais stated, "We have had our share of difficulties, our crisis of growth and all which that implies concerning adaptation to changing conditions. But it was proven in 1979 that the Community is a sound organization, not only viable but necessary to the well-being and progress of the member municipalities."[15] He made it quite clear that his objectives for the MUC were to improve its existing services and have it play a major role in promoting the eco-

11. For details on the MCM and other left-wing municipal groups in Montreal, see Henry Milner, *Politics in the New Quebec* (Toronto: McClelland and Stewart, 1978), Ch. 10, and 'The M.C.M.: Back to the Drawing Board," *City Magazine* (April 1979), pp. 37–41. Also see Jean Desjardins, "Le Rassemblement des citoyens de Montréal" (M.A. thesis, Université Laval, 1979).

12. *La Presse* (Montreal), August 1, 1978.

13. Montreal, *Résultats, Elections 1978* (Montreal: 1978), p. 1. See also Ludger Beauregard, *Les elections municipales de Montréal: Une étude de géographie electorale* (Département de géographie, Université de Montréal, 1980).

14. *Le Devoir*, August 1, 1978.

15. Montreal Urban Community, *1979 Annual Report*, p. 2.

nomic well-being of the Island of Montreal. DesMarais was presiding over an institution that, in his words, had "attained its cruising speed"[16] and was not about to change course.

The MUC: Accomplishments and Failures

During its existence, the MUC has figured in a great deal of local political discussion and debate, but with very little public awareness of either its accomplishments or failures. Admittedly, the MUC has no record of accomplishments to compare with Metro Toronto's suburban development achievements in the 1950s or with those of Metro Winnipeg in transportation, water supply, sewers, and parks during the 1960s.[17] The MUC's overall record is not that impressive largely because of a multitude of jurisdictional and political disputes. Nevertheless, it has had at least some appreciable impact in four subject areas: property assessment, air and water quality, public transit, and regional planning.

Property Assessment

The MUC was supposed to standardize property assessments among the various municipalities on the Island of Montreal, but the original MUC assessment department found this task impossible due to lack of suburban cooperation.[18] In late 1971, however, as part of an overall provincial reform of the assessment system, the government passed legislation placing all municipal assessment on the Island of Montreal under the exclusive control of the MUC. The new MUC department, comprising mainly assessors transferred from the City of Montreal, officially absorbed the relevant departments of the member municipalities on January 1, 1972, and the first common assessment roll had been presented by the end of the year.[19] The MUC then had adequate administrative machinery to ensure, in theory at least, that all property on the Island of Montreal would eventually be assessed using consistent procedures and standards.

Although the unification of the various municipal assessment departments created a great deal of bitterness in some quarters, it certainly was no cause for general public concern, because it was

16. *Le Devoir*, July 10, 1980.

17. Albert Rose, *Governing Metropolitan Toronto* (Berkeley: University of California Press, 1972), Ch. 3, and S. George Rich, "Metropolitan Winnipeg: The First Ten Years," in *Urban Problems: A Canadian Reader*, ed. Ralph R. Krueger and R. Charles Bryfogle (Toronto: Holt, Rinehart and Winston, 1971), pp. 363–67.

18. MUC, *1970 Annual Report*.

19. MUC, *1972 Annual Report*, pp. 14–15.

more a bureaucratic power struggle than anything else. Suburban mayors were eager to retain control over their own assessment establishments. In some respects, they were responding to the desires of their employees, who did not wish their own positions and procedures radically changed. The mayors were also responding to their personal preference not to preside over the disappearance of their local municipal civil service. Furthermore, they were genuinely and justifiably concerned about the efficiency and accessibility of a vast metropolitan assessment department dominated by former Montreal officials unfamiliar with suburban conditions.

But hovering above these aspects of the squabble was an important matter of principle: all MUC municipalities should have their property assessed in exactly the same way so that each would pay its fair share of MUC costs. Those in the City of Montreal and the provincial government who advocated unification could always appeal to that principle. Rightly or wrongly, suburban politicians who opposed an islandwide assessment department could not escape the suspicion that, regardless of their public pronouncements, they were trying to subvert the basic principle of equal property assessment.

The Quality of Air and Water

One of the MUC's most notable successes has been its substantial reduction of air pollution on the Island of Montreal, accomplished through a series of bylaws regulating motor vehicle and industrial emissions, heating fuels, and domestic incinerators.[20] All are enforced by the MUC's air purification and food inspection department.

Water pollution has been a much more difficult problem. Most of the water surrounding the Island of Montreal is so polluted that it is a hazard to public health,[21] largely due to the dumping of sewage and industrial wastes into the Ottawa River and into upstream sections of the St. Lawrence River system. In addition, each day the Montreal area contributes more than 500 million gallons of completely untreated sewage to the surrounding waters.[22] In 1971 the Quebec Water Board ordered the MUC to build a purification plant to treat sewage discharged by municipalities within the MUC area.[23] Construction of the integrated sewer system was begun in 1974 and is still proceeding. The plant itself has been built in the northeast corner of the island at

20. The figures that attest to this are presented in MUC, *Annual Reports, 1971– 1979.*

21. MUC, Planning Department, *Proposals for Urban Development* (Montreal: 1973), pp. 94–95.

22. Boyce Richardson, *The Future of Canadian Cities* (Toronto: New Press, 1972), p. 228.

23. MUC, *1970 Annual Report,* pp. 10–11.

Rivière-des-Prairies. More than two-thirds of the estimated cost ($1.5 billion in 1980) is being paid by the provincial government.[24] The earliest possible completion date is 1986, but ultimately this depends almost exclusively on provincial decisions concerning the granting of funds.

Even when the plant is in operation, the water discharged into the St. Lawrence at the eastern tip of the Island of Montreal will still be quite polluted. Because the river's flow is strong at that point, however, it is claimed that no great environmental damage will result.[25] In any event, although the scheme is far from perfect, it will greatly improve the quality of the water surrounding Montreal.

The island's water supply comes from six distinct systems, all operated by individual municipalities. The City of Montreal's is by far the largest. It provides water for virtually all the territory in the central and eastern portions of the island. Five municipalities (Dorval, Lachine, Pierrefonds, Pointe-Claire, and Sainte-Anne-de-Bellevue) supply the western portion.[26]

Intermunicipal negotiations over water supply have been bitter and controversial, particularly regarding the water the City of Montreal has supplied to its neighboring municipalities. As early as 1970 some suburban mayors were urging that the MUC take over the municipal water supply function, and late that year the MUC water purification department began the necessary studies.[27] This work was complicated in March 1973 by a provincial government decision to allow Pierrefonds to expand its water supply capability to meet the growing requirements of the island's northwestern section.[28] This decision reduced the likelihood of integrating the island's water supply in the foreseeable future.

Most issues of air- and water-pollution control and water supply produce noticeable splits between the West Island and the other MUC municipalities. The western municipalities have never been much affected by air pollution and consider locally managed water supply and sewage systems generally cheaper and more efficient. Given the West Island's separation from the central part of the MUC by two airports (Dorval and Cartierville), their case has some validity. This geographic reality is reflected in the water supply system, but the separation of the western municipalities has not been acknowledged with respect to sewage, as the engineers have successfully convinced

24. MUC, *1980 Annual Report* (Montreal: 1981), p. 44.
25. *Le Devoir,* April 6, 1973.
26. For a map of the water supply system, see "Carte 5" in Quebec, Ministère des Affaires municipales, *L'urbanisation dans la conurbation montréalaise* (Quebec: 1977).
27. MUC, *1970 Annual Report.*
28. *News and Chronicle* (Pointe-Claire, Quebec), March 15, 1973.

local and provincial politicians to build an expensive integrated system for the entire island.

Public Transit

The MUC's authority to build extensions to the subway system, control traffic on main thoroughfares, and operate the public transit network (through the MUCTC) seemed likely to make it the major agent of transportation planning in metropolitan Montreal. In its early years the MUC seemed in full control. By 1973 it had launched a plan to add 61 new subway stations and 32 more miles of track to the original network of 28 stations and 14 miles of track.

The province then asserted itself. In May 1976, after the system's extension to the new Olympic site was largely completed, the province's Liberal government announced that it would not continue subsidizing construction of the extensions until it had completed a thorough study of the public transportation needs for the entire metropolitan area.[29] After defeating the Liberals in the provincial election of November 1976, the new *Parti québécois* government found itself with the responsibility of resolving public transit issues in metropolitan Montreal. Because these matters were not really subjects of partisan dispute, the new government simply continued with the studies called for by the Liberals.

Meanwhile, the MUC executive committee, having seen the fate of the subway extension program transferred to provincial hands, began looking for other ways to improve public transit. In early 1979 a plan was worked out to integrate the declining commuter train service on the West Island with the bus and subway network of the MUCTC. In return for this, and for a limited extension of MUCTC bus service, the 12 West Island municipalities in the MUC would for the first time start paying their share of the MUCTC deficits.[30] But when Montreal officials estimated that the net effect of these changes would be to increase the MUCTC deficit by more than the West Island contributions, Mayor Drapeau saw to it that the plan was scuttled.[31] This is an excellent illustration of the difficulties of getting both Montreal and the suburbs to support any new MUC policy initiative.

These circumstances made provincial intervention inevitable. In late 1979 the government announced that effective January 1980 the West Island municipalities would begin to share MUCTC deficits;[32] that the province would pay 100 percent of the cost of future extensions to the subway system; and that existing rail lines in the West

29. *The Montreal Star*, May 20, 1976.
30. *The Gazette* (Montreal), May 30, 1979.
31. *Le Devoir*, June 20, 1979.
32. Ibid., November 21, 1979.

Island and elsewhere would be used to create a "regional metro" fully integrated with the MUCTC system.[33] Financially, this meant a $1 billion commitment, spread over five years. Regardless of whether the plan is actually carried out in full, its announcement emphasizes the MUC's complete loss of control over planning for public transit in the Montreal area.

Regional Planning

The MUC's greatest failure was in regional planning, precisely the field in which its political authority as a metropolitan government was most needed. In 1973 the MUC planning department, staffed largely by former City of Montreal planners, released a vague but visually appealing document called *Proposals for Urban Development*. It called for three major new suburban parks that, together with five large existing parks in the City of Montreal, would constitute a geographically balanced network controlled and financed by the MUC. It also proposed the establishment of two major "satellite centers," one based on the Fairview Shopping Centre in the West Island and on *Galéries d'Anjou* in the east. Intensive development, including high-rise office buildings and apartments, would be encouraged in the satellite centers and generally prohibited elsewhere. This would supposedly ease the pressure on the central business districts, bring some order to suburban development, and facilitate the creation of new public transit networks. Other major proposals included integration of the subway and commuter rail lines and a halt to expansion of the island's expressway system.

The proposals underwent two separate investigations by committees of MUC councillors, and in 1976 a bylaw was drafted to implement the main provisions of the plan. Suburban mayors raised strong objections, primarily because the bylaw meant strict limitations on the density of future suburban development, except in the proposed satellite centers.

By this time the Conference of Montreal Suburban Mayors (CMSM)—successor organization to the Inter-municipal Co-ordinating Committee—had hired a full-time staff and had become highly articulate in expressing suburban interests. The CMSM dispatched three of its members to Europe to study suburban development patterns and subsequently hired one of Quebec's most prestigious planning consultants to provide further advice. Next, the mayors announced that good planning for Montreal would include the encouragement of higher-density development in the traditional commercial sectors of the older suburban municipalities.[34]

33. *The Gazette*, December 18, 1979.
34. Conférence des Maires de la Banlieue de Montréal, "Aménagement du Territoire de la Communauté urbaine de Montréal" (Montreal, September 14, 1976).

Although the debate between the suburban mayors and the MUC planners was muddled and incomplete, some of the major issues were at least raised. Should development in Montreal be concentrated, to maintain the economic health of the central city? Or should orderly decentralization be encouraged, to reduce transit problems and create self-sufficient suburban areas? Should shopping centers be recognized as the real foci of suburban communities, around which public transit should be oriented? Or should they continue to serve only car owners? Should undeveloped land be put aside for major parks, or is it too valuable for such use?

Unfortunately, there was no serious effort to give these issues intensive public debate. Neither Mayor Drapeau nor anyone else showed significant interest. Knowledgeable observers knew there was little chance a meaningful bylaw could ever be approved and thus saw no reason to become excited about the various arguments. Toward the end of 1976 it became apparent that the suburbs simply would not approve the satellite center bylaw in anything like its drafted form; consequently, it was quietly dropped.

Even if the MUC had managed to agree on a plan for its territory, further provincial involvement was inevitable, primarily because the MUC lacked significant control over the north-south axis of urban development. Following the construction of the Champlain Bridge in the early 1960s, the south shore experienced a massive boom in suburban development. To the north on Île-Jésus, the City of Laval had emerged from a difficult beginning and by the 1970s was waging a vigorous campaign to attract industrial and residential development.

North of Laval lay yet another band of outer suburban development anchored in the west by the new municipality of Mirabel, which the federal government chose as the location for Montreal's second international airport in 1969. Ottawa's choice of Mirabel was probably the single most important decision affecting metropolitan Montreal's physical development made by any level of government after 1945. The federal decision was reached against the express opposition of Quebec's provincial government, which wanted the airport located to the southeast of Montreal. Although the City of Montreal's planning department was represented on the site selection task force, there were no other mechanisms for involving any of the area's municipalities.[35] By choosing Mirabel, the federal government single-handedly ensured that metropolitan Montreal's northern section would be the main focus of new industrial development and that future

---

35. Roger Gosselin and Jean-Pierre Brassard, *Mirabel: Site Selection Process and Decision*, Case Program in Canadian Public Administration (Toronto: Institute of Public Administration of Canada, 1977), p. 5.

provincial investments in roads and public transit would also be heavily focused on that area.

The original provincial opposition to Ottawa's choice of the Mirabel location was advanced by Premier Bertrand's *Union nationale* government. When Premier Bourassa came to office in 1970 as head of a Liberal government, the federal government found that it had a more amenable partner. In particular, the Bourassa government was willing to become involved in planning the roads, industrial parks, and other facilities that must accompany any modern airport. Despite the provincial government's eventual participation, the fact remains that the federal government made the first crucial decision on Mirabel's location with virtually no consideration of the policy preferences of other levels of government.

After the *Parti québécois* came to power in 1976 it seemed much less interested than the Liberals in using Mirabel airport as an anchor for developing the north-shore area. This was, no doubt, partly due to a general antipathy to cooperation with the federal government but was also grounded in a carefully considered policy for urban development in metropolitan Montreal, based on a 1977 document in which the new government outlined the huge costs involved in allowing the continuation of urban sprawl far beyond the Island of Montreal.[36]

The provincial government opted to consolidate urban development on the island itself and in a few other well-established areas, notably Laval to the north and Longueuil to the south. The PQ strategy was intended to avoid providing far-flung suburbs with expensive sewers, roads, and public transit and to protect Quebec's valuable farmland. While the MUC planners wanted to protect the City of Montreal by limiting suburban growth on the island itself, the provincial planners seemed more concerned with protecting the economic well-being of the island as a whole by preventing extensive suburban growth to the north and south of the island. Considering the inability of the MUC to finance major projects on its own, it is not surprising that recent MUC planning documents have echoed provincial policy.[37]

Provincial dominance was further confirmed in 1979 when the government gave a grant of $10,540,000 to the MUC for the establishment of a network of metropolitan parks.[38] Such parks had been discussed within the MUC since 1973, but it was not until provincial funds were made available that any action was taken. As with public

---

36. Quebec, *L'urbanisation.* For more details see Gérard Divay and Marcel Gandreau, "L'Agglomération de Montréal: Velléités de concentration et tendances centrifuges," *Canadian Journal of Regional Science,* vol. 5 (1982): 83–98.

37. Communauté Urbaine de Montréal, *Rapport du sous-comité des objectifs du schéma d'aménagement* (Montreal: 1978), and *Schéma d'aménagement: Concept préliminaire* (Montreal: 1982).

38. *Municipalité 1979* (August-September 1979), p. 7.

transit, the provincial government, not the MUC, is now the main
agent of regional planning in metropolitan Montreal.

The Montreal Urban Community Police Department

The MUC's general ineffectiveness can best be understood by
recalling that the main immediate reason for its creation was the need
to help the City of Montreal with its spiralling police costs. The MUC
Act stated that as of January 1, 1970, all island police costs would be
pooled. A portion of these expenditures would be covered by special
provincial grants and by a special surtax on all properties in the MUC
whose taxable assessments were over $100,000.[39] The remaining
amount would be paid by each member municipality in proportion to
its share of the total taxable property within the MUC.

This system lasted only two years, 1970 and 1971, during which
the MUC municipalities spent $167,200,000 on policing, $137,800,000
of which was covered by ordinary municipal revenues. The intermunicipal transfers resulting from the police-cost financing formula
show the City of Montreal receiving $52,800,000 from the MUC to
help cover its police costs, representing 40 percent of the city's total
police expenditures for 1970–71.[40] These figures demonstrate that
from the very beginning the MUC did in fact serve its original intended purpose—to redistribute financial resources from the suburbs
to the City of Montreal.

Three suburbs—Verdun, Sainte-Anne-de-Bellevue and Saint-
Pierre—also profited from these provisions, but only in the relatively
modest amount of $633,204. All other MUC municipalities lost as a
result of the transfers. According to the terms of the cost-sharing arrangements, each municipality's loss depended on two variables: (1)
the total assessed value of its taxable property; and (2) total expenditures for its own police force. The effect of each variable will be
discussed in turn.

1. *Taxable property.* Because total MUC police costs were
   shared on the basis of each municipality's proportion of total
   taxable property, it follows that a higher municipal share of
   such property would result in a higher policing bill. For example, a suburban municipality with 8 percent of total taxable property would pay 8 percent of its own, and everybody
   else's, police costs. If its share of taxable assessed property
   went up, its share of total police costs would also rise.

39. The surtax provisions were added later. See Quebec, *Statutes* (1971), Ch. 90,
Section 18.
40. Figures in these paragraphs derive from financial data found in Montreal
Urban Community, *1972 Budget* and *1973 Budget*, pp. 48.2 and 49, respectively.

2. *Police expenditures.* Under the police-cost sharing system, municipalities continued to run their own police forces. Costs incurred for their own forces were deducted from their share of total MUC costs. This effectively meant that each dollar spent on local policing was one less dollar contributed to municipalities that benefited from the system (mainly Montreal).[41]

Problems with Police-Cost Sharing

As we have seen, this system was designed primarily to channel funds from suburban municipalities to the City of Montreal, which it succeeded in doing. But problems arose from the way the various suburban municipalities shared the burden. Twelve of the 28 suburban municipalities paid less per capita toward subsidizing Montreal's police costs than the overall suburban per capita average. This in itself was hardly cause for concern, especially if the suburbs paying less were the ones with limited financial resources, that is, low per capita taxable property levels. In fact, however, four of these 12 municipalities—Hampstead, Montreal West, Senneville, and Westmount—had per capita taxable property levels *above* the suburban average.

The apparent anomaly is explained by the fact that each of these municipalities had very high police costs, even when these costs were expressed as a proportion of the municipality's total taxable property. This reflected their emphasis on an extravagant "service style" policing, like that often found in wealthy American suburbs.[42] The cost-sharing system not only allowed these municipalities to maintain such extravagant police forces but also implicitly encouraged them to do so. The Public Security Council—established by the 1969 MUC legislation to control the police forces—tried to block excessive and unusual increases in local police expenditures, but it did not force significant cutbacks from existing levels of service, which meant that the system was actually perpetuating existing inequities in levels of police protection. In short, the sharing of police costs was not the great mechanism for distributive justice that Robert Lussier, provincial minister in charge of the original MUC legislation, made it out to be.

Jacques Benjamin reports that Lussier considered the policy a way of tilting the financial balance on the Island of Montreal toward the francophone majority.[43] If Montreal is compared with the suburbs

41. This is fully explained in Claude-André Séguin, "Re-organizing the Provision of Urban Public Services: The Case of the Montreal Urban Community Police" (Ph.D. diss., Syracuse University, 1978), p. 195.
42. See James Q. Wilson, *Varieties of Police Behavior* (Cambridge: Harvard University Press, 1968).
43. *La Communauté urbaine de Montréal: Une réforme ratée* (Montreal: L'Aurore, 1975), pp. 18, 30.

as a whole, the policy does have this effect. But if the distribution of the burden *among* the suburban municipalities is considered, francophone suburbanites appear unfairly treated. The overwhelmingly anglophone residents of Senneville, Montreal West, Hampstead, and Westmount simply were not paying their share.

This inequity is one of many reasons that total unification of the police forces was inevitable. If the cost-sharing procedure of 1970 and 1971 had been continued much longer, its inequitable features would soon have become obvious, and demands to reduce police expenditures in the wealthy anglophone municipalities would have grown. The original inequity was temporarily disguised by the fact that at the outset virtually all suburban municipalities, even the wealthy ones, faced impressive increases in police costs due to the funds required by the City of Montreal.

Police Force Unification

The difficulties with the pooling of police costs were the main reason for the complete unification of the island's police departments. Such a course was recommended by the Public Security Council in late 1970 on the basis of a study supervised by Guy Tardif, then a criminologist at the University of Montreal.[44] Following a stormy debate on March 2, 1971, the MUC council approved in principle the plan for police unification, with nine suburbs voting against.[45] The only reason more did not oppose was that mayors Dawson of Mount Royal and Ryan of Montreal North convinced the council that unification was inevitable anyway, so the more advantageous suburban strategy would be to influence the way it was implemented. After the council vote, opposition to unification was transferred to the hearings of the Quebec Municipal Commission, which, under the MUC Act, had to approve before the plan could take effect.

The commission's decision was never publicly released, principally because procedural flaws were found in the drafting of the unification plan. This gave the provincial cabinet an opportunity to take control, particularly the justice minister, Jérôme Choquette. On September 23, 1971, Choquette announced that he would introduce a bill to unify the police forces of the MUC through provincial legislation.[46] By December 23, 1971, the bill had completed all stages in the legislative process, and on January 1, 1972, the Montreal Urban Community Police Department came into being.[47]

---

44. Montreal Urban Community, Public Security Council, *Report on Police Integration* (Montreal: 1970). From 1976 to 1980 Tardif was Quebec's minister of municipal affairs.

45. Montreal Urban Community, *Minutes of the Council*, March 2, 1971.

46. *Le Devoir*, September 24, 1971.

47. Quebec, *Statutes* (1971), Ch. 93.

The new law had many dramatic effects, an important one being removal of virtually all of Mayor Drapeau's control over Montreal's police.[48] For the MUC, the most immediate and important effect was a vast complication of the budget-making process. By law, the 1972 MUC budget had to provide for refunding police costs to municipalities for the period September 1, 1970, to December 31, 1971. It also had to provide funds for the unified force for the calendar year 1972. In short, the MUC budget had to provide for a 28-month period,[49] which meant either staggering increases in local tax rates or highly unusual government-sanctioned borrowing to cover what were really current operating costs.[50] Under these circumstances, the suburbs exercised their veto in the MUC council and refused to approve the budget.

Quebec Municipal Commission: 1972 MUC Budget

Although in most democratic political systems, budgets proposed by the executive branch must be approved by elected representatives in the legislature, the legislation establishing the MUC did not reflect this principle. Provisions of the MUC Act—which mirrored those of the charter of the City of Montreal—placed the executive committee in the dominant budgetary position.[51] Once approved by the executive committee, the budget had to be presented to council for debate, but council approval was not necessary. After a set period of time, the budget was deemed approved regardless of the council's actions.

This was how the 1972 MUC budget got its legal authority. From the suburban point of view, the one redeeming feature of this draconian system was the possibility of appealing to the Quebec Municipal Commission. The arguments could relate only to the *substance* of the budget, not to the *process* by which it came into force. Under these rules, 20 suburban municipalities drew up a formal case against the budget's main provisions.

At one stage of the proceedings, lawyers for the City of Montreal introduced evidence that only 40 percent of the citizens in the appellant municipalities were French speaking. Presumably, the point was that the appellants did not really represent Montreal's population; con-

---

48. This was done by placing the PSC in direct control of the MUC police and altering its composition such that half of its members, including the chair, were provincial appointees. In 1977 the authority of the PSC was reduced, and the number of provincial appointees was reduced to one. But Mayor Drapeau was no farther ahead, because the suburbs had the same representation as the city—three members each. See ibid. (1977), Ch. 71. Further changes in 1982 are discussed later in this chapter.

49. Ibid. (1971), Ch. 93, Sections 6, 57.

50. Ibid., Ch. 92, Section 9. Such borrowing was authorized by this statute.

51. Ibid. (1969), Ch. 84, Section 248, as amended by ibid. (1971), Ch. 92, Section 86.

sequently, their arguments need not be taken seriously. The presiding judge ruled this part of Montreal's submission out of order but did allow evidence that the appellant municipalities' citizens were of a much higher socioeconomic status than residents in the rest of the island.[52] On February 11, 1972, the commission handed down its ruling. It approved the budget but also recommended that the government establish a study committee to review the structures, finances, and services of the MUC.[53] The suburbs interpreted this as confirmation of commission sympathy with many of their complaints. On March 9 the government established the committee and appointed as its chair Lawrence Hanigan, chair of the MUC executive committee.[54] The study committee's work is discussed later in this chapter.

Language and Policing

Police force unification caused considerable concern among anglophones. The new arrangements meant there would be no more anglophone-controlled police forces on the Island of Montreal. Nevertheless, despite the abolition of these important symbols of anglophone autonomy, there was little overt anglophone opposition. Anglophone suburban politicians realized that unification was an inevitable result of pooling the island's police costs.

The two-stage unification process, set in motion by the original uncertainty of the *Union nationale*, was and is unparalleled elsewhere in Canada. Moreover, the actual process of implementing police unification on Montreal Island was much more difficult than in Metropolitan Toronto or Winnipeg Unicity. In fact, the literature on these two cities scarcely mentions policing. Metropolitan Toronto's 13 police departments were amalgamated by special provincial legislation passed in 1957 in response to a recommendation from a Metro Council committee chaired by a suburban mayor.[55] The whole process was orderly and noncontroversial. There was little serious opposition to the notion that one metropolitan force would be more effective and efficient in fighting crime, managing traffic, and protecting the population. Police forces in metropolitan Winnipeg were legally amalgamated with the creation of Unicity in 1971, and effective amalgamation took place in October 1974. The policing issue did not play an important role in the public debate on the creation of Unicity.

In Montreal, debates about the implementation of police unifica-

52. *Le Devoir*, February 7, 1972.

53. Quebec, Commission municipale du Québec, *Budget de la Communauté urbaine de Montréal pour l'année 1972* (Quebec: 1972).

54. *Le Devoir*, March 10, 1972.

55. Rose, *Governing Metropolitan Toronto*, p. 36.

tion dragged on well into 1978.[56] At the center of the discussion were questions about who should have political control over the force, how it should relate to local municipalities, and how the boundaries for police station areas should be determined.[57] Once again, however, there was little overt public discussion of the language issue, although it did surface in connection with a number of specific problems that were particularly evident in Westmount. Thus, when the City of Westmount disputed the need for a centralized police communications network, one of its technical consultants made the seemingly obvious point that any plan for such a network would have to specify under what circumstances one or the other of the two languages could be used.[58]

Another problem was the number of suburban anglophone police officers who felt they had no future in an MUC force. A departing Westmount policeman said this: "The roads for advancement are closed here. . . . I couldn't work in a professional capacity . . . within the French milieu. . . . If it [the force] had remained Westmount's I don't think I would have left."[59] On another occasion a prominent member of the Westmount Municipal Association complained about police-citizen "communication problems" by saying that "unilingual French is no good when 80 percent of the population which the police are dealing with is English."[60] But these problems and concerns were not publicly articulated by local anglophone politicians, who remained uninvolved in linguistic issues, thereby maintaining their valuable alliances with francophone interests. In short, anglophone suburban concerns about the linguistic implications of police unification did not even figure in the public debate let alone become openly resolved.

Attempts at Municipal Consolidation

Linguistic cleavage is not particularly evident in the ordinary operations of the MUC because the MUC does not have jurisdiction

56. For a summary of the developments see Quebec, *Rapport du groupe de travail sur l'organisation et les functions policières* (Quebec: 1978), Ch. 18. For a valuable analysis of the effects of unification on various municipalities see Divay and Collin, *La Communauté*, pp. 67–80. See also Séguin, "Re-organizing," *passim*.

57. Important documents relating to this issue are: Montreal Urban Community Police Department, *Allocation of the Human and Physical Resources* (Montreal: 1974), and Quebec, Commission de police du Québec, *Décisions . . . relative au Service de la police de la C.U.M.* (Quebec: 1975).

58. W. Ornstein, "Project of Centralization of Radio Communications on the Territory of the Montreal Urban Community" (Report prepared for the City of Westmount, May 12, 1972), p. 10.

59. *Westmount Examiner*, May 16, 1974.

60. Ibid., May 15, 1975.

over subjects of immediate relevance to the lives of French and English Montrealers.[61] Had the MUC dealt with such matters as schools, housing, urban renewal, libraries, and social services, more overt conflict along linguistic lines might have been expected. The fact that the MUC was not given such jurisdiction is, of course, partly attributable to the concern about the language division. (In contrast to the MUC, Metro Toronto is deeply involved in such functions as housing, libraries, and social services.)[62]

In any event, there is virtually no direct evidence of overt French-English conflict among MUC suburban municipalities. Admittedly, Jacques Benjamin's book on the MUC refers to the way ethnic differences cause anglophone mayors to be exceptionally vigilant in protecting their municipalities against a loss of identity within a powerful MUC,[63] but voting behavior within the MUC council between 1970 and 1976 shows anglophone suburbs with only a marginally higher propensity to vote against the City of Montreal than francophone suburbs.[64] In short, it is extremely difficult to demonstrate any clear effect of ethnic (i.e., linguistic) differences on the day-to-day politics of the MUC.

Disputes within the MUC have centered mainly around the relative power, on fairly technical issues, of Montreal and suburban politicians and their dependent bureaucracies. They have generally not sparked great public concern. To the extent that the MUC has seemed to make highly visible decisions—such as the subway extensions—it has soon become apparent that the provincial government had the final say.

The MUC is unlikely to become an independently significant political institution unless it gets the kind of provincially imposed restructuring that Toronto got in 1967 and Winnipeg in 1971. Thus, until the MUC's smaller suburban municipalities are amalgamated and the City of Montreal's territory reduced, a fair and democratic representation system working through the political structures of the MUC will be impossible. Without such a system, crucial political decisions cannot be made at the metropolitan level. Whereas it is never easy to alter municipal boundaries, even in places like Toronto and Winnipeg, it is still more difficult in Montreal, where a major boundary change can shift French or English residents from a majority

61. See Oliver P. Williams, "Life-style Values and Political Decentralization in Metropolitan Areas," in *Community Politics: A Behavioural Approach*, ed. Terry N. Clark et al. (London: Collier-Macmillan, 1971), pp. 56–64.

62. Ontario, *Report of the Royal Commission on Metropolitan Toronto* (Toronto: 1977), Chs. 12, 19, 20.

63. Benjamin, *La Communauté*, pp. 43–44.

64. Divay and Collin, *La Communauté*, p. 167.

position in the old municipality to a minority position in the new. In such circumstances, boundary change is understandably sensitive, and the importance of the linguistic cleavage becomes clear.

The Westmount "Bourg" Plan

When it introduced the MUC Act in 1969, the *Union nationale* government seemed to recognize both the need for boundary restructuring and its inherent political dangers. Instead of presenting a plan for such revisions, the government included this provision in the act: "Within five years of the coming into force of this Act [i.e., January 1, 1975], the Community shall prepare and submit to the Minister a project for re-arranging the territorial limits of the municipalities."[65] These original requirements of the MUC Act were not met, and as 1975 approached, the law had to be amended to delete any reference to the deadline.[66]

Nevertheless, the original provision provoked a considerable amount of activity. Between 1971 and 1973 various suburban municipalities published three reports on future boundary arrangements. The first and most comprehensive was released by the City of Westmount in January 1971. It proposed the abolition of existing boundaries and the establishment of 13 "bourgs" with populations between 10,000 and 250,000.[67] The bourg boundaries would be based on natural and artificial physical barriers as much as possible, the most significant being the east-west Metropolitan Boulevard.

The Westmount plan was well publicized, particularly among other suburban politicians, who invariably supported its main principles. In contrast, Drapeau and Saulnier were extremely negative, finding no merit whatever in the proposals. Both politicians based their attack on linguistic arguments. Saulnier said, "The richest municipality on the Island wants to reduce the French influence in Canada's metropolis and try to dilute the French population of the Island in the midst of new English municipalities."[68]

The allegation that Westmount was consciously trying to gerrymander the proposed boundaries to favor anglophones was a serious charge whose validity would be hard to prove. But judging the proposal's effect on francophone influence is more easily done. In one respect, the proposal would actually strengthen French influence. Table 5 shows that in 1971, 14 of the 29 MUC municipalities had

65. Quebec, *Statutes* (1969), Ch. 84, Section 195.
66. Ibid. (1974), Ch. 82, Section 14.
67. Westmount, *Local Government in the Montreal Metropolitan Area* (Westmount: 1971).
68. *Gazette*, January 28, 1971.

Table 5– MUC Population Using French as Main Home Language, 1971 and 1981

	Population		Percent French	
	1971	1981[a]	1971	1981
French majority municipalities				
Anjou	33,895	37,350	83.6	82.8
Lachine	44,440	37,520	55.1	60.8
LaSalle	72,905	76,300	50.0	50.7
Montreal	1,214,380	1,018,610[b]	67.5	67.2
Montreal East	5,060	3,780	83.1	88.3
Montreal North	89,135	94,915	82.2	79.5
Outremont	28,630	24,340	58.2	66.6
Pointe-aux-Trembles	35,555	(36,270)[b]	91.1	(93.1)
Saint-Léonard	52,040	79,430	62.8	54.8
Saint-Pierre	6,795	5,305	79.1	81.2
Saint-Raphael-de-l'Île-Bizard	2,930	6,560	91.0	80.4
Sainte-Anne-de-Bellevue	5,035	3,980	57.3	56.0
Sainte-Geneviève	2,870	2,575	84.5	84.7
Verdun	74,695	61,290	61.1	65.6
TOTAL	1,668,365	1,451,955		
French minority municipalities				
Baie-d'Urfé	3,880	3,675	6.4	15.6
Beaconsfield	19,450	19,615	8.7	16.7
Côte-Saint-Luc	24,375	27,530	5.0	8.3
Dollard-des-Ormeaux	25,220	39,940	16.9	23.2
Dorval	20,465	17,720	28.3	30.5
Hampstead	7,030	7,600	7.5	10.3
Kirkland	2,860	10,475	17.0	25.0
Montreal West	6,365	5,515	3.3	5.8
Mount Royal	21,570	19,250	30.0	36.5
Pierrefonds	33,015	38,390	31.1	42.3
Pointe-Claire	27,305	24,570	13.8	18.7
Roxboro	7,635	6,290	32.8	40.0
Saint-Laurent	62,940	65,900	42.2	43.1
Senneville	1,375	1,220	35.6	37.6
Westmount	23,570	20,480	15.3	16.7
TOTAL	287,055	308,170		

Source: Canada, *1971 Census of Canada*, Cat. 75–704 (CT–4B) and Canada, *1981 Census of Canada*, Cat. 95–943 (vol. 3—Profile Series B).

[a]The 1981 home-language percentages do not include the "inmate" population because in 1981 "inmates" were not asked this question. An inmate is a resident of an "institutional" collective dwelling other than staff members and their families. Such dwellings include children's homes, special care homes for the elderly and chronically ill, hospitals, treatment centers, penitentiaries, and jails. (See Canada, *1981 Census of Canada*, Cat. 99–901, p. 28.)

[b]1981 figures for Montreal include populations of Pointe-aux-Trembles and Saint-Jean-de-Dieu, which were annexed to Montreal in 1980 and 1982, respectively. Saint-Jean-de-Dieu, which consisted exclusively of a psychiatric hospital in the east end of the island, was never a member of the MUC.

French-speaking majorities, whereas 9 of the 13 bourgs would have francophone majorities.[69]

On the other hand, Westmount's plan would reduce the. total population in municipalities with francophone majorities. This was mainly due to the size of the francophone-controlled City of Montreal, which meant there were 1,668,365 people in municipalities with francophones in the majority. Under Westmount's plan this would be reduced to 1,383,575, the francophone municipalities of Saint-Pierre, Outremont, Lachine, and Sainte-Anne-de-Bellevue being absorbed by anglophone-controlled bourgs as well as Montreal's anglophone areas of Notre-Dame-de-Grâce and Côte-des-Neiges. Part of Saint-Laurent would be the only area with large concentrations of anglophones in a francophone-controlled area. With this perspective, Saulnier's accusation against the plan makes more sense.

Lachine's Seven Cities Plan

In June 1972 the City of Lachine published a report calling for the creation of seven new cities within the MUC.[70] Only three of the seven proposed municipalities would be controlled by francophones, and the three would have only 1,339,925 people within their boundaries. Even so, the Lachine plan had two features that might have made it more attractive to francophones than the Westmount plan. First, it provided for a strong, francophone-dominated City of Montreal, with just under half of the island's total population. Second, it called for Montreal to absorb the two wealthy anglophone suburbs of Westmount and Mount Royal. In general, though, the Lachine report was not taken seriously, perhaps because it proposed that the second-largest city on the island be called Lachine.

West Island Fusion

A less comprehensive but more realistic proposal was made in June 1971 when the West Island Fusion Committee released its report. It recommended creation of a new West Island city containing all island municipalities west of Dorval and Saint-Laurent.[71] The report was not greeted with much enthusiasm by the francophone municipalities of Sainte-Anne-de-Bellevue and Sainte-Geneviève, and the

69. These calculations were made by relating the boundaries of the proposed bourgs as closely as possible to the existing census tracts and using data concerning language used most often in the home. The data came from Canada, *1971 Census of Canada*, Cat. 95–704 (CT–4B).

70. Roger Pominville Ltée., *Une étude de regroupement municipale* (Montreal: 1972).

71. Fusion Study Committee of West Island Mayors, *The Status Quo or Municipal Fusion* (Montreal: 1971).

francophone mayor of Pierrefonds led the opposition to fusion using a variety of arguments. Like the plan's proponents, he studiously ignored the linguistic composition of the proposed new city, but it was obvious, however, that the francophone municipalities were not eager to be absorbed by a new city with less than 25 percent of the population francophones.

The provincial government's initial reaction was favorable, on the other hand, because the plan meshed well with its stated objective for 1972; that is, to create five, six, or seven new cities within the MUC's territory.[72] But it was not long before the provincial government grew more sensitive to the desires of West Island francophones and more aware of the political dangers of allowing West Island anglophones to consolidate their position in one huge municipality.[73] In any event, after the release of the Hanigan report in May 1973, the West Island fusion proposals were dead.

Hanigan's Suggested Mergers

The Hanigan committee was established following the hearings of the Quebec Municipal Commission on the 1972 MUC budget. The records of one of its main subcommittees show Mayor Dawson of Mount Royal once again successful in blocking any recommendation involving creation of a West Island city and the forced absorption of the inner suburbs by the City of Montreal.[74] The report of the full committee called for preserving all municipalities with more than 20,000 inhabitants. As a short-term objective, the committee recommended seven immediate mergers affecting 16 municipalities.[75] The West Island francophone municipalities as well as francophone Ile-Bizard would be absorbed into anglophone-controlled municipalities, and Montreal West, the only anglophone municipality to lose its identity, would be annexed by an otherwise untouched City of Montreal.

In general, these proposals were much less damaging to the francophone position than any of the others, but no action was taken, even on these innocuous recommendations.[76] By this time the Bourassa government had become aware of the way in which any reorga-

72. Report of interview given by municipal affairs minister Maurice Tessier, *Le Devoir*, December 3, 1971.

73. André Dubois, "La Communauté urbaine de Montréal: les forces en présence" (M.A. thesis, University of Montreal, 1974), p. 194.

74. Quebec, Comité d'étude de la CUM, *Rapport du sous-comité: Structures administratives* (Quebec: 1973), Ch. 3.

75. Quebec, *Report of the Study Committee on the Montreal Urban Community* (Quebec: 1973), p. 14.

76. They were, however, endorsed by the Castonguay task force in 1976. See Quebec, *L'urbanisation au Québec: Rapport du groupe de travail* (Quebec: 1976), p. 147.

nization of municipal boundaries would provoke political protest from anglophones and francophones alike. Consequently, it came out against *all* forced municipal mergers. Even the election of the *Parti québécois* in 1976—which might have been expected to herald the end of provincial concern for anglophone suburban autonomy—brought no change in the provincial position.

Tinkering with MUC Structures

In July 1980 the PQ government, at the urging of the MUC suburbs, committed itself to reviewing the legislative framework in which the community was operating. When the resulting legislation was passed in June 1982, it was clear that the suburbs had made major gains. Simultaneous with the suburban victory at the provincial level, Mayor Drapeau was weakening their political base by absorbing one of their number. The annexation of Pointe-aux-Trembles meant that the City of Montreal had bolstered its territorial control of the eastern tip of the island and had forestalled the danger that its population figures might soon slip below 50 percent of the MUC total.

In its attempts to reform the MUC, the main objective of the Conference of Montreal Suburban Mayors was to obtain city-suburban parity on the MUC executive committee while not surrendering the suburban veto on the MUC council. The main justification for parity was that the combined suburban property-tax base had just about equalled that of the city, and hence the suburbs were paying about as much for MUC services as the city itself.[77] The suburbs acknowledged that only about 44 percent of the MUC population lived within their borders,[78] but an extrapolation from past censuses confirmed their contention that it would not be long until the population figures were equal as well. Mayor Drapeau was notably uncooperative with the government's attempts to encourage an internal MUC consensus on significant reform proposals. He simply maintained that the city deserved its dominant position within the MUC and that no major

77. Following passage of Quebec's new municipal finance law (Quebec, *Statutes* [1979], Ch. 72), it is difficult to calculate each municipality's exact contributions to MUC finances. This is because most provincially owned properties—which were previously tax exempt—are now effectively subjected to municipal taxation and are included in calculations determining each municipality's share of total MUC property assessment. In 1981 suburban municipalities contained about 51 percent of the assessed value of all MUC taxable property (excluding government property) but only 44 percent of the assessed value of all property. See Communauté urbaine de Montréal, *Annual Report 1981* (Montreal: 1982), p. 21.

78. According to the 1981 federal census, the City of Montreal's population was 980,354, and that of the MUC was 1,760,122. Canada, Statistics Canada, *1981 Census of Canada*, Cat. 93–905 (Ottawa· Minister of Supply and Services, 1982).

changes were required. However, when the PQ government was re-elected in April 1981—with its 1980 independence referendum well behind it—the government had no particular reason to cater to the wishes of Jean Drapeau. Because some francophone suburban mayors had supported the PQ and because the CMSM had carried out an effective lobbying campaign, the minister of municipal affairs, Jacques Léonard, in fact became quite willing to move toward the suburban position.

This became clear in December 1981, when Léonard released his proposals for change.[79] Because they did nothing to change municipal boundaries and functions, the proposals were hardly revolutionary. Nevertheless, they did provide for parity on the executive committee, and mainly for this reason, they outraged Mayor Drapeau, who claimed that the proposals reduced Quebec's metropolis to the level of a mere suburb, just one among many.[80] Despite Drapeau's impressive performance at the parliamentary hearings,[81] the government held firm.

Bill 46, approved by the National Assembly in June 1982, contained the following main provisions.[82]

1. Voting procedures on the MUC council were changed such that only weighted votes would henceforth be counted. For a motion to be adopted it now has to receive one-half the total weighted votes cast by both the City of Montreal councillors and the suburban mayors. This change has the effect of drastically reducing the power within the council of mayors from small municipalities. Because most such suburbs are English speaking, this change presumably furthers the government's stated objective of advancing metropolitan Montreal's role as the major French-speaking urban center in North America.[83]

2. The MUC budget, as proposed by the executive committee, will no longer automatically be in force if not approved by the council before a specified date.

3. The MUC council will now have five permanent commissions: finance, public security, public transit, environment, and planning. Commission meetings are to be public (un-

79. Quebec, Ministère des Affaires municipales, *Une nouvelle Communauté: La Réforme de la Communauté urbaine de Montréal* (Quebec: 1980).

80. *Le Devoir*, January 5, 1982.

81. Quebec, l'Assemblée nationale, *Journal des Débats*, Commissions parlementaires, 3e Session, 32e Législature, Commission permanente des affairs municipales, 46 (March 3, 1982): B2397–B2436.

82. Quebec, National Assembly, Bill 46: *An Act to Amend the Act Respecting the Communauté urbaine de Montréal* (Quebec: 1982).

83. Quebec, *Une nouvelle Communauté*, p. 26.

like those of the executive committee), but the public security commission can meet in private as long as it holds at least two public meetings each year. Except for the one on public security, each commission is composed of no more than seven members, with at least two coming from the city and two from the suburbs. The council elects the chair and vice-chair of each commission, one of whom will be from the city and the other from the suburbs.

4. The executive committee has 13 members: the 10 chairs and vice-chairs of the council's commissions, the chair and vice-chair of the council itself, and a chair of the executive committee chosen by the council from among its members. The chair of the executive committee has to resign his municipal position on taking office but will not have to run again for municipal office if his four-year term is being renewed. In cases of ties in executive committee votes, the chair will cast the deciding vote. He remains a member of the MUC council, casting one vote only.

5. If four or more of either the city or suburban representatives on the executive committee vote against the position of the majority, a decision on the issue in question will be suspended until the next meeting. If the veto still holds, the issue is referred to the council, where the veto is sustained only if it is supported by two-thirds of the weighted votes.

6. To choose a chair of the executive committee, the MUC council will have to pass the appropriate motion in the normal way, that is, it will require half the weighted votes of both city and suburban representatives. If no motion succeeds, the procedure changes at the council's next meeting. This time two-thirds of the total weighted council votes are required to elect a chair. If this second meeting fails to resolve the issue, the provincial government has the right to name the chair itself.

7. A new administrative position of director-general is created. All heads of MUC departments, except the director of the police department, are to report to the executive committee chair through the director-general.

8. All regulations passed by the Montreal Urban Community Transportation Commission (MUCTC), including those relating to fares and bus routes, now have to be approved by the MUC council. The MUCTC is to be mainly concerned with internal administrative matters, and the public transport commission of the council is to be concerned with advising the council on policy questions and with hearing complaints from the public.

9. The Public Security Council becomes the public security commission of the council, but unlike other such commissions, it is to have one member from outside the MUC council chosen by the provincial government. The other six members, chosen by the council, are to be split equally between the city and the suburbs. Rather than reporting to the new public security commission, the director of the police department now reports directly to the MUC executive committee.

10. The MUC is given new authority in land-use planning. Provisions of the new 1979 provincial planning law[84] now apply to the planning functions within the jurisdiction of the MUC. Nevertheless, the City of Montreal still retains its own unique planning procedures, which are quite different from those that apply to other municipalities.

During the debate on Bill 46 the major protagonists were the minister of municipal affairs, supported by the CMSM, and Mayor Drapeau, supported by a wide array of political forces within the City of Montreal, including the opposition municipal parties and many PQ members of the National Assembly representing constituencies within the City of Montreal. Although the Liberals opposed the bill on third reading, they did support the government's position concerning parity on the executive committee.

Pointe-aux-Trembles Annexation

Rather than meekly accept defeat, Drapeau launched an especially effective counterattack. Just as the city's political strength within the MUC was being reduced, he carried out Montreal's first major annexation since 1964. By absorbing Pointe-aux-Trembles he added 36,720 new residents to the City of Montreal[85] and consolidated the city's presence on the eastern tip of the island.

Pointe-aux-Trembles had long been in financial difficulty and as a result had come close to being annexed in the past. Although Mayor Bernard Benoît had been president of the CMSM, his successor Maurice Vanier was more concerned with tax rates and services within Pointe-aux-Trembles than with the virtues of suburban autonomy. In early 1983 Mayor Vanier's council decided that annexation—to Anjou, Montreal East, or Montreal—was the solution. Only the City of Montreal seemed willing to absorb the debts and problems of Pointe-aux-Trembles, and by the end of March agreement between the two

---

84. Quebec, *Statutes* (1979), Ch. 51.
85. Canada, *1981 Census*, Cat. 93–905. This meant that the city's population was once again more than one million. See footnote 78.

councils was reached. As well as paying general property taxes at the city's lower rate, Pointe-aux-Trembles residents were offered a comprehensive plan of local improvements and a three-year exemption from the city's special taxes such as that levied to pay the deficit from the Olympic Games.

In these circumstances it is not surprising that the opponents of annexation failed in their attempt to overturn the apparently attractive arrangements. They used their legal right to force a referendum on annexation, but on May 17, 1982, 4731 Pointe-aux-Trembles citizens (58.7 percent) voted yes to annexation, and 3336 expressed their disapproval.[86] Shortly thereafter, the minister of municipal affairs approved the annexation, and the municipality of Pointe-aux-Trembles was no more.[87]

As a result of the annexation, the Pointe-aux-Trembles ward of the City of Montreal was given three representatives on city council, bringing the total membership to 58, including the mayor. These 58 members of the city council and the mayors of the remaining 27 suburbs constitute the MUC council.

The Suburban Alliance

The annexation of Pointe-aux-Trembles took place despite provincial government policy rather than because of it. The most significant feature of the 1982 changes in the MUC legislation was that they did not in any way affect municipal boundaries. Once again, the existing municipalities survived intact. Why have municipal boundaries within the MUC been so resistant to change despite the pressure for reform and the examples of Toronto and Winnipeg? Why do 28 MUC municipalities still survive when the constituent units of the Quebec Urban Community and the Outaouais Regional Community have been reduced from 26 to 13 and from 32 to 8, respectively?[88] Only the linguistic cleavage can explain the continued existence of so many municipalities on the Island of Montreal. Any provincial government contemplating a revision of municipal boundaries must make the kinds of calculations discussed here. Not surprisingly, the various permutations and combinations have profoundly discouraged all cautious policymakers.

But the explanation does not end there. The existing suburbs have themselves consistently maintained a powerful political alliance, but because it is motivated by self-preservation it is more likely to oppose political change than initiate it. A closer look at the alliance

---

86. *Le Devoir*, May 19 and 20, 1982.

87. *Le Devoir*, June 25, 1982.

88. For the 1970 boundaries see Quebec, *Annuaire du Québec* (Quebec: 1971), pp. 27, 31. For information on the restructured QUC see *Municipalité '79* (January 1979). For the ORC see *Municipalité '77* (June 1977).

will help explain the impact of language differences on metropolitan Montreal's municipal structure. The alliance's fundamental assumption is that every municipality has the right to continue to exist. Any other position would sacrifice the political support of any municipality whose continued existence was threatened. In this respect, the alliance is not unusual—most suburban municipalities virtually anywhere would subscribe to it.

In Montreal, however, the alliance is unique because of the municipalities' special motivations and the unusual fervor with which they support the assumption. Anglophone municipalities support it because many of their citizens fear they could be swallowed by the francophone City of Montreal and lose both their position as a linguistic majority and their cherished patterns of responsible, efficient, service-oriented local government. West Island francophone municipalities also support the assumption for fear of losing their identities in an anglophone West Island city. Other francophone municipalities support it because their leaders do not generally wish to lose power over local political systems that have been valuable sources of political influence, patronage, or even personal profit.

Given these relationships, the anglophone suburbs' cause does not appear to be an exclusively anglophone position. The most eloquent spokesmen for suburban autonomy have in fact been mayors of francophone suburbs.[89] From their viewpoint, the alliance enables them to associate themselves politically with municipalities whose record for honesty and efficiency in local government has been generally more impressive than their own. Furthermore, any proposal to abolish francophone municipalities can be portrayed as discriminatory, unless it also calls for the abolition of English municipalities at the same time.

In short, the alliance described is almost wholly symbiotic, with mayors of anglophone and francophone suburban municipalities tied inextricably to each other's interests. This also makes it extremely difficult for the provincial government or the City of Montreal to take any action against the combined strength of the suburbs. Isolated attacks on any particular suburb or group of suburbs are inevitably interpreted as an implied attack on all of them. Moreover, an attack on all the suburbs means a challenge of a greater political force than even the government of Quebec is accustomed to tackle, a force made up of elements that no other provincial government in Canada has to confront. These circumstances help explain why the MUC still contains 28 independent municipalities.[90]

89. Since 1970 all five presidents of the Conference of Montreal Suburban Mayors have been francophones, even though half the member municipalities have anglophone majorities.

90. Technically, the MUC contains 29 municipalities. But one, Dorval Island, has a population of 15 and for MUC purposes is considered part of Dorval.

8

The Reorganization of Montreal's School Boards

Quebec's system of public education before the Quiet Revolution of the 1960s was described in Chapter 4. Its main features were: (1) there was virtually no central provincial control over education; (2) all schools were effectively either Catholic or Protestant; and (3) both Catholics and Protestants had a great deal of autonomy in governing their own school systems through their local school boards. No sector of Quebec life was more affected by the Quiet Revolution than education. In a few short years after 1960 many of the system's best-known characteristics had changed beyond recognition, and most of these changes had a dramatic impact on the Island of Montreal's complex network of educational institutions. Nevertheless, in this chapter we will see how—despite the immense pressures for secularization brought about by the Quiet Revolution—the system of governing Montreal's schools, which was based above all on the distinction between Catholic and Protestant, has survived remarkably unscathed.

The Parent Report

During its first year in office the Liberal provincial government of Jean Lesage established a royal commission "to study the organization and financing of education in the Province of Quebec, report its findings and opinions and submit its recommendations as regards measures to be taken to ensure the progress of education in the Province."[1] The commission, in existence from 1961 to 1966, was to provide the framework for the total overhaul of Quebec's educational system. Its chair was the Rt. Rev. Alphonse-Marie Parent, vice-rector of Laval University in Quebec City.

The commission's first objective was to address the reform of educational structures at the provincial level. Throughout most of

1. Quebec, *Report of the Royal Commission on Education in the Province of Quebec* (Quebec: 1963), vol. 1, p. viii.

Quebec's history, its educational system had been directed by two independent committees of a body called the Council of Public Instruction. The council as a whole rarely met, giving its Catholic and Protestant committees a free hand in running their respective systems. All school boards were under the jurisdiction of one committee or the other.

The system was nominally held together by a provincial department of education headed by a civil servant known as the superintendent of public instruction. The superintendent was inevitably a Catholic and was concerned almost exclusively with the Catholic side of the system, whereas the associate superintendent was a Protestant and was given great freedom in the supervision of all Protestant schools. The superintendent reported to the government through a cabinet minister designated for that purpose, usually the provincial secretary. For eight years after 1867 Quebec was actually blessed with a cabinet minister with the title "minister of education." But in 1875 the provincial legislature abolished the post on the grounds that education was not suited to the meddling of politicians.[2]

The Parent commission was convinced that this venerable system was incapable of carrying out the reforms necessary to adapt French Quebec education to the needs of modern society. Accordingly, in 1963 it recommended that the superintendent be replaced by a cabinet minister[3] and that the council of public instruction be replaced by an advisory body to be known as the superior council of education. The superior council would have both Catholic and Protestant committees, but most of its work would be done by the entire body meeting together.[4] The government immediately announced its intention to implement these recommendations. From June 1963 until final passage of the legislation in March 1964 there was an intense public debate over the government's proposals.[5] Finally, on May 13, 1964, Paul Gérin-Lajoie, the cabinet minister who had been directing the government's educational policies, became Quebec's first modern minister of education.[6]

While these changes were taking place in Quebec City, the Parent commission was studying what it called the system's "pedagogical structure." In 1964 it published a blueprint for a system in which all students in Quebec would for the first time follow roughly the same course of study in the same types of institutions. The government

2. Ibid., p. 16.
3. Ibid., p. 88.
4. Ibid., pp. 118–19.
5. See Paul Gérin-Lajoie, *Pourquoi le Bill 60* (Montreal: Editions du jour, 1963), and Léon Dion, *Le Bill 60 et la societé québécoise* (Montreal: Editions HMH, 1967).
6. Quebec, Ministère de l'Education, *Premier rapport du Ministre de l'Education* (Quebec: 1965), p. 1.

accepted most of the proposed changes, and during the late 1960s educational institutions throughout the province, especially at the post-secondary level, experienced drastic structural change. One result of these reforms was the preparation of many more francophone youths for highly skilled jobs or for entrance to a university. When neither the jobs nor the university places materialized, the resulting frustration fuelled many of the nationalist riots and demonstrations of the late 1960s.[7]

Secularization of School Boards

The final volumes of the Parent report were released during the provincial election campaign of 1966. They dealt mainly with educational structures and finance at the local level. Their most important recommendation was that school boards lose their classification as Protestant or Catholic and therefore no longer have any confessional status. The commission members did not, however, wish to do away with the confessional nature of individual schools, nor did they wish to eliminate the distinction between French and English schools. They wanted parents to be able to choose from among six types of institutions, involving different combinations of language and religion. The schools could be either English or French in language and Catholic, Protestant, or nonconfessional in religion. The full range of choices would probably be available only in large cities.[8]

For the Island of Montreal, the commission members recommended that the existing 24 Catholic and 15 Protestant school boards[9] be replaced by seven new boards, each responsible for all elementary and secondary education in its respective area. Under this plan the English would have clearly been in control of two boards, thus placing 145,005 francophones, including the citizens of Outremont, in a minority situation. Anglophones placed in a minority situation would have numbered 234,145, most of them in Saint-Laurent, Verdun, La-Salle, and the south-central part of the City of Montreal.[10]

The plan also called for the establishment of a council of school development to be made up of government appointees and representatives of the seven boards. The council would have jurisdiction over such matters as collection and distribution of property taxes and government grants, the wages and salaries of personnel, school transportation, and various other auxiliary services.[11] The commission did not

7. Robert Chodos and Nick Auf der Maur, *Quebec: A Chronicle, 1968–1972* (Toronto: James Lewis and Samuel, 1972), p. 13.

8. Quebec, *Royal Commission on Education,* vol. 4, p. 85.

9. Ibid., pp. 187–89.

10. Calculations made from ibid., final pages, and Canada, Statistics Canada, *1971 Census of Canada,* Cat. 95–734 (CT–4B), pp. 2–45.

11. Quebec, *Royal Commission on Education,* vol. 4, pp. 203–4.

really address itself to the constitutional and political problems involved in abolishing institutions perceived as being important protectors of different confessional and linguistic groups. It protected itself on this question by recommending that confessional matters in individual schools be under the jurisdiction of school committees elected by parents.[12] But this hardly seemed sufficient to French Catholics who feared any form of secularization or those English Protestants who viewed their school boards as their last line of defense against the aggressive francophone majority.

During the period immediately after the recommendations were published, the one concerning Montreal received only limited public attention, but there was much more concern with the confessional issue in the province as a whole. The fact that the 1966 provincial election campaign was in progress discouraged dispassionate debate on this and most other matters connected with educational reform. When the election was over, however, and the new *Union nationale* government had taken office, the issues raised by the Parent report had to be faced. Not surprisingly, the new government never seriously considered abolishing the traditional confessional identity of school boards outside the Montreal area. For the Island of Montreal, where the situation was far more complex and where the *Union nationale* had little political support, the government had no clear idea what policy to follow.

The Pagé Report

Because of its general policy against imposing educational reforms on unwilling communities, the *Union nationale* government chose not to act on the Montreal issue before further consultation with the leaders of various educational interest groups. On September 30, 1967, the government created the council for school reorganization on the Island of Montreal.[13] In its final form the council consisted of 18 members. Nine were appointed by the school boards: four from the Montreal Catholic School Commission (MCSC)—two French, one Irish, one Italian; two from other Catholic school boards; two from the Protestant School Board of Greater Montreal (PSBGM); and one from the Protestant Lakeshore Regional Board. Five represented the teachers' organizations: three from the French Catholic groups and one each from the English Catholics and Protestants. Four were from parent groups: two from the French Catholics and

12. Ibid., p. 171.
13. Quebec, Department of Education, *Report of the Council for School Reorganization on the Island of Montreal* (Quebec: 1968), p. 11.

one each from the English Catholics and Protestants.[14] In short, the council's membership was carefully balanced and thoroughly representative. These virtues, however, made it unwieldy and unlikely ever to reach agreement. At its first meeting it elected as chairman Joseph Pagé, vice-chairman of the MCSC.[15]

In early 1968 the council finally came to grips with its main problem—the nature of Montreal's future school boards. Chairman Pagé put forth a proposal that would in effect perpetuate the status quo. He called for two types of school boards: one serving all Catholics of any language and all non-Catholics who wished to be educated in French, and one serving all Protestants and all non-Catholics and non-Protestants who wished to be educated in English. Each type of school board would operate confessional and nonconfessional schools and French and English schools, depending on parental demand.[16] A uniform tax rate would be set by a metropolitan school council; citizens would choose which type of board they wished to be electors for; and parents could choose the type of school their children would attend.[17] Although the proposal appeared clumsy and unwieldy, it had the virtues of offending no major group and of causing virtually no administrative disruption.

From February until June 1968 the council studied other proposals submitted by various interest groups.[18] Most, including the MCSC, favored having a dual network of school boards in which language alone would be the distinguishing factor.[19] In supporting this arrangement the PSBGM emphasized the need to replace existing constitutional guarantees for denominational school boards for similar guarantees related to language.

The only major opposition to linguistic school boards came from English-speaking Catholics, because the arrangement would have dismantled the distinct English Catholic system built up within the MCSC. English Catholics were particularly upset that the MCSC had taken its position by a 3–2 vote, with the chair casting the deciding ballot, in the absence of the only anglophone commissioner. Furthermore, there had been no consultation with anglophone teachers or parents.[20] Although the anglophone Catholic opposition to this pro-

14. Ibid., pp. 12–14.
15. Quebec, Department of Education, Council for School Reorganization on the Island of Montreal, *Minutes*, Meeting of October 13, 1968.
16. Quebec, *Minutes*, Meeting of January 29, 1968.
17. Ibid.
18. For an analysis of the 32 briefs presented, see Louise Bigras, "Analyse du contenu des reponses au questionnaire du Counseil de restructuration scolaire de l'Ile de Montréal sur certaines recommandations du Rapport Parent" (Quebec: Ministère de l'education, 1968).
19. Ibid., Meeting of April 8, 1968.
20. Ibid., Meeting of May 6, 1968. See the copy of a letter from Kevin Quinn attached to these minutes.

posal was vehement, the group as a whole was not clear about what alternative it preferred. The federation of English-speaking Catholic teachers argued for separate school boards for anglophone Catholics, whereas John McIlhone, the top anglophone MCSC administrator, supported the proposals of the Parent commission, of which he had been a member.[21] He no doubt assumed that in a unified system English Catholics could benefit from associating themselves with English Protestants on some matters, and with French Catholics on others.

At its June 5 meeting the council for school reorganization made a final decision about the type of school board system it would recommend. The PSBGM representatives voted for the Pagé proposal on the grounds that there was no likelihood of constitutional protection for any other type of arrangement. Except for Pagé himself, no one else supported this proposal. The representative of the Verdun Catholic School Commission was the only supporter of a system that would have one set of school boards for Catholics and another set for all others. The anglophone Catholic teachers' representative was also alone in supporting a plan for three types of boards: French, English Catholic, and English non-Catholic. John McIlhone and two of the parent representatives supported the Parent proposals for unified boards. The remaining eight members present all supported linguistic school boards,[22] and this became the fundamental policy on which the rest of the council's work was based.

The council eventually recommended nine French boards and four English. The French boards would provide both Catholic and "pluralist" schools, and the English would provide three different types: Catholic, "pluralist," and Protestant.[23] By this time all the Protestants and the one Jew on the council had rallied to the PSBGM position, holding that linguistic boards were not a satisfactory substitute for the existing confessional arrangements unless accompanied by appropriate constitutional guarantees. They all joined in presenting a minority statement to this effect.[24]

In a similar fashion the two Irish Catholics united to sign a minority statement supporting McIlhone's consistent pleadings for a unified system. They were joined by the representative from the Le Royer regional board. Their statement was accompanied by a map showing the division of the island into 11 different school board areas.[25]

Finally, there was a separate statement from the Verdun representative, insisting that the confessional division was still the ideal

21. Ibid.
22. Ibid., Meeting of June 5, 1968.
23. Quebec, *Report of the Council*, pp. 75–76.
24. Ibid., p. 131.
25. Ibid., pp. 141–45.

structural arrangement.[26] The plethora of 12 minority reports virtually destroyed any credibility the majority recommendation might have had. This was further reinforced when Chairman Pagé publicly declared in October 1969 that even he did not support the majority position of his own council. Moreover, by this time he was no longer supporting his original proposal but instead had rallied to the unified school board position.[27]

Other major council recommendations supported the Parent proposals on school committees and the establishment of an islandwide body comprising one representative from each of the 13 proposed boards.[28] This latter body, the school council for the Island of Montreal, was to control taxation, financing, planning, coordination, and certain common services.[29] This proposal itself inspired two minority statements urging clarification and limitation of the school council's role on which eight of the nine signatures were those of anglophones.[30]

Although the Pagé report majority recommendations were supported editorially in *Le Devoir* as being more judicious, flexible, and realistic than the Parent proposals,[31] few people ever took them seriously. The work of the council for school reorganization on the Island of Montreal deserves attention not because of its lasting influence but because of the particularly vivid way it exposed the many alternatives, difficulties, and frictions inherent in any attempt to change Montreal's traditional patterns of school administration.

Bill 62: Eleven Unified School Boards

Unfortunately for Pagé's council, its work on school board reorganization had been completely overshadowed by the conflict in Saint-Léonard about Italian immigrant children's access to English-language schools.[32] Consequently, the *Union nationale* government of Premier Bertrand was forced to consider the Pagé report within the context of this explosive political problem. The government's legislation on school board reorganization in Montreal, Bill 62, was part of a wider policy worked out by the provincial cabinet, including Bill 63, the controversial legislation guaranteeing parents the right to choose either French or English schools for their children.

In return for the support of Bill 63 by the education minister

26. Ibid., pp. 146–51.
27. Quebec, Assemblée Nationale, *Débats* 8 (1969): B4402–3.
28. Quebec, *Report of the Council*, pp. 75–76.
29. Ibid., p. 58.
30. Ibid., pp. 164–67.
31. *Le Devoir*, November 11, 1975.
32. See Ch. 5.

Jean-Guy Cardinal, Premier Bertrand agreed to Cardinal's view that the Parent recommendations for unified school boards on the Island of Montreal should be followed.[33] Bill 62, introduced on November 4, 1969,[34] called for 11 unified school boards. Francophones would have comprised a majority in seven of the proposed boards, anglophones in two, and two would have had no majority linguistic group. Compared with the Parent recommendations for only seven unified boards, Bill 62 would slightly reduce the numbers in both linguistic groups that would find themselves in a minority situation under the new boards.[35]

Under Bill 62 the boards were to have six to nine members each, elected every four years. One-third were to be chosen by the school committees and two-thirds by universal suffrage.[36] The rest of the bill largely followed the Parent recommendations, although there was an important difference concerning the proposed areawide school council. Bill 62 called for a council of 11 school board representatives and four others, but all would be named by the government.[37] The school council would have a great deal of financial power, particularly because it would assume the ownership of all school buildings and land. Bill 62 did provide for six different types of linguistic and confessional schools, but at the level of the school boards and the school council there were few provisions for recognizing the political and administrative needs of the district linguistic and confessional groups.

Opposition Grows

Although Cardinal was committed to the bill's passage before the forthcoming provincial general election, it was referred to the legislature's education committee prior to second reading.[38] At the committee's first meeting René Lévesque suggested that it would be preferable to have separate school boards for anglophones and francophones. The school council, he claimed, could ensure that anglophones would no longer be in a superior financial situation.[39] (Despite Lévesque's expressed preference for linguistic school boards, the PQ was later to express fervent opposition to this alternative.) This was the last time Bill 62 was debated during the 1969 session.

When the education committee convened early in 1970 to study

33. John E. Parisella, "Pressure Group Politics: Case Study of the St. Léonard Crisis" (M. A. thesis, McGill University, 1971), p. 161.

34. Quebec, *Débats* 8 (1969): 3509.

35. Calculated from ibid., p. B4417, and Canada, *1971 Census*, Cat. 95–734, pp. 2–45.

36. Pierre Fournier, "A Political Analysis of School Reorganization in Montreal" (M. A. thesis, McGill University, 1971), p. 34.

37. Ibid., pp. 33–35.

38. Quebec, *Débats* 8 (1969): 3512.

39. Ibid., p. B3983.

Bill 62, a number of public hearings were held. Sixteen different presentations were made, four from groups concerned exclusively with school taxes. Nine of the remaining 12 groups were anglophone, and all opposed the principle of unified boards. Many suggested that the Pagé proposals were much more desirable and realistic. One Liberal member of the committee pointed out that English-Catholic schools had always existed on a satisfactory basis within the MCSC. If this had been the case for anglophones within a Catholic board, why could the same not be true within unified boards? John Parker, Montreal city councillor and principal of a Protestant school, gave an answer that demonstrates impressive insight into the complicated reality of education in Montreal:

> You are talking about a situation where there is an English catholic section belonging to the Montreal Catholic School Commission, but in an island situation where there is also a PSBGM [i.e., Protestant school system], which is a constant reminder that English quality education is available and which provided some kind of encouragement to the Catholic School Commissions of Greater Montreal to continue to provide quality to its English adherents.[40]

Within unified boards this role-model effect would no longer exist; hence, according to Parker, anglophones would inevitably experience a reduction in educational standards. No advocate of unified boards ever attempted to rebut this fascinating assertion.

Meanwhile, Montreal's Protestant educators conducted what the *Montreal Star* called "an insidious campaign" to spread anxiety and confusion among anglophone parents.[41] Typical was the claim by Stanley Frost, a vice-principal of McGill University, that "Bill 62 virtually spells the end of the English language teaching profession in Quebec."[42] This assertion was based on the unsubstantiated assumption that Protestant teachers' unions could not function within the unified structure. Unlike the Saint-Léonard crisis, which only affected Catholics, Bill 62 struck at the heart of the Protestant educational establishment. Although it would not have led to the abolition of English-language schools, it would have drastically reduced the power of Protestant administrators. Led by McGill's principal, Rocke Robertson, Protestant educational leaders formed the Association for the Reform of Education, a short-lived group devoted to mobilizing anglophone protest.

During this time the most effective argument for linguistic boards

40. Ibid., vol. 9 (1970): B7.
41. *Montreal Star*, February 28, 1970.
42. *The Gazette*, February 3, 1970.

was expressed cautiously and moderately in a series of three articles by Claude Ryan, the director of the influential newspaper *Le Devoir*.[43] Ryan pointed out that Bill 62 completely ignored the social reality of the two distinct linguistic communities in Montreal. His arguments would undoubtedly have received more francophone support if public attitudes had not already been so hardened by the Saint-Léonard crisis and Bill 63. Bill 62 was generally perceived as a symbolic reassertion of francophone power, and few were willing to consider in dispassionate terms whether it was actually in the long-term interest of francophone Montrealers.

At meetings on March 4 and 11, 1970, the education committee of the National Assembly heard representatives of the MCSC. Six of its seven members now favored unified boards, although they also insisted on more confessional and linguistic guarantees than Bill 62 provided.[44] The one dissenter was the same member who had been the main force behind the MCSC's previous policy favoring linguistic school boards. He claimed that francophone Catholics would lose out if the Protestant and Catholic systems were unified. Francophones could best be served by having their own financially secure school boards, rather than being thrust into the same system with the more advanced anglophones.[45]

The MCSC testimony was not completed before Premier Bertrand unexpectedly dissolved the National Assembly and called an early election for April 29, thereby ensuring that Bill 62 would proceed no further and leaving Bill 63 standing alone on the statute books. Not only had the Bertrand government guaranteed freedom of access to English-language schools but it had also failed in its objective of abolishing Protestant school boards. For Jean-Guy Cardinal, one of the strongest Quebec nationalists within the *Union nationale*, this was a most unsatisfactory conclusion to his term as minister of education.

●

The Liberal Proposal: Bill 28

Because the principle of unified school boards for Montreal was generally accepted by the major political parties, Bill 62 was not an important issue in the 1970 election campaign. Montreal anglophones voted overwhelmingly Liberal in the undoubted expectation that Robert Bourassa would treat them more kindly than anyone else. In some respects they were right. Guy St. Pierre, the new minister of education, was certainly more sympathetic to anglophone concerns

43. *Le Devoir*, February 6, 7, and 9, 1970.
44. Quebec, *Débats* 9 (1970): 167.
45. Ibid., pp. B174–B176.

than was Jean-Guy Cardinal. Although St. Pierre was determined to continue Cardinal's policy of creating unified school boards on the Island of Montreal, he made a great effort to do so only with the consent of anglophone educational leaders.[46] He was also anxious to ensure that his plan could survive any possible constitutional challenge, whether by Protestants or ardent Catholics. These considerations explain why St. Pierre's new version of Bill 62, called Bill 28, was not officially made public until July 6, 1971.[47]

In most respects Bill 28 simply reintroduced the main provisions of Bill 62. For example, the boundaries of the 11 proposed unified school boards were exactly the same in both bills. But there were also a number of significant differences. According to St. Pierre's plan, each board would consist of 15 members elected by universal franchise unless the election resulted in the linguistic minority not being represented, in which case the minister of education could appoint two additional members to represent the minority. Each school board would also be required to appoint two deputy directors-general, one anglophone and one francophone. The directors of academic, student, and personnel services would each be required to have an assistant whose mother tongue, whether English or French, was different from that of the director.

Each board would also have both a Protestant and a Catholic committee made up of delegates from the relevant school committees. These committees could insist that the board appoint officials who would be responsible for Catholic and Protestant education within the board's schools. The areawide school council would consist of one representative chosen by and from each of the 11 unified school boards and four appointed by the minister of education. Unlike Bill 62, Bill 28 did not state that the school council would assume ownership of the real estate of the various boards. All these changes were clearly aimed at building in safeguards for the minority, thus reducing anglophone opposition to the bill.

Bill 28 in Committee

Determined to take all possible steps to gain support, St. Pierre decided to send his bill to the education committee of the National Assembly prior to its second reading so that extensive public hearings could be conducted. From September 28 until November 18, 1971, the committee met for 50 hours and heard 39 separate presentations. Ten were from groups concerned only with minor issues affecting their

46. Fournier stresses the importance of the way anglophone business and education interests affected St. Pierre's thinking during the period from mid-1970 to mid-1971. See Fournier, "A Political Analysis," pp. 101–7.

47. Quebec, *Débats* 11 (1971)· 3058–59.

specialized membership or from miscellaneous groups whose positions on the issue had little political significance.

The other 29 presentations fell into 5 major categories, grouped by source. (1) Those from Catholic school boards, and associations of francophone Catholic school administrators, generally supported the government's position. (2) The trade union federations and francophone nationalist organizations and teachers' unions supported unified school boards but opposed any special guarantees for minority groups. (3) Anglophone Catholic organizations generally wanted unified boards with stronger minority guarantees, and they wanted fewer and larger boards so that anglophone Catholics would have more viable school systems within each. (4) The archbishop of Montreal and various francophone Catholic organizations ardently defended the need for a strengthened confessional school system. (5) The Protestant organizations argued for separate French and English networks of school boards.

The Protestants were the greatest source of opposition, despite St. Pierre's considerable effort to gain their support. Many Protestant presentations pointed out that if unified boards were actually established, many anglophones who thus found themselves in a minority would move into the jurisdiction of school board areas in which anglophones dominated. The tendency for the West Island to become an anglophone ghetto would thus be greatly strengthened.

The most important Protestant presentation came from the PSBGM, which urged two separate networks of school boards based on language. Unlike most other groups, it did not hesitate to raise the issue of Section 93 of the BNA Act. Its spokesman, Samuel Godinsky, argued that lawyers for the PSBGM were convinced that the bill was unconstitutional.[48] Liberal, *Union nationale,* and *Parti québécois* members all disapproved of Godinsky's introduction of the constitutional issue, and one Liberal member, William Tetley, pointed out that it was probably unconstitutional for Godinsky, a Jew, to be a member of the PSBGM.[49] Although he made a brief defense of the constitutionality of his own position, Godinsky's case was not convincing. If nothing else, this episode demonstrated the inherent dangers in making arguments based on the BNA Act.

Perhaps realizing this, the Montreal Teachers' Association specifically stated that it did not favor the use of the BNA Act in debates about the desirability of Bill 28.[50] Although the teachers thus disagreed with their employers on the matter of tactics, it is important to note that they were in full agreement on the vital issues. Thus, both

48. Ibid., p. B4576.
49. Ibid., p. B4707.
50. Ibid., p. B4582.

the PSBGM and its teachers opposed unified boards and supported linguistic boards. Despite their usually different interests, the various components of the Protestant educational system came together in the face of this obvious threat to their continued existence.

Throughout the hearings the only political party that consistently opposed Bill 28 was the small *Ralliement créditiste*, which objected to the abolition of confessional school boards. Like the nationalist organizations and trade unions, the PQ opposed the bill because it gave too many concessions to minority linguistic and religious groups and, more importantly, because it did nothing to limit immigrants' access to English-language schools. The PQ supported the *principle* of unified school boards. As the hearings went on, however, PQ education critic Claude Charron focused his attention more and more on the need to repeal Bill 63 and to include in Bill 28 provisions restricting English schools to students whose parents were long-standing members of Quebec's anglophone minority. The official position of the PQ became clear on December 7, when its leaders held a press conference to announce that they would introduce many amendments to the bill to implement their linguistic objectives.[51] On the linguistic issue Bill 28 was now under attack on two distinct fronts: from the PQ and its supporters for not going far enough in recognizing and protecting the majority position of the French language, and from anglophone and Protestant groups for abolishing their historic rights.

On December 8, 13, and 14, Bill 28 was given detailed clause-by-clause study in the education committee, and it became obvious that the government could not get the bill through before Christmas without substantial concessions to the PQ on the language issue. Charron, with the assistance of some other PQ members, began what in effect was a systematic filibuster. Meanwhile, various francophone nationalist and labor organizations sponsored demonstrations against Bill 28 in both Montreal and Quebec City. On December 11 Claude Ryan of *Le Devoir* came out in favor of the PQ position. In an important editorial he supported their suggestion that Bill 28 be amended so that only children having English as a mother tongue or who are already enrolled in English schools would be permitted education in English.[52]

The Bill Is Abandoned

In a matter of days the government's position had become virtually untenable. St. Pierre had tried to present the legislation primarily as a matter of administrative rationalization, in which religious and linguistic rights would still be protected. But by linking Bill 28 to the

51. Pierre Beauchamp, "La restructuration scolaire de l'Ile de Montréal" (M. A. thesis, University of Montreal, 1973), p. 23.
52. *Le Devoir*, December 11, 1971.

need to repeal Bill 63, the PQ effectively shifted the focus of debate. No longer could Bill 28 be portrayed as simply another administrative reform. It was henceforth inextricably entwined with all the emotional and controversial arguments about how to protect the French language in North America. When the bill came back for debate in the National Assembly on December 21 and 22, 1971, all opposition parties spoke at length against its passage in the existing form, and the government could do little to stop them. On December 23 the government announced that debate on Bill 28 would be suspended.[53] Like Bill 62, Bill 28 had been abandoned.

The most thoughtful comments on the failure of Bill 28 came from Claude Ryan in *Le Devoir*. He pointed out that recent events had shown school reform to be impossible in Montreal without an overall consensus. He suggested that the government's resolve had been shaken not only by the PQ and other nationalists but also by the Roman Catholic church.[54] If the church had supported the bill, the government might have been prepared to continue the debate immediately after Christmas.

In his presentation to the National Assembly's education committee,[55] the archbishop of Montreal's official representative had expressed mild opposition to unified school boards. He simply claimed that they were not needed at present and that more limited reforms should be made immediately while this more drastic innovation was studied in detail. Ryan's point in his editorial was that the church's opposition, though much more subtle than that of the nationalists, was probably just as important. Lacking church approval, the government had failed to obtain the support of any of the major interests affected by the proposed legislation.

Disagreement among francophones was the immediate cause of the bill's abandonment. Despite their unity, Protestant anglophones appeared to be more the beneficiaries of its defeat than its cause. Nevertheless, a deeper analysis suggests that, were it not for the anglophone influence bolstered by an appeal to the constitution, St. Pierre would have had to make far fewer concessions to linguistic and confessional minorities. Moreover, if the 1970 Liberal electoral promise to provide 100,000 new jobs had not been so dependent on the anglophone-dominated private sector, St. Pierre might have been able to ignore anglophone protests and accept the PQ position on language policy. Under these hypothetical circumstances, with the PQ as allies, perhaps he could also have ignored objections of the church. The debate over Bill 28 is an excellent illustration of the great delicacy of

53. Ibid., December 24, 1971.
54. Ibid., December 28, 1971.
55. Quebec, *Débats* 11 (1971): B4659–61.

the political balance among Montreal's linguistic and confessional groups.

Bill 71: The School Council of the Island of Montreal

Soon after the government's forced retreat on Bill 28, Premier Bourassa shuffled his cabinet. Guy St. Pierre was replaced as education minister by François Cloutier, who also continued his previous task of overseeing the development of a comprehensive language policy. Cloutier was not eager to revive Bill 28. He wanted to avoid the political difficulties confronted by St. Pierre and was genuinely suspicious of any policy to create unified boards.[56] Accordingly, despite his public support of such a policy during the Bill 28 debate, Cloutier now voiced his fear that unified boards would encourage the formation of linguistic ghettos and that immigrants would flock to anglophone areas to ensure top-quality English-language education for their children.

Cloutier also criticized the complex administrative system that unified boards would need. In short, he was convinced that unification would neither improve the position of French Canadians nor help reduce linguistic tensions. Although Cloutier was always careful to acknowledge that unification might be appropriate in the future, his arguments against it seemed likely to remain powerful for many years to come.

Throughout 1972 Cloutier's staff worked on a new, less ambitious scheme that would not involve the creation of unified school boards (unlike Bills 62 and 28). The staff acted in very close consultation with leaders of Montreal's various educational groupings, and the finished product was finally unveiled on December 1 as Bill 71.[57] The new bill's main purpose was to establish an areawide school council with the same functions provided for in Bill 28. Bill 71 reduced the number of school boards on the island from 33 to eight. Six of these were to be Catholic and two Protestant. The bill did not affect the boundaries or internal structures of the MCSC, which continued unchanged as one of the six Catholic districts. Seventeen suburban districts were consolidated to form the other five Catholic boards.[58]

On the Protestant side, the existing PSBGM was theoretically abolished along with its 10 suburban constituent boards, all to be absorbed by the Protestant Board of School Commissioners of the City

56. François Cloutier, *L'enjeu: Memoires politiques 1970–1976* (Montreal: Stanké, 1978), p. 115.
57. Quebec, *Débats* 12 (1972): 2908–10.
58. Quebec. *Statutes* (1972), Ch. 60, Schedule A.

of Montreal, which changed its name to the Protestant School Board of Greater Montreal and extended its territory to include that of the old PSBGM.[59] In reality, however, the administrative structure of the PSBGM was allowed to continue very much as before. The unusual way Bill 71 described the rationalization of the PSBGM was undoubtedly prompted by a wish to avoid disturbing the constitutional position of Montreal's Protestants. The second Protestant board included the part of the West Island not covered by the PSBGM.

Bill 71's boundaries for the eight boards are shown in Map 4, and characteristics of the student population in their territories (in 1972 and 1979) are shown in Table 6. Each of the six new boards was to choose a member to sit on the school council, and the MCSC and the PSBGM were to choose six and two, respectively. The government would appoint three additional members.[60]

Cloutier did not pretend that this restructuring of the boards was final. Thus, one of the bill's provisions called on the school council "to make an intensive and objective study of the factors pertinent to an adequate school reorganization" and to submit a plan to the minister by December 31, 1975.[61] Considering the failure of two successive ministers of education to produce an acceptable plan, this requirement obviously placed a heavy burden on the new school council.

Bill 71 was clearly designed to be acceptable to almost all the island's major educational interests. The Roman Catholic church and its devout adherents were satisfied by the retention of confessional school boards; the MCSC and the PSBGM by the lack of tampering with their boundaries; the PQ and other nationalist groups by the acknowledgment that a final solution could not be decided without an overall language policy; and Protestant businessmen by the retention of the administration of their children's schools.[62]

The only dissatisfied group was the anglophone Catholics. Because all members of the new boards were to be elected by universal franchise, anglophone Catholics no longer had any guarantee of representation on the MCSC. Although there were more Catholics than Protestants attending anglophone schools on the island (see Table 6), the anglophone Catholics were given no official recognition, whereas the Protestants had two school boards of their own and a guarantee of at least three representatives on the school council. An organization called the Committee for the Co-ordination of Anglophone Catholic Education—comprising parents', teachers', and principals' groups—conducted a vigorous campaign to convince Cloutier to establish two

59. Ibid., Schedule B.
60. Ibid., Section 3.
61. Ibid., Section 7. This deadline was extended by one year by Bill 42 (1976). The same bill postponed the scheduled 1976 school board elections until 1977.
62. Beauchamp, "La restructuration scolaire," p. 32.

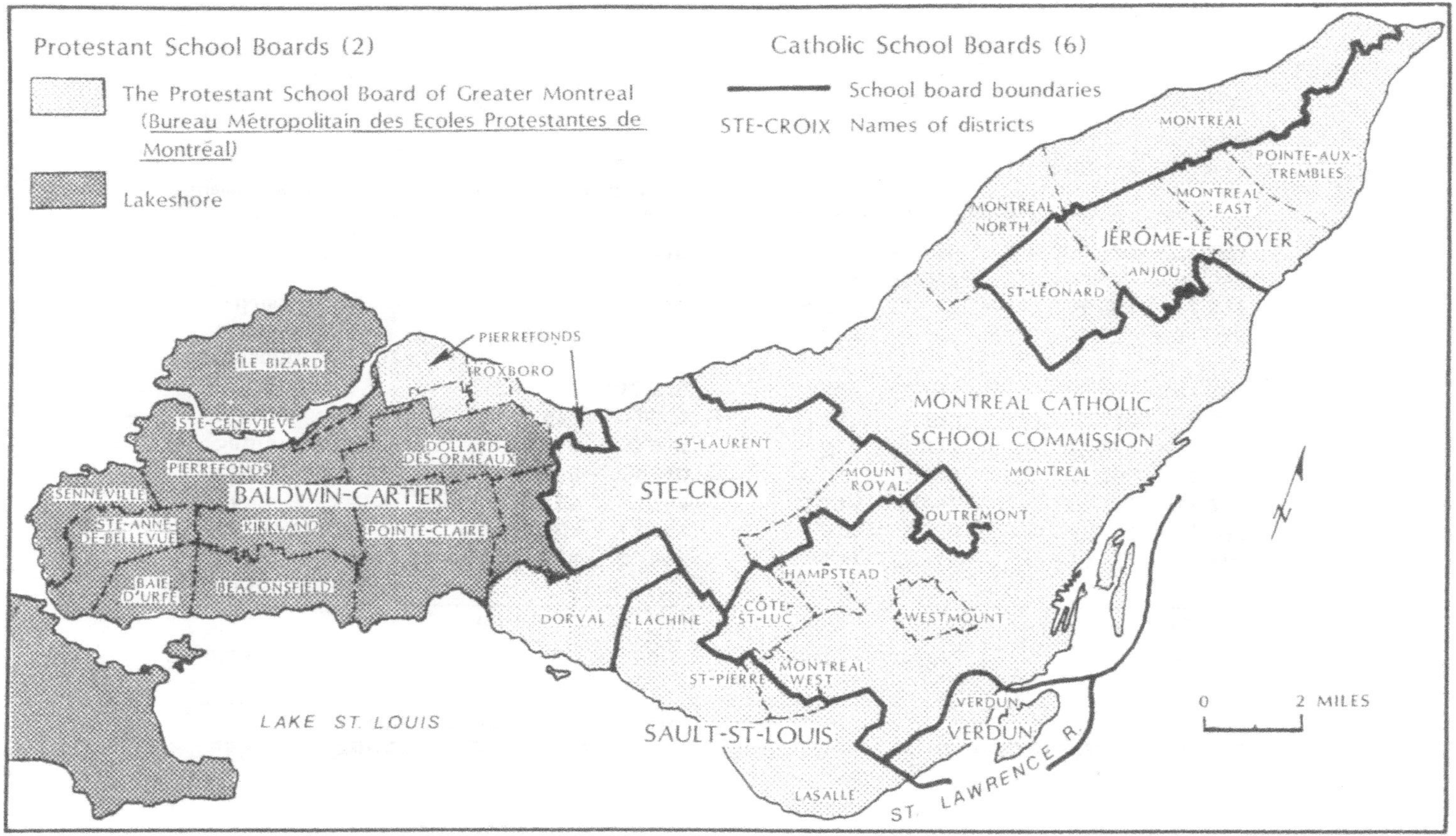

Map 4

Catholic and Protestant School Boards in Montreal Resulting from Bill 71, 1972

Source: The School Council of the Island of Montreal Newsletter, Vol. 2, no. 2 (March 1974), pp. 6–7.

Table 6— Student Population in School Commission Territories Established by Bill 71, 1972–1973 and 1981–1982

School Board	Pupils in French Schools		Pupils in English Schools		Totals	
	1972–1973	1981–1982	1972–1973	1981–1982	1972–1973	1981–1982
Catholic						
MCSC	164,125	91,656	44,450	22,914	208,575	114,570
Le Royer	25,303	17,247	5,812	5,950	31,115	23,197
Baldwin-Cartier	10,185	10,744	9,597	6,537	19,782	17,281
Sault-Saint-Louis	14,568	9,940	6,885	4,439	21,453	14,379
Sainte-Croix	11,210	6,958	4,013	1,938	15,223	8,896
Verdun	9,977	5,500	2,337	997	12,314	6,477
TOTAL	235,368	142,045	73,094	42,755	308,462	184,800
Protestant						
PSBGM	1,064	4,167	54,613	30,101	55,677	34,268
Lakeshore	—	398	14,281	11,923	14,281	12,321
TOTAL	1,064	4,565	68,894	42,024	69,958	46,589
GRAND TOTALS	236,432	146,610	141,988	84,779	378,420	231,389

Source: Adapted from data in *Le Devoir*, January 11, 1973, and in School Council of the Island of Montreal, Résumé, Report of Council Meeting of December 21, 1981.

separate school boards for Montreal's anglophone Catholics.[63] The campaign failed when Cloutier firmly refused their demands on the grounds that if he yielded on this he would soon face justified requests from other groups, most notably the Jews, for their own separate systems.[64]

Bill 71: Passage and Implementation

All three opposition parties opposed Bill 71 in the National Assembly. Jean-Guy Cardinal of the *Union Nationale* accused the government of shirking its responsibility by delegating the problem of further restructuring to the school council.[65] The *Ralliement créditiste* spokesman said the bill was being rushed through without adequate public debate.[66] Claude Charron of the *Parti québécois* maintained that the bill's provisions had been dictated by Montreal's anglophone minority.[67]

During the clause-by-clause study, the PQ and UN repeatedly proposed amendments to strengthen the position of French in Montreal's educational system. All were defeated by the Liberal majority. Cloutier refused to accept proposals to make the school council officially French, arguing that in practice French would be its predominant language.[68] There was also considerable debate about the apparent overrepresentation of Protestants and underrepresentation of the MCSC on the school council and about the council's role in equalizing school resources. Compared to the Bill 28 debate, however, the atmosphere was extremely calm and cooperative, and on December 21, 1972, the bill became law.[69]

Although the new law seemed modest in comparison with Bills 62 and 28, it had profound effects on Montreal's educational system. Starting in 1973, all individual property owners on the island were subject to one uniform school tax, and all companies were subject to another.[70] In June 1973 residents covered by the MCSC and the old Protestant School Commissioners of the City of Montreal experienced

---

63. See the committee's full-page advertisement in *The Montreal Star*, December 4, 1972.

64. *Le Devoir*, December 8, 1972.

65. Quebec, *Débats* 12 (1972): 2988.

66. Ibid., p. 2994.

67. Ibid., p. 2996.

68. Ibid., p. B7294.

69. Quebec, *Statutes* (1972), Ch. 60.

70. In 1979 Quebec's system for local government financing was changed so that school boards lost virtually all their taxing authority. Almost all funds for education are now provided directly by the provincial government. See "Dossier: La réforme de la fiscalité municipale est en vigeur," *Municipalité Québec* (January–February 1980): 23–42.

their first elections for school board members. Although the voting turnout throughout the island was only about 25 percent, there were some lively contests. After what seemed a disproportionately high anglophone turnout, anglophone Catholics won three of the 19 MCSC seats.[71] Their fears of losing all their representation as a result of Bill 71 had proven unjustified.

Bill 71 also affected the legal position of the Jews. It repealed the 1931 law that had ratified the agreement between the Protestants and the Jewish School Commission.[72] The new law gave Jews and other minority religious groups throughout the island equal rights within the school board of their choice. Desirable as these changes obviously were, they raised constitutional difficulties. We saw in Chapter 4 how the highest court in the British Empire ruled a Quebec law allowing Jews to sit on the Montreal Protestant school board to be in violation of Section 93 of the British North American Act, in the Hirsch decision of 1928. Because the new PSBGM is legally a continuation of the old City of Montreal Protestant school board, and because no subsequent changes have been made to Section 93,[73] the provisions of Bill 71 treating all religious groups equally might well be unconstitutional. If in the future the matter were taken to a Canadian court, however, that aspect of the Hirsch ruling might, of course, be overturned.

School Board Reorganization: An Unresolved Problem

In early 1977, after yet another lengthy study and debate of the issue, the school council finally recommended retention of the existing confessional system.[74] This was not because of any great attachment to the system but simply because a council majority voted down *every other possible alternative*, once again demonstrating the divisiveness of the whole issue.

In June 1982 the PQ government presented its solution to the problem.[75] The main feature of the government's policy involved es-

---

71. *Le Devoir*, June 19, 1973. For a good account of the MCSC elections see Lise Duval and Jean-Pierre Tremblay, *Le projet de restructuration scolaire de l'Ile de Montréal et la question linguistique au Québec* (Quebec, International Centre for Research on Bilingualism, 1974), Ch. 3.

72. Quebec, *Statutes* (1972), Ch. 60, Section 27.

73. Section 29 of Canada's Constitution Act (1982) states: "Nothing in this charter abrogates or derogates from any right or privileges guaranteed by or under the Constitution of Canada in respect of denominational, separate or dissentient schools."

74. School Council of the Island of Montreal, *Résumé*, January 31, 1977.

75. Quebec, Ministère de l'Education, *L'Ecole québécoise: une école communautaire et responsable* (Quebec: 1982). For an analysis of recent public opinion surveys concerning school reorganization, see Guy Pelletier and Claude Tessard, *La population québécoise face à la restructuration scolaire* (Montreal: Guérin, 1982).

tablishing each public school in the province as a corporate body in its own right, most of whose directors would be elected by parents. Individual schools would decide their own confessional status (Catholic, Protestant, or nonconfessional) and language (French or English). School boards would continue to exist but henceforth would no longer be elected by universal suffrage. Most school board members would be delegates from the governing bodies of the individual schools.

School boards on the island would be organized on the basis of language. There would be eight French-language boards and five English ones. There was no intent to abolish rights protected by Section 93 of the BNA Act. In Montreal this meant that Protestants and Catholics living within the territory served by the City of Montreal's Catholic and Protestant boards in 1867 would maintain their right to perpetuate their confessional school boards if they so desired. Because these confessional boards would presumably benefit only from the level of government assistance available in 1867, the right to maintain them appears in practice to have little substance.

Quite predictably, the proposals were met with howls of protests, particularly from anglophone groups and school board organizations that preferred the status quo. By early 1984 the government still had not proceeded with legislation on the subject, and the fate of the latest plan for school board reorganization was far from clear.

There are three main factors that have forced any governing party in Quebec to attempt some kind of school board reform, particularly in Montreal. First, some parents of children attending French-Catholic schools, acting through officially recognized parents' committees, have attempted to deconfessionalize their own schools while acknowledging that they continue to fall under the jurisdiction of the MCSC. In April 1980, however, the Quebec Superior Court ruled such action unconstitutional as a violation of Section 93 of the BNA Act.[76] But as the lapsed Catholic and non-Catholic element among the francophones continues to grow, the pressures to create a nonconfessional network of French schools inevitably increase.[77]

Second, many French-Catholic educators are increasingly disturbed by the fact that their own clientele is shrinking drastically, whereas the number of children in French Protestant schools is increasing. Convinced that Protestant educators are fostering this sector to protect their own positions, most francophones see no need for a

76. *Le Devoir*, April 18, 1980.
77. For further details, see Henry Milner, "Notre-Dame-des-Neiges: A Neighbourhood Battles for Its School," *Montreal Review* 5 (December 1980–January 1981): 17, 21; and "The Deconfessionalization of Montreal's School System: The Rights of Entrenched Minorities Versus the Capacity of Institutions to Evolve with Their Community" (Paper presented to the 1981 Annual Meeting of the Canadian Political Science Association).

full-scale Protestant network of French schools. Finally, the school population as a whole is shrinking, increasing the need to close selected schools on a planned and rational basis. As long as every area is served by two quite independent Catholic and Protestant school boards—each with French and English schools—such a policy is virtually impossible to implement.

It is important to note the remarkable similarity of current pressures for reorganizing Montreal's school boards to those felt in 1966 by members of the Parent royal commission, which originally recommended the establishment of unified school boards. The francophone members of the Parent commission were not ardent nationalists, and even the anglophone members (both prominent educators) supported the unified concept, concluding that the unified boards would be the most effective mechanisms to govern a remodeled Montreal school system offering more educational choice, not less. The Parent report wanted families to be able to choose among French and English schools as well as among Catholic, Protestant, and neutral schools. Because the establishment of six separate networks of school boards was clearly unrealistic, the commission recommended one kind of school board that would operate six different kinds of schools.

In 1969, when the *Union nationale* government moved to implement the Parent proposal in Montreal, political circumstances had changed. The Saint-Léonard school crisis had taken place, and in Bill 63 the government had confirmed the right of all parents to choose the language of education of their children. Bill 62, the legislation for unified school boards, was explicitly introduced not only as an organizational reform measure but also as a way of appeasing nationalist elements in the province (and the cabinet) that had objected to Bill 63's liberal provisions. Under these circumstances it is not surprising that the debate quickly became embroiled in the larger issues of non-francophones' roles in an increasingly French Quebec.

With Bill 28, introduced in 1971, the Liberal government tried to show that it was also not afraid to take on the anglophone educational establishment. But the Liberals placed much more emphasis on organizational rationality to justify their bill. By this time, however, few in Quebec were willing to debate the measure in these terms. Nationalists, anglophones, and fervent Catholics all objected to the symbolic significance of Bill 28, even if they were not fully familiar with its substance. The role of the proponents of Catholic confessional school boards in forcing the abandonment of Bill 28 must not be underestimated. But it must also be remembered that were it not for the strident demands for linguistic autonomy by English Catholics and Protestants, the demands for distinct Catholic school boards could much more easily have been accommodated.

Three successive efforts to reorganize Montreal's school system failed: the *Union nationale* tried in 1969, the Liberals in 1971, and the School Council of the Island of Montreal in 1977. Complex political interests and alignments based on both language and religion made it impossible to mobilize a clear majority behind any single option. The *Parti québécois* government faces the same difficulties and realities as its predecessors. In the last decade and a half the need for change has probably increased, but the positions of the linguistic and religious interests seem to have hardened. Consensus is likely to be even more elusive than before.

9

Social Services

Chapter 4 described the evolution of Quebec's social service system prior to the Quiet Revolution. Even more than education, the social service system was severely fragmented, with French Catholics, English Catholics, Jews, and Protestants each operating their own network of institutions and coordination virtually nonexistent. In the early 1960s the provincial government was preoccupied with educational reform, and the social services were not a top priority. When the government became concerned, ministers gave more attention to questions of income maintenance than to ways of improving personal social services like child protection, community organization, and various forms of family counseling and assistance. But by the late 1960s the old practices and institutions were under the most wide-ranging scrutiny, and drastic structural changes had been made by the mid-1970s. In short, reforming Montreal's social service system seemed a much easier task than reforming its school boards.

The Castonguay-Nepveu Commission and Bill 65

Shortly after taking office in 1966, Jean-Paul Cloutier, the *Union nationale* minister who headed both the health and social welfare departments, announced the appointment of a commission of inquiry to study the "entire field of health and social welfare."[1] The first chair was Claude Castonguay, a Quebec City actuary who left the commission in 1970 to enter politics as Robert Bourassa's minister of social affairs.[2] From 1970 onward the chair was Gérard Nepveu, a civil servant who had first been appointed as the commission's secretary. Although the subject matter of the Castonguay-Nepveu commission was extremely broad, our principal concern is

---

1. Quebec, *Report of the Commission of Inquiry on Health and Social Welfare* (Quebec: 1967), vol. 1, p. ix.
2. Ibid., vol. 6, p. 6.

with the political and administrative organization of the province's social services.[3]

The commission's recommendations on these matters were made public in 1972. It suggested that Quebec's social service organization be based on 12 administrative regions, the one for Montreal covering the territory of the Montreal Urban Community and the City of Laval.[4] Each of the 12 regions would have one major social service organization known as a "center for the delivery of personal adjustment services." Because of their large populations, the Montreal and Quebec City regions would have an unspecified number of extra centers.[5] "Community centers" would also be established to serve populations of between 15,000 and 40,000, providing day-care centers, community organization workers, and various other preventative social services. In Montreal, certain community centers would be designated to work with each of the city's main ethnic communities.[6] Apart from this one reference to Montreal's heterogeneous ethnic composition, the commission did not suggest how Montreal's existing social service system might be adapted to the proposal for a unified, monolithic system.

The commission also recommended that all residential social service institutions be thoroughly integrated into the new system. Each region would have a network of institutions to serve the handicapped, those requiring specialized care, the elderly, orphans, and those temporarily in need of refuge and assistance.[7] All these institutions and the two kinds of social service centers would come under the administrative control of a "regional social services office."[8]

Unfortunately for the commission, its recommendations on the social services were issued after the government had already implemented a massive reorganization, dealing with both Quebec's health and social services. This had been done under the leadership of Claude Castonguay, whose first legislative project in late 1970 was merging the ministries of health and social services into a new ministry of social affairs. Castonguay justified this action as leading to more efficient delivery of both kinds of services.[9] Because the commission's

3. For an analysis of changes in the health services see Marc Renaud, "The Political Economy of the Quebec State Interventions in Health: Reform or Revolution" (Ph. D. diss., University of Wisconsin-Madison, 1976); Sidney S. Lee, *Quebec's Health System: A Decade of Change, 1967–77* (Toronto: Institute of Public Administration of Canada, 1979); and Frédéric Lesemann, *Du pain et des services: La réforme de la santé et des services sociaux au Québec* (Montreal: Editions cooperatives Albert Saint-Martin, 1981).

4. Quebec, *Report on Health and Social Welfare*, vol. 6 (tome 1), p. 131.

5. Ibid., pp. 222–23.

6. Ibid., p. 228.

7. Ibid., vol. 6 (tome 2), pp. 53–55.

8. Ibid., p. 57.

9. Quebec, Assemblée Nationale, *Débats* 10 (1970): 1890.

social service recommendations had assumed the continuation of the two separate ministries, the government's subsequent implementation efforts understandably did not follow the commission's proposals.

The First Version of Bill 65

In July 1971 Castonguay announced the government's plan for reorganizing the province's health and social services. His proposed law, Bill 65, stated that the administration of all these services was to be completely reorganized and decentralized. "Regional offices of social affairs" were to be established to decentralize the administration and control of both health and social services.[10] Bill 65 also stated that "local community service centers" would be established as the main local point of delivery for social services as well as for day-to-day care. As the commission recommended, residential social service institutions were to be totally subsidized and wholly public; no longer would they be run by religious or charitable foundations relying on a combination of public and private funds. Private institutions could remain but would receive no subsidies. "Social service centers" were to be established in each region, corresponding to the commission's centers for the delivery of personal adjustment services.[11]

Hearings on the main principles of Bill 65 were held by the social affairs committee of the National Assembly from August 24 to December 2, 1971. Sixty-one organizations or individuals made oral presentations, and another 21 groups submitted written briefs.[12] Many briefs came from professional groups concerned with the extent of government interference in professional activities as well as a good many submitted by individual institutions anxious about Bill 65's effect on their own activities. The overriding concern of most groups was that the government would establish excessively complex and bureaucratic mechanisms of control. There was a dual fear that the proposed regional offices would either be under the direct control of the ministry, and therefore simply another source of "red tape," or else that the regional offices would have too much freedom and therefore be able to interfere arbitrarily in the operations of individual institutions.

Montreal: A Special Case?

Only a few of the briefs dealt directly with the unique problems of delivering social services on the Island of Montreal. But the com-

10. Ibid., vol. 11 (1971): 3281–82.
11. Ibid.
12. For a general analysis of the briefs presented, see Vincent Lemieux, François Renaud, and Brigitte von Schoenberg, *Les conseils régionaux de la santé et des services sociaux: Une analyse politique* (Département de science politique, Université Laval, 1974), pp. 26–33.

mittee did hear separate pleas for continued autonomy for Montreal's French Catholics, English Catholics, and Jews. Pierre Hurteau, the director of the *Société d'adoption et de protection de l'enfance de Montréal*, was upset that Bill 65 did not provide for the distinct ethnic, cultural, and linguistic characteristics of the population.[13] He suggested that Quebec could learn from the experience of Holland, where the state officially recognizes the plural nature of the society and provides for special representation of Catholics and Protestants. Hurteau considered Montreal especially suited for such representation, although he recognized that it might not be necessary in other parts of the province.[14] With what seems in retrospect uncanny foresight, Hurteau commented: "It could be bizarre indeed if, in Quebec, only the Jewish minority is able to maintain confessional services."[15] No other Montreal French Catholic took such a firm stand in favor of maintaining French-Catholic social service structures. Most others accepted the need for state-controlled secular structures (although all did not accept the government proposals for bringing this about).

Montreal's English Catholics made only one presentation to the committee, by Richard Macklem, chair of the social agency called Catholic Family and Children's Services and the North American director of the operations of Rolls-Royce. He seemed more concerned with language than religion: "The main thrust of all these recommendations is to demonstrate the need for a continuation of English language services for clients who speak that language."[16]

Castonguay responded that social service legislation in Quebec had never taken language into account and said he assumed that Bill 65 would not affect established practices concerning the language in which Montreal's various health and social services were delivered.[17] Castonguay was readily supported by the parliamentary leader of the *Parti québécois*, Camille Laurin, who said the minister was quite correct in deliberately omitting any reference to language. He commented that the problem "really has not arisen practically."[18] Of course, it had not arisen until then because there had been separate social service agencies for each of the four main ethnic-linguistic groups. The English Catholics were clearly quite justified in their fear that Bill 65 would not only change the structures but also the practices under which English-speaking Catholics were served by English-speaking personnel.

A joint brief from several Jewish organizations in Montreal

13. Quebec, *Débats* 11 (1971): B3609.
14. Ibid., p. B3623.
15. Ibid., p. B3614 (author's trans.).
16. Ibid., p. B5338.
17. Ibid., p. B5339.
18. Ibid.

pleaded with the government to allow their separate institutions for health and social services to continue. Their spokesman stated that experience in other cities had shown that unified, nonsectarian agencies could not deal with the special needs of the Jewish family.[19] Although Castonguay made no promises to the Jews, spokesmen for the *Union nationale* and *Créditiste* parties stated their support for the idea of separate social services for francophones, Jews, and "anglo-saxons."[20] The committee hearings did not, however, produce a single Protestant "anglo-saxon" demand for the maintenance of any kind of ethnic or linguistic social service structure. The English-Protestant social work establishment was so unaccustomed to having to defend itself that it was unprepared and ill equipped to respond in public to the government's proposals.

Castonguay Makes Concessions

Following the committee hearings, Castonguay presented a completely revised version of Bill 65,[21] the most notable new feature being virtual abandonment of the idea of powerful regional offices. Instead, these were replaced by "regional councils of health and social services," made up mainly of representatives from the various institutions under the jurisdiction of each council. Their chief role was as a link between the ministry and the various establishments.[22] This change represented a major concession to professionals and administrators who had protested so strenuously against the imposition of another layer of governmental control. The new councils, however, were to be much weaker than the proposed regional offices, so further centralization of provincial control in Quebec City seemed inevitable.

The new version of Bill 65 provoked little debate and became law on December 24, 1971. Although less disruptive of the status quo than originally envisioned, the bill opened hitherto private boards of directors of the province's health and social service institutions to membership representing a much broader range of the population; it brought all institutions under much closer governmental control; and it established the new regional councils. The more detailed changes resulting from the bill's implementation, particularly as it affected Montreal, were not known for another 10 to 15 months.

19. Ibid., p. B4843.
20. Ibid., p. B4845.
21. Ibid., p. B4885.
22. Lemieux, Renaud, and von Schoenberg, *Les conseils régionaux*, pp. 33–35.

The Council of Health and Social Services of Metropolitan Montreal

Although the boundaries of the territories to be covered by each regional council were not stated in Bill 65, by mid-1972 it was clear that the Montreal region would comprise the territory originally suggested for social service organization in the Castonguay-Nepveu Report, that is, the MUC and the City of Laval. The Council of Health and Social Services of Metropolitan Montreal opened its doors in late 1972[23] but was not fully operational until March 1973, when its board of directors was complete and its first director-general took office.

The council's official functions are the same as those of the province's other regional health and social service councils and are relatively few in number. It has a general responsibility to promote cooperation, planning, and citizen participation and to supervise the elections for the boards of directors of the various health and social service institutions. It also receives complaints about services these institutions provide and makes recommendations based on these complaints, promotes the setting up of common services, and carries out special tasks assigned by the minister.[24] In recent years the importance of these special council tasks has grown considerably, so much so that by 1980 the councils throughout Quebec had taken on a good many of the regional responsibilities of the provincial social affairs ministry. For example, the Montreal council is now determining admissions policies to various residential institutions, developing a regional information system for health and social services, and working out ways of improving the ambulance system.[25]

The environment in which the Montreal regional council operates differs completely from that of the other regional councils. The Montreal council has the largest population (36 percent of the province) and the smallest territory. Its health and social service facilities are larger, more complex, and more specialized than those found elsewhere.[26] In a study of the province's regional councils, three *Université Laval* researchers found the Montreal council to have the most difficulty penetrating the independence of the existing institu-

23. For an account of these early months, see Council of Health and Social Services of Metropolitan Montreal, *Annual Report 1972* (Montreal: 1973).

24. Quebec, *Statutes* (1971), Ch. 48, Sections 16, 17. Also see Claude E. Forget, "Développement et implantation des services de santé et des services sociaux au Québec," *Canadian Public Administration* 17 (1974): 32–35.

25. Conseil de la santé et des services sociaux de Montréal métropolitain, *Rapport annuel 1980–81* (Montreal: 1981), pp. 9–10.

26. Conseil de la santé et des services sociaux de Montréal métropolitain, *Rapport annuel 1974* (Montreal: 1975), pp. 5–10.

tions and making contact with the population.[27] The first problem was undoubtedly caused by the fact that so many of its institutions were large and important, accustomed to dealing directly with the ministry's top levels. The second problem resulted simply from the size and heterogeneity of a population that was also being confronted with a number of other new metropolitan structures at the same time.

Language Issues

Nothing in Bill 65 or the regulations issued under it acknowledged that, unlike other regional councils, Montreal's council contains both French and English networks of health and social services, each separate and complete in itself. Research for the Gendron commission on language policy, conducted immediately before the implementation of Bill 65, showed the extent of this linguistic separation. First, the study found no such thing in Montreal as a totally bilingual hospital. All could be classified as either French or English, although both hospitals and administrators made special efforts to ensure that employees providing outpatient or emergency services could function in both languages.[28]

Although hospital records concerning the linguistic preferences of their patients are inexact, there seemed to be a definite tendency for English hospitals to admit higher proportions of francophone patients than French hospitals did of anglophone patients.[29] Nevertheless, personnel in French hospitals seemed to have a greater ability to communicate in English than personnel in English hospitals had in French.[30] These are not surprising findings, reflecting the fact that Montreal's francophone majority is more bilingual than the anglophone minority. They may also reflect a belief among francophones in the superiority of English hospitals. In other words, some bilingual francophone doctors and patients may choose English hospitals for medical reasons, even if they cannot make full use of their preferred language.

27. Lemieux, Renaud, and von Schoenberg, *Les conseils régionaux*, Chs. 7, 8. Lemieux et al. identify the various regional councils only by randomly selected letters. This is an attempt to preserve their individual anonymity in a study that was government sponsored and that dealt with certain delicate issues. However, on page 157, a table concerning responses to a questionnaire shows that metropolitan Montreal was the only region for which there were 17 responses. In other tables concerning the questionnaire in the study, the N for Region E is consistently 17. This together with certain statements in the study concerning the nature of Region E lead to the unmistakable conclusion that it is in fact metropolitan Montreal.

28. Claude Gousse, *Pratiques et usages linguistiques de la clientele québécoise en rapport avec des organismes de service: Une approche qualitative*, Etude E-18 de la Commission d'enquête sur la situation de la langue française et sur les droits linguistiques au Québec (Quebec, l'Editeur officiel, 1973).

29. Ibid., pp. 20–21.

30. Ibid., p. 39.

The same study found a similar linguistic division among Montreal's social service agencies. But because these agencies do not have to meet the kinds of emergency demands that hospitals do, they have even less incentive to operate bilingually.[31] While noting that linguistic practices had generally been quite stable, the researcher noted a tendency for French agencies to become more openly unilingual, whereas English agencies shifted toward at least an image of bilingualism. This was done by sending senior personnel to French courses and by hiring bilingual secretaries who could use French to direct stray francophones to agencies operating in their own language.[32]

English institutions are likely to become more bilingual in the years ahead as a natural outgrowth of the many changes in Quebec since 1960. Bilingualism was especially encouraged by recent Quebec provincial laws governing qualifications for professional accreditation. In 1970 the Quebec legislature passed a bill requiring all non-Canadians seeking admission to a Quebec professional corporation to possess a working knowledge of French.[33] In practical terms this made it extremely difficult for English hospitals to continue recruiting qualified nurses from such places as Britain and the British West Indies. In 1973 the legislature took this policy one step further when it approved a new Professional Code, stating that beginning July 1, 1976, Canadian citizens must be able to work in French in order to practice a profession in Quebec.[34] Although this rule did not apply to those already in a professional corporation prior to its adoption, unilingual anglophone doctors, nurses, and social workers will obviously become increasingly rare as time goes on.

Despite this, there is every likelihood that both francophones and anglophones will continue to prefer institutions that are efficient and unilingual rather than cumbersome and bilingual. Montrealers will still want separate networks of health and social service establishments, but everyone acknowledges that there must be communication and cooperation between the two. Communication between the two networks previously took place almost exclusively in English, if it occurred at all. The Professional Code and other language laws intend to ensure that future communication will be in French. If nothing else, the creation of the Montreal regional council has provided an official forum for the discussion of such cooperative policies and to some extent for their implementation.

31. Ibid., p. 119.
32. Ibid., p. 122.
33. René Dussault and Louis Borgeat, "La réforme des professions au Québec," *Canadian Public Administration* 18 (1974): 418.
34. Ibid., pp. 420–21.

Social Service Centers for Montreal

The process of reorganizing Montreal's social service agencies in accordance with Bill 65 was fundamentally different from the establishment of the regional council. The latter involved creation of a new coordinating institution, which did not itself deliver services to the public. In contrast, the reorganization of the social service agencies meant the government must tamper with agencies that had been in existence for decades and that were deeply rooted in the city's ethnic and religious communities. From the very beginning the government wanted agencies throughout the province to be intimately involved in the reorganization process. To this end it accepted a proposal from the *Féderation des services sociaux à la famille du Québec* that organizing committees, comprising representatives from each affected agency, be established in each of the province's 12 social affairs regions. These committees were to be coordinated by a "provincial mission" that included five members each from the Ministry of Social Affairs and the *Féderation*. The mission began work in January 1973.[35] One of its first acts was hiring professional consultants to assist the various regions.

Language-Based Task Forces

In Montreal the mission hired a consultant for the French-language sector and another for the English. Consequently, from the very beginning the reorganization process tended toward linguistic separation. When the Montreal regional committee met for the first time on February 15, it delegated future preparations to a joint committee made up of the executive directors of all the agencies. This group in turn recommended that "for purposes of efficiency" the work of the committee be done by two separate language-based task forces. Consequently, each executive director found himself in either the French task force or the English task force.[36] In mid-March and early April both task forces met separately.

After study, the anglophone task force concluded that the most desirable organizational alternatives were those not calling for any separation of structures by language. They settled on two possible models considered consistent with this objective. The first was the creation of five to seven territorially based social service centers for Montreal, each drawing on a population of 200,000 to 500,000. These

35. John R. Walker, "Implementation of Social Service Center, Ch. 48 (Bill 65)," Mimeographed.

36. P. A. Dufays, "Progress Report, Anglophone Planning Task Force, Region 6A Montreal" (Mimeographed, April 24, 1973), p. 5.

centers would be coordinated by a kind of "superboard," conceivably the Montreal regional council.

The second alternative was for one social service center to cover the whole region, but with its work decentralized to various regional units, each having its own board of directors. The anglophones noted that the working language would be French under both alternatives but emphasized that services would have to be provided in the client's language.[37]

The francophone task force faced similar alternatives to those confronting the anglophones but opted for separating structures by language. It proposed two separate social service centers, one francophone and one anglophone. The francophone center would be relatively centralized, the local units not having their own boards of directors. It also proposed a joint regional committee to coordinate the work of the two centers.[38]

It is not entirely clear why the two task forces took their respective positions, but the following speculation provides useful clues. Anglophones undoubtedly believed that if they advocated anything save linguistic integration they would be open to the charge of trying to protect their privileged autonomy. Most anglophone social workers traditionally took "progressive" positions within their community and had no desire to align themselves with the generally conservative forces intent on defending anglophone rights. Furthermore, as professionals, they were already having to work more and more in a French environment. Given the government's policy as expressed in Bill 65, it is not surprising that the anglophones saw little choice but to contribute constructively to an integrated system.

The French social work establishment was under no such constraints. It saw grave difficulties in an integrated system and was frank in pointing them out. First, under a truly integrated system more francophone social workers would need to be able to deal with English-speaking clients. Because many such social workers were fervent Quebec nationalists, the prospect of having to adapt to these clients was not attractive. Equally unpleasant was the prospect of absorbing large numbers of anglophone social workers into institutions that had been wholly French speaking.

Another serious problem of a unified system concerned the internal divisions within each linguistic group. Competing unions had organized their own bargaining units in the various French-speaking agencies. In part, this reflected considerable disagreement within the profession about the roles the union should be playing. The English group was divided by severe internal jealousies over different concep-

37. Ibid., p. 17.
38. Ibid., p. 18.

tions of the social role of the profession as well as by different religious persuasions. The French did not want to add these disputes to those already simmering within their own group.

The two task forces held a joint meeting on April 6 and tentatively agreed to support the francophone position. Although the decision could not have been a major disappointment to most anglophone social workers, it undoubtedly left the English Catholics and the Jews in an ambiguous position. Under the anglophones' integrated alternative, all anglophones would be in the minority, which would probably leave relatively more autonomy to the smaller religious components of the English-speaking minority. But under the francophones' alternative of separate centers, these minorities would have been asked to subject themselves to the secular anglophone majority. Jewish Family Services made it clear that, at least for the short term, it would not participate in such an arrangement and would therefore remain out of the system altogether.[39] It is important to understand that none of this maneuvering was done in public. There were no public hearings or meetings, and very few Montrealers were aware of what was happening. To this day it is difficult for a researcher to determine the precise course of events.

Three Centers: French, English, and Jewish

On April 16, 1973, the two consultants to the Montreal committee met with Claude Castonguay and his senior officials to present the conclusions of the two task forces. Castonguay saw no difficulty in establishing language-based social service centers in Montreal. He explicitly noted that such a policy was bound to appear reasonable, given the difficulties encountered in the educational sphere.[40] There is no available evidence that, even at this stage, the ministry itself had developed a carefully considered policy for Montreal. Castonguay was obviously acting as a careful politician responding to recent political events and not as an administrator concerned primarily with orderly organizational charts. By the end of the meeting it was clear that the government was willing to establish both a French and an English social service center for Montreal and even a Jewish center if the Jews agreed to conform fully to the other provisions of Bill 65.[41]

Once Castonguay had given his approval, there was nothing to stop the implementation of the francophone task force position. On July 1, 1973, two social service centers—*Montréal Métropolitain* and Ville Marie—officially came into being.[42] Despite its name, Ville

39. Ibid., p. 19.
40. Ibid., p. 20. See Ch. 8 for the debate on educational structures.
41. Ibid.
42. Ville Marie Social Service Centre, *Newsletter*, July 3, 1973.

Marie is the anglophone center. It absorbed six agencies, including Catholic Family and Children's Services. The Jewish agency declined to participate and continued its activities as a private institution. *Montréal Métropolitain* absorbed eight existing agencies. Both public centers have subsequently taken over the administration of hospital and school social workers operating in their respective languages.

In 1974 the Jewish agency decided, for financial reasons, that it should enter the public sector. This involved the legal separation of the agency from Allied Jewish Community Services and the creation of a new legal entity, the Jewish Family Services Social Service Center. These changes were made after "an agonizing process of evaluation, appraisal, and negotiation."[43] In the agency's last annual report as a private body its officers asked several questions that vividly express Jewish concern about the entire process of social service reorganization: "Is life within the public sector in fact incongruent with our tradition? Can our ethnically and culturally-laden vitality survive the incursions of government bureaucracy? Will the human responses be diluted by computerized anonymity? Can the persistent tradition transcend technocratic values?"[44] The agency maintains that, if these questions are not answered satisfactorily in years to come, it will remove itself from the public sector and once again rely on charitable support through Allied Jewish Community Services. By initially refusing to join the anglophone center, it appears that the Jews protected their independence and subsequently were able to enter the public sector in their own right. They also say they have enough community support to leave again, if this proves absolutely necessary. Many English Catholics would have preferred a parallel option, but it was never open to them. They lacked the necessary support from both the government and their own community.

Montreal has three social service centers, each with its own board of directors in accordance with the provisions of Bill 65. In the remainder of the province outside Montreal, however, planners and administrators in the Ministry of Social Affairs successfully merged all social service agencies into a single social service center for each region. Hospitals, residential institutions, and local community service centers each name two of the board members, and associated universities, if any, name one. The clinical and nonclinical staff each has a single representative, and two representatives are chosen by clients. The provincial government chooses two more, "after consultation with the most representative socio-economic groups in the terri-

43. Jewish Family Services, *110th Annual Report, 1863–1973* (Montreal: 1974), p. 4.

44. Ibid.

tory served by the center."[45] The professional head of the center, the director-general, is also a member.

Setting up the boards in this way has virtually eliminated the role of religious orders and middle-class volunteers in helping govern social service agencies, which generally ensures that board members are closely connected to the health and social services system because of their involvement in associated institutions. Although their class backgrounds are undoubtedly more diverse than those of the previous private boards, the new members are less likely to take independent positions in opposition to major provincial government policies.

In Montreal this observation originally applied to all three social service centers, but as it began to feel its position being threatened, Ville Marie's board became increasingly outspoken in its defense of English-language services. This was particularly evident after the *Parti québécois* came to office in 1976.

Sectorization

In 1977 a new wave of change seemed likely to be forced on social service centers. The Ministry of Social Affairs, now led by Denis Lazure of the *Parti québécois*, began to insist that Montreal's social service arrangements were unsatisfactory, because they precluded the kind of territorially based planning and budgeting being carried out in Quebec City for the province's 11 other social service centers. Lazure claimed that the "sociocultural" basis of the three social service centers adopted in 1973 was only a temporary measure and did not properly reflect the wholly public character of the province's new social service system. He argued that the social centers in Montreal would soon have to be changed so that every social service center in the province would have a clearly defined territory.[46] Only then would the province's central administrators have accurate population figures for use in a statistically consistent way to compare the budgets, personnel figures, and services of all the social service centers.

In July 1977 Montreal's three social service centers responded by arguing that everybody's interests could best be served by establishing an administrative commission to further coordinate their respective activities.[47] But this was not good enough for the Ministry of Social Affairs. On October 17 an associate deputy minister wrote the social service centers, saying that as a minimum requirement each center

45. Quebec, *Statutes* (1971), Ch. 48, Section 52.
46. Ville Marie Social Service Centre, *Report to C.S.A.C. Membership on Change of Status Discussions* (May 1978), p. 2.
47. Ibid.

would have to have an "exclusive zone responsibility" for the population of part of the Montreal region. This division of responsibility would facilitate government policies favoring parity in the financing of the centers, and it would "identify clearly for the population a single spokesman responsible globally for specialized social services."[48]

Following this directive from the ministry, all three social service centers agreed to sit on a strengthened coordinating committee established under the regional council. Its mandate was to prepare a plan for the implementation of "sectorization," the process whereby the territory of the MUC and the City of Laval would be divided among the three centers. In theory this committee was expected to assume that after sectorization all three centers would be able to serve clients in French, English, or whatever other languages might be required.

In practice, of course, each center saw itself as continuing to reflect the needs of francophones, anglophones, and Jews rather than the population of particular territories. This was especially true of Ville Marie and Jewish Family Services, both of which consistently held that even after sectorization, contractual arrangements would have to be worked out among the centers so that anglophones and Jews living outside the territories of their respective centers could continue to be served by "their own" organization.[49]

As noted earlier, in 1972 the francophone social service establishment favored separate French and English social service networks. But by 1978 their position had changed, and the *Montréal Métropolitain* social service center was now being led by a group of social service administrators who shared the modernizing perspectives of the Ministry of Social Affairs and who recognized the need for planning and budgeting on a territorial basis. Furthermore, they realized that with a generous allocation of territory the financial resources available to their center were bound to increase.

Drawing Linguistic Boundaries

When the social service center coordinating committee began work in 1978 it launched an operation unprecedented in the history of Montreal. For official public purposes, it was in effect drawing the territorial boundaries of the francophone, anglophone, and Jewish

48. Letter from Aubert Ouelett, sous-ministre adjoint à la programmation, Ministère des Affaires sociales, to Jean-Claude Deschênes, directeur-general, Conseil de la santé et des services sociaux de la région de Montréal métropolitain, October 17, 1977.

49. See VMSSC, *Preliminary Proposal: Territorial Designation for V.M.S.S.C.* (April 26, 1978), pp. 2–3; and Memo from Leon Ouaknine, Director-General, Jewish Family Services Social Service Centre, to Comité Inter-CSS., October 20, 1978.

populations of metropolitan Montreal. Not surprisingly, committee members had great difficulty reaching agreement.

At the heart of the matter was the controversy over Quebec's language policy. What should be done with Montreal's immigrant population? With considerable justification, Ville Marie argued that its constituent agencies were the ones that made initial contact with most of the newer immigrant groups and that these contacts were stronger and lasted longer than those of the other social service centers.[50] But this line of argument clearly was contrary to the spirit of the new language legislation. The purpose of Bill 101 was to ensure that the immigrant groups formed associations with French institutions rather than with English institutions. Consequently, Ville Marie's arguments never had a real chance of being seriously considered.

A related controversy involved the census data to be used when trying to define anglophone and francophone areas. Ville Marie wanted to use "home-language" figures, arguing that they represented the actual language preference of people in each area and that the client's personal preference should be the key determinant in deciding the language for delivery of the social service.[51] Home-language figures gave more strength to anglophones than any other language indicator in Montreal because they included all immigrant families who used English as their main language. *Montréal Métropolitain* wanted to use "mother-tongue" figures, arguing that everyone not having English as his or her first language was part of its natural client group.[52]

Both of the two larger social service centers acknowledged that the Jewish Family Services Social Service Center should have its territorial base in the municipalities of Côte-Saint-Luc and Hampstead and in immediately surrounding areas of the City of Montreal. But the representatives of the Jewish social service center did not share the others' concern with boundaries. Instead, they wanted clear recognition that their organization would, in practice, have the chief responsibility for Montreal's Jewish population, regardless of boundaries.[53]

Both Ville Marie and the Jewish social service center realized that the larger the territory they claimed, the less likely they were to have an anglophone or Jewish majority within it. How could they remain primarily anglophone or Jewish in these circumstances? This problem was never dealt with satisfactorily. Both were willing to adjust to providing services for French Catholics, but due to the way they defined their principal objectives, it was clear they did not anticipate francophones (in the case of Ville Marie) or non-Jews (in the

50. VMSSC, *Territorial Presentation: Stage II* (May 11, 1978), p. 5.
51. Ibid.
52. Centre de services sociaux Montréal métropolitain, *Proposition pour délimiter le territoire du C.S.S.S.M.M.* (March 30, 1978), p. 3.
53. Memo from Leon Ouaknine, October 20, 1978.

case of Jewish Family Services) ever occupying a majority of the positions in the senior management or boards of directors.

On the other hand, if the anglophone and Jewish social service centers tried to protect their majority status by accepting smaller territories in which their main client groups clearly predominated, they faced cuts in funding from the provincial government. In summary, there were penalties for being too large or too small, and consequently the goal was a territorial base just large enough to support the centers' current establishment.

When *Montréal Métropolitain* and Ville Marie presented their territorial claims, they overlapped in huge areas of the Island of Montreal. Both claimed the main immigrant area in the island's center as well as the Verdun-LaSalle area in the southwest.[54] *Montréal Métropolitain* wanted to resolve boundary questions before considering any future cooperative arrangements among the three social service centers. It was willing to trade off one area for another to arrive at a territorial compromise.[55] But Ville Marie insisted that territorial decisions could not be made final until other matters were determined, such as how Ville Marie would relate to anglophones living outside its defined territory. Discussions of the territorial issue continued throughout 1978 and 1979.[56]

An important factor forcing the social service centers to accept some kind of territorial division was implementation of a new provincial Youth Protection Act.[57] This law came into force on January 15, 1979, entrusting social service centers with clear responsibilities to protect children against abuse. To administer the act, the territorial jurisdiction of each center had to be made explicit. For example, the MUC Police had to know whom to contact when confronted with children who were apparent victims of beatings or other forms of undue hardship. Accordingly, for youth protection purposes, the social service centers agreed on the boundaries shown in Map 5, but these boundaries were not recognized as the final settlement for all social service purposes.

LaSalle was the area of greatest dispute because it was equally divided between francophones and anglophones. The battle for LaSalle was complex and bitter. The eventual settlement, requiring Lazure's direct intervention, effectively allocated LaSalle to *Montréal Métropolitain*. In return it was officially acknowledged that even

54. See maps 1 and 2 in VMSSC, *Territorial Presentation: Stage II*.
55. Conseil de la santé et des services sociaux de Montréal métropolitain, *Rencontre C.S.S.M.M.-C.S.S.V.M.: Procès-Verbaux* (August 29, 1978), p. 2.
56. Conseil de la santé et des services sociaux de Montréal métropolitain, *Comité Inter-C.S.S.: Procès-Verbaux* (1978–79).
57. Quebec, *Statutes* (1977), Ch. 20.

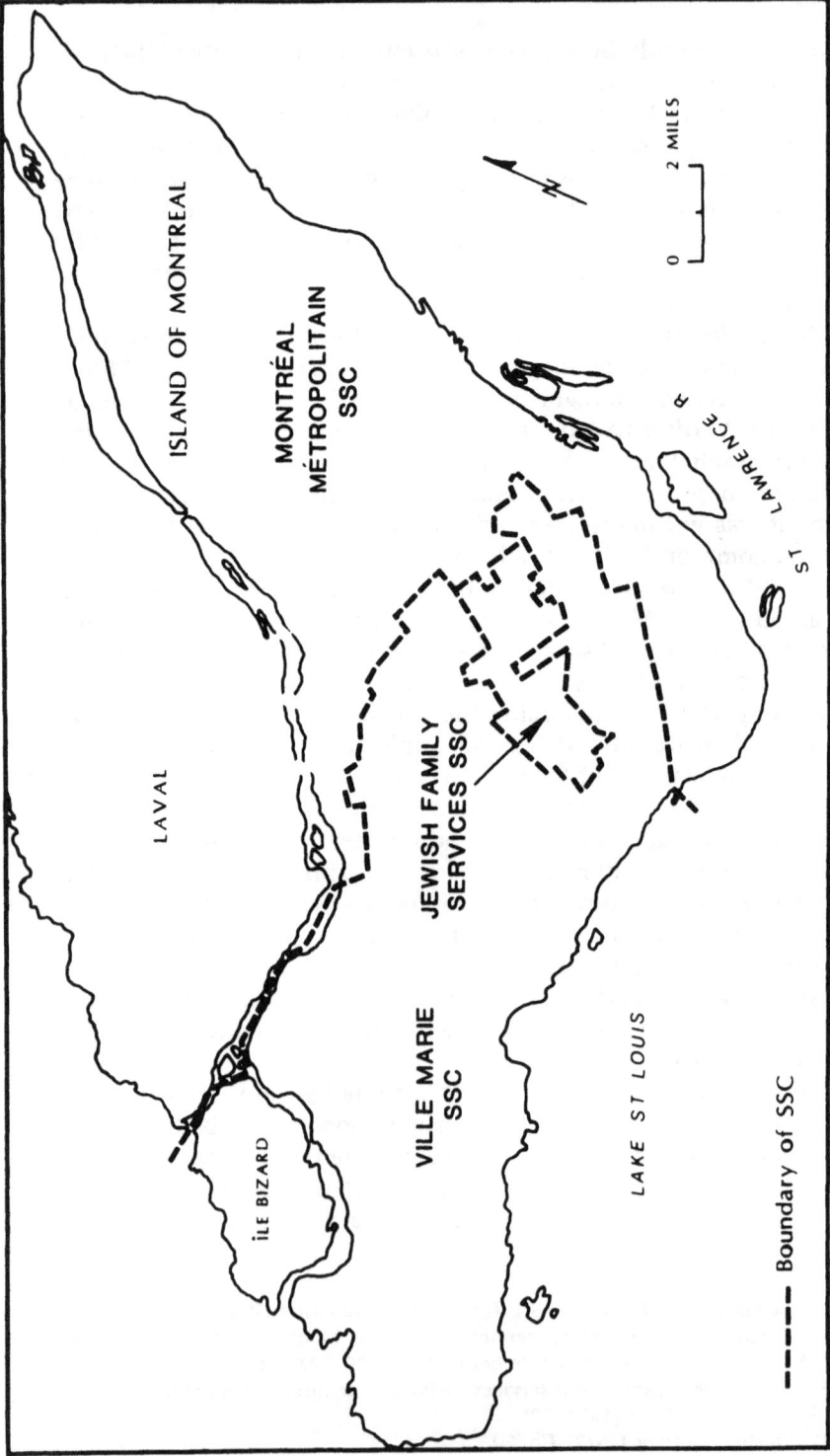

Map 5

The Territories of the Montreal Social Service Centers (SSC), 1980

Source: Derived from map drawn for Centre de recherche en Aménagement Régional. Université de Sherbrooke. 1979. Amended to reflect 1980 SSC boundary settlement.

ISLAND OF MONTREAL

MONTRÉAL
MÉTROPOLITAIN
SSC

LAVAL

JEWISH FAMILY
SERVICES SSC

VILLE MARIE
SSC

ÎLE BIZARD

LAKE ST LOUIS

ST LAWRENCE R

0   2 MILES

━ ━ ━ Boundary of SSC

with sectorization "the socio-cultural reality of each social service center must be respected." The administrative responsibility for minority groups in each center's territory would rest with that center, which would also be expected to serve its minority outside the center's own boundaries by making service arrangements with other centers.[58] Ville Marie and Jewish Family Services considered this a significant victory.

Although it is still unclear how or when sectorization will be implemented, the basic policy has been established and the boundaries adopted. Depending on the arrangements worked out among the three social service centers, the boundaries may never really have much political significance, although their existence is sure to pacify statisticians and planners in Quebec City.

For the student of Montreal's local government, however, the creation of these boundaries is a major development, especially because each social service center has now been officially guaranteed that its "sociocultural reality" is to be respected. This means that for one set of government functions at least, Montreal has three distinct territories—one each for the French, the English, and the Jewish.

The Private Politics of Public Social Services

As recently as the late 1960s, social services in Montreal were handled by a complex array of highly autonomous agencies, most of which had deep roots in one of Montreal's distinct linguistic or religious communities. Government control was minimal, although its financial contributions were rising rapidly. The agencies were nominally governed by volunteer boards of directors, but in practice the full-time professionals had considerable freedom to shape policies and programs in accordance with their own view of their agency's mission. Although this arrangement allowed the development of very high-quality social work practice, it also, of course, contributed to the emergence of inequities and duplication. By 1970 it was obvious that social services were due for provincially sponsored rationalization and modernization.

The Castonguay-Nepveu commission was to health what the Parent commission was to education. It proposed a complete framework for change, much of it implemented—admittedly in a milder form—by Castonguay himself while he was minister of social affairs from 1970 to 1973. Unlike the Parent commission, Castonguay gave no special

---

58. Letter from Denis Lazure, Minister of Social Affairs, to Madame Alphonsine Howlett, President of the Board of Directors, VMSSC, February 29, 1980.

treatment to metropolitan Montreal. At the beginning, at least, he assumed that Montreal's public social services system could be identical in structure to those of other regions in the province. When he was charged with actually implementing this policy, he made significant adjustments to account for Montreal's obvious social heterogeneity. In fact, he presided over the creation of separate social service centers for francophones and anglophones, and shortly afterward he approved another one for Montreal's Jewish population.

Later in the 1970s pressure came from the provincial government and from Montreal's francophone social service centers to restructure Montreal's social services on a territorial basis. The move toward sectorization—which effectively created Montreal's first official ethnic and linguistic boundaries—has been the least-known aspect of recent institutional change.

The mainly private controversy about social services organization deserves to be better understood, because it adds a particularly vivid dimension to our knowledge of the way the linguistic cleavage affected the organization of Montreal's local governmental institutions. As this is the main concern of the entire book, a reexamination of this issue forms the basis of the concluding chapter.

10

Conclusion: Language Differences and Metropolitan Reform in Montreal

Until the late 1960s Quebec's provincial government kept aloof from debate over the structure of local political power in metropolitan Montreal. Before 1960 both the Liberal and *Union nationale* governments were either unable or unwilling to do anything that would upset the privileged position of Quebec's anglophones. Considering the reformist credentials of the Lesage Liberal government of 1960–66, one might have expected it to address this matter openly. Except for a few threatening speeches by René Lévesque, however, this never happened. Although the Lesage Liberals encouraged a redistribution of wealth from English to French with policies that increased provincial subsidies to local school boards, they made no attempt to change existing local institutions within Montreal. The Lesage Liberals were in fact preoccupied with rationalizing and modernizing government at the provincial level, a necessary first step in attempting to exert francophone political power.

Their reluctance in Montreal's case contrasted sharply with their policies for other parts of the province, where they began regionalizing school boards and amalgamating many small municipalities. Even on Île-Jésus, just north of Montreal, they merged 13 municipalities into the new City of Laval. We can conclude that the Lesage Liberals were simply not ready to confront the complex social and political forces on the Island of Montreal, the province's one area where anglophone strength was obviously concentrated. Had they remained in office beyond 1966, however, they like their successors would have had to deal with the problems of restructuring local governmental institutions in Montreal. By the late 1960s it was no longer an accepted principle of Quebec politics that the provincial government could not tamper with anglophone interests.

The MUC: Continuing Stalemate

The first in a series of dramatic local institutional changes— creation of the Montreal Urban Community—was a direct response to a peculiar kind of service crisis rather than the result of a well-planned effort to rationalize local organizations. Because of political violence in the late 1960s, Montreal needed effective policing more than any other Canadian city. In October 1969 the city's police made it clear that the city would get no policing unless they were paid adequately. Both city and province were under severe financial pressure, and neither had anything to lose by alienating suburban voters.

Accordingly, the *Union nationale* government decided to force the suburbs to help pay the extra costs. To make this policy look like something other than outright confiscation of suburban funds, the government created the Montreal Urban Community, which began existence as little more than a channel to redistribute the costs of policing the Island of Montreal. Its creation was justified on the grounds that it would soon become a multifunctional metropolitan government capable of providing services to benefit suburban areas as well as the central city.

Compared to the metropolitan governments in Winnipeg and Toronto, the development of the Montreal Urban Community has not been impressive. Nevertheless, with strong financial assistance from other levels of government the MUC has managed to launch massive extensions to the subway system and to begin constructing a sewage treatment plant and new collector sewers. Because of the obvious need for both these major capital projects, neither has generated much public controversy, although the subway extension has led to the inevitable debates among specialists about the most appropriate technology and location of routes.

Apart from the abolition of local police forces, the MUC's existence has caused no significant decline in local autonomy. This is particularly noticeable in the MUC's total inability to carry out any significant form of metropolitan land-use planning, although this was one of its original functions. The suburbs have blocked all attempts to introduce an official plan that would in any way restrict their authority to control land use in their territories.

Montreal's experience contrasts with that of Toronto and Winnipeg, where the provincial governments overruled the suburban municipalities and their desire to retain control of land-use planning. This happened in Toronto and Winnipeg largely as a consequence of drastic municipal boundary changes that created much larger and more heterogeneous municipal units, rather than because of any explicit decision to remove planning from local jurisdictions. In principle, the government of Quebec also believed in restructuring municipal boundaries, just as much as the governments of Ontario and Manitoba. If so, how did the MUC municipalities retain both their full power and their existing boundaries? They maintained their powers by using their veto in the MUC council, and they perpetuated their existence and unchanged boundaries by entering into the powerful, mutually protective alliance described at the end of Chapter 7.

The strength of the suburban veto in the MUC is best explained by recalling that without it the city would have had absolute control. Since 1960 policy has been governed exclusively by Jean Drapeau's Civic Party, with its vast majority of the Montreal city council seats. Accordingly, it is not surprising that francophone and anglophone suburbs have been especially eager to protect themselves from Drapeau's "municipal imperialism" and have joined together in the Conference of Montreal Suburban Mayors for just this purpose.

The peculiar force of the language division is not seen in the conference or in relation to the frequent use of the suburban veto. It is best seen in the provincial government's inability, after many years of study, to achieve some degree of rationality in municipal boundaries. Any significant boundary change also changes the linguistic balance within the municipalities, and *many* such changes would in fact transform some citizens from a linguistic majority in their old municipality to a minority in the new municipality. Most politicians believe the political difficulties attending such projected changes would be serious enough to outweigh any gains in organizational rationality. This is how linguistic cleavages make Montreal's experience with metropolitan government vastly different from Toronto's or Winnipeg's.

The Policing Controversy

Since the MUC's establishment, the problem of police organization has been extremely sensitive. The discussion in Chapter 7 concerning the unification of the island's municipal police forces described the discontent generated in Montreal's English municipalities, particularly Westmount, by the loss of their local community forces. Although the extent to which linguistic issues fueled this discontent is extremely difficult to assess, a few points are obvious. For example, the sense of "belonging" on the part of an anglophone police officer in a predominately English-speaking suburban force is substantially different from what it would be in a francophone-dominated MUC force. Similarly, measures to ensure police officers' fluency in English would be stricter among English-speaking suburban officials than among officials of the MUC.

Police unification was carried out despite language differences, although much more slowly and with greater political difficulties than in Toronto and Winnipeg. The case for unification was initially argued in the 1970 Public Security Council report with the emphasis primarily on rational organization. But the political decision to integrate was made by Justice Minister Jérôme Choquette, who based his justification mostly on the need to improve the ability of police to fight the growing menace of organized crime. This argument rested on the assumption that dealing effectively with criminals working in large organizations requires police who are similarly organized. The suburbs countered that most police work does not involve fighting organized crime, but this rather obvious point could not compete with the rhetoric of a dedicated crime-buster.

Unification was also encouraged by the fact that costs were pooled as of July 1, 1970. Once municipalities were paying police costs in proportion to their share of the island's taxable assessment, formal administrative unification of the forces inevitably followed. Carrying out Montreal's police unification in two stages—first financial and then administrative—rather than in one stage, as in Toronto and Winnipeg, greatly facilitated the ultimate result.

Uniqueness of Social Services

The impact of linguistic cleavage was clearest in the reorganization of Montreal's social service institutions. The initial reform plan, with a common pattern for the entire province, was altered because of Montreal's unique linguistic makeup. Instead of the provincewide practice of having only a single social service center in a given territory, the government soon saw the wisdom of two centers in Montreal—one for anglophones and one for francophones. By initially staying out of the anglophone system, the Jews were eventually able to have their own social service network also recognized as a third public social service center, but this does not alter the fact that the fundamental decision on reorganization in Montreal was based on language.

Why was the language criterion so readily adopted for social services? There are four plausible explanations. First, the provision of personal social services was not a highly visible government activity. Unlike education, social services have never caused great political dispute among ethnic, language, or religious groups; consequently, there are no statutory or constitutional guarantees respecting the acquired rights of any particular group. In short, social service administrators, civil servants, and politicians have been able to accommodate each other's interests without the glare of publicity— the process could almost be called secret. Accommodations are invariably easier for both sides when each step in the process does not require the negotiators to justify themselves publicly to their respective constituencies.

Second, there is general agreement that social services must be provided in the language of the client. Nobody has ever argued that anything is gained for individuals or society by counseling clients on personal and family problems in a language other than their own. This leads to the conclusion that language-based administrative structures are appropriate for these services.

Education is viewed very differently. Thus, many people in both language groups argue that students gain from immersion in an educational environment in which a language other than their mother tongue predominates. On the other hand, some Quebec nationalists in Montreal have countered that the very existence of English schools subverts French language and culture.

Third, there was no clear reason that social service administration in a densely populated urban area like Montreal needed to be divided up on a territorial basis. Police administration is different, because it would be disastrous for two police forces—one English and one French—to operate in the same territory and with the same legal authority. Consequently, a single police force must in some way cope with the languages used in the area in which it operates. When a region has two or more language groups, with clusters of people speaking predominantly one language, both the territory and the principal language of a police force take on great significance. In contrast, there is no reason that social services (or education) cannot be provided by two or more linguistic networks operating in the same territory. Although this might be thought costly, in fact a single system of social service institutions, with internal bilingualism, would be at least as expensive and perhaps more so.

Fourth, there are social class considerations. Personal social services are theoretically available to all members of society, but in fact the clientele's background is overwhelmingly low income. Consequently, separate English social service agencies—unlike school systems or wealthy municipalities—are not seen as bastions of anglophone privilege. True, when social service agencies were primarily financed by private philanthropy, English Montreal had better social services than French. But under the Bill 65 reforms the agencies were to be completely public, and funding was to be based on demonstrated need. In short, social service agencies are not considered symbols of economic superiority, nor do they assist in developing future economic elites.

All these four factors helped ensure the political feasibility of language-based social service centers. Admittedly, the three centers are now assigned their own specific territories, but in addition the provincial government still explicitly recognizes the special responsibility each has for a particular sociocultural community, without regard to territory.

School Boards: Pressure from Quebec Nationalists

Some special features of the debate about educational structures in Montreal have already been discussed. Although language-based school boards might theoretically have been as sensible as language-based social service agencies, the attendant political considerations were quite different. Language use in schools is a key determinant of future language patterns in society as a whole, and school programs and policies can be of great importance in perpetuating ethnic group identity. Consequently, the school system was highly visible to all segments of the community. The political importance of schools is underlined by the religious-group guarantees enshrined in Section 93 of the British North America Act. Although access to English-language schools can logically be separated from the question of school board organization, we saw in Chapter 8 how the two issues were soon closely linked in public discussion. Most of the spokesmen for francophone Quebec nationalism argued against separate French and English school boards. Lacking agreement on any other alternative, and because many French Catholics still insisted on the need for Catholic administrative structures, the limited reorganization that was effected in 1973 left in place the basic elements of a system that has persisted for more than a century.

The francophone nationalists intervened in the debate over educational structures to a far greater degree than on any other issue treated in this book. Their efforts with education had relatively little success, but their political victories in other fields in the past decade—most notably with the language law, Bill 101—have been very impressive. The proven capability of Quebec to build a thoroughly French province within federal Canada has diminished, if not removed, one of the original reasons that the political movement for Quebec's independence became so potent.

French-English Relations: Two Models for the Future

One model of future French-English relations in Quebec assumes that the seemingly inexorable trend toward an almost totally French-speaking society is likely to cause still more anglophones to leave. Those who stay will become thoroughly bilingual and thoroughly integrated into the social, political, and economic life of French-speaking Montreal. If this happens, there will presumably be little continued anglophone resistance to the kinds of nationalist demands for local structural change expressed during debates over Montreal's school board organization. The provincial government could implement such changes, and the end result would resemble Toronto's and Winnipeg's major reforms and boundary changes.

In other words, in such a thoroughly French Quebec, we could expect the demands of organizational rationality to prevail, in this case fueled by nationalism. In addition to having a unified police force on the Island of Montreal, there would also be a single public educational system; a single social services system; and despite continued suburban opposition, a drastic restructuring of municipal boundaries, without reference to remaining small pockets of anglophones.

This scenario assumes the beginning of an end to the social conflict that has persisted since Montreal's conquest in 1760, or at least its dramatic reduction. Francophones would still be influenced by American and English-Canadian political and economic developments but would be largely free from direct local evidence that they were once a conquered people. Chapter 2 noted that Lewis Coser defined a social conflict as "a struggle in which the aims of the opponents are to neutralize, injure, or eliminate their rivals."[1] Although the use of English will never be eliminated in Montreal, the end result would be the elimination of anglophones as a distinct collectivity.

The passage of the Constitution Act of 1982—agreed to by the federal government and all provinces except Quebec—is unlikely to be of much assistance to Quebec anglophones.[2] It overrides Quebec's language legislation (Bill 101) on only one relatively minor point. The new constitutional provisions say parents living in Quebec who received their education in English in *Canada* have the right to send their children to English-language schools, whereas Bill 101 restricts that right to parents educated in English in *Quebec*.

The political importance of the imposition of the Constitution Act on Quebec relates not so much to its actual provision but to the way it was approved. For decades Quebec provincial politicians from all parties have believed that constitutional change in Canada required their consent. The country, they claimed, is based on a pact between English and French, and the government of Quebec represents the French more legitimately than any other institution. But the new constitutional arrangements were not approved by Quebec, nor does the new constitution's amending formula require Quebec's approval for major future changes. In short, Quebec was simply treated as another province, not as a unique province that represents one of Canada's two founding peoples. In approving the constitution in this way, many Quebec francophones see the English-speaking provinces as having refused to recognize the government of Quebec as the prin-

1. Lewis Coser, *The Functions of Social Conflict* (Glencoe, Ill.: Free Press, 1956), p. 8.

2. For a useful commentary see David Milne, *The New Canadian Constitution* (Toronto: Lorimer, 1982). For the British Parliament the statute is officially known as the Canada Act (Section 4), but in Canada its official title is the Constitution Act (Section 1).

cipal institution to represent French-speaking Canadians. If English Canada thus fails to recognize Quebec's special position in Canada, why should Quebec francophones recognize any special position for the anglophone minority in Quebec? The implied answer obviously supports the first model, an almost totally French-speaking society.

The second model of future French-English relations is based on a different interpretation of recent events that are seen as not necessarily having set Quebec on an inexorable path toward a French-speaking society with the near extinction of English as one goal. Instead, recent developments are seen not as the source of continuing bitterness but as the first signs that the contentious issue of Quebec's relationship with the rest of Canada has been settled. According to this view, now that Quebec's constitutional status has lost prominence as a political issue there will be fewer Quebec nationalists intent on obliterating Montreal's English institutions.

With pressures thus reduced, English-speaking Montrealers committed to staying in Quebec would no longer have their energies diverted by the fight against separatism and consequently would then be able to give priority to organizing politically as a linguistic minority. Anglophones could develop institutions they could use for negotiation and exerting influence on matters affecting their linguistic minority interests. Coser's analysis suggests that such organization could meet the implicit requirements of the francophone majority by providing, for example, recognized minority spokespersons who could act as a clear political link between the minority and the francophone leadership.[3] Given enlightened and skillful leadership on both sides, such a development could reduce French-English tensions by defining the terms of a continued anglophone presence in Quebec.

The objective of the kind of organization projected would *not* be insistence on perpetuating anglophone economic dominance but rather on maintaining a limited network of local anglophone institutions. Schools and social services would probably be of greatest concern, but also included might be the protection of the right of certain municipal units (those with high levels of anglophone population) to conduct their internal affairs in English. Such arrangements would still require various metropolitan agencies to provide for continuing contacts with and coordination among the various institutions. Bodies like the Montreal Urban Community, the School Council of the Island of Montreal, and the Council of Health and Social Services of Metropolitan Montreal would insure French and English local administrators against the total isolation from each other that they experienced before 1960.

---

3. Coser, *Social Conflict*, p. 129. There is evidence that such anglophone organizations and leaders are emerging. Alliance Quebec is probably the most important example.

Any such new recognition of the desirability of fostering certain kinds of English public institutions would, of course, occur within a province clearly recognized as being fundamentally French. The use of French, and *only* French, as Quebec's common public language now seems assured, regardless of the province's political future. Once francophone Quebeckers are fully aware of this, they will probably be willing to reach a new accommodation with Montreal's anglophone population.

Such a new accommodation could involve guarantees that anglophones could continue to control and organize their own local services, while it continued to permit existing institutions and boundaries to be changed through negotiation. Achievement of such a linguistic-cultural accommodation would, in fact, be a much greater political accomplishment than anything done in Toronto or Winnipeg. It would merit the attention not only of students of metropolitan reorganization but also of all who are concerned with the peaceful settlement of human conflict.

Appendix: Political Parties in Canada, Quebec, and Montreal

Federal

The Liberal Party: With its tradition of alternating between English- and French-speaking leaders, the Liberals have been Canada's dominant political party throughout most of the twentieth century, their strongest base of support being in Quebec. The party has held office in the years 1896–1911, 1921–26, 1926–30, 1935–57, 1963–79, and 1980–84. Within Quebec its strong support for a bilingual Canada has attracted francophones and anglophones alike. From 1968 until 1984 its leader was Pierre Elliott Trudeau. The current leader is John Turner.

The Progressive Conservative Party: The adjective "Progressive" was added in 1942. After providing Canada's first prime minister, Sir John A. Macdonald (1867–73 and 1878–91), the party has been notably less successful, in large part because in Quebec it has often been perceived as anti-French. In this century it held office in 1911–21, 1926 (for a few months), 1930–35, 1957–63, 1979–80, and 1984–. It has never had a French-Canadian leader, although the current PC prime minister, Brian Mulroney, is fluently bilingual and from Quebec.

The New Democratic Party: The NDP was founded in 1961 as the result of an alliance between the socialist Co-operative Commonwealth Federation and the Canadian labor movement. Although strong in western Canada and parts of Ontario, it has never elected a member from Quebec and has virtually no presence in provincial politics.

The Créditistes: Under their populist leader Réal Caouette, the Quebec branch of the Social Credit sprang to prominence in the 1960s by winning dozens of seats in rural and small-town Quebec. Its strength declined throughout the 1970s. In the election of 1980 the party failed to elect any candidates and now appears moribund.

Provincial

The Quebec Liberal Party: Originally part of the same organization as the federal Liberals, the Quebec Liberals established their own

Seats Won by Various Parties in Quebec Provincial Elections, 1944–1981

Election	Liberal	UN	PQ	Cred.	Others	Total
1944	37	48			6	91
1948	8	82			2	92
1952	23	68			1	92
1956	20	72			1	93
1960	51	43			1	95
1962	63	31			1	95
1966	51	56			1	108
1970	72	17	7	12		108
1973	102		6	2		110
1976	27	11	70	1	1	110
1981	42		80			122

autonomous organizational structure in 1964 under the leadership of Premier Jean Lesage (1960–66). Prior to Lesage the party held office this century from 1897 to 1936 and from 1939 to 1944. The Liberals were in office again from 1970 to 1976 under the leadership of Robert Bourassa. Because of its usual opposition to Quebec nationalism, the party in recent years has attracted the almost unanimous support of Quebec anglophones. From 1978 to 1982 its leader was Claude Ryan, formerly well known as editor of the newspaper *Le Devoir*. Ryan was a frequent critic of the federal Liberals, especially in constitutional matters; this combined with his party's loss in the 1981 provincial election hastened his resignation. His successor is Robert Bourassa.

The Union nationale *(UN)*: Founded in 1935 by provincial Conservative leader Maurice Duplessis as an alliance between his party and dissident Liberals, Duplessis soon converted it into a powerful electoral machine that governed the province from 1936 to 1939 and from 1944 to 1960 in accordance with conservative and nationalist principles. The party held office once again in the late 1960s, first under Daniel Johnson (1966–68) and then under Jean-Jacques Bertrand (1968–70). After winning no seats in the general election of 1973 it experienced a brief resurgence in 1976. In 1981 it was once again completely eliminated.

The Parti québécois *(PQ)*: In 1967 René Lévesque, a former provincial cabinet minister, quit the Quebec Liberal Party because it refused to adopt his position favoring a sovereign Quebec linked economically with the rest of Canada. Lévesque's new organization, the *Mouvement Souveraineté-Association*, merged in 1968 with the *Ralliement national*, a right-wing separatist party, to form the *Parti québécois*, headed by Lévesque. Following the merger, the left-wing separatist party, the *Rassemblement pour l'indépendance nationale*, disbanded and most of its members joined the PQ. Since 1976

Lévesque has led a PQ government in Quebec, but he has been unable to advance toward independence because he failed to win the 1980 Quebec referendum in which he asked for a mandate to begin sovereignty negotiations with the federal government.

The Créditistes: Even more than their federal counterparts, the provincial *Créditistes* have gone through various name changes and splits as a result of factional bickering. With a rural and small-town electoral base, the group managed in 1970 to win 12 of 110 National Assembly seats, but it has been in decline ever since. In 1981 it did not win any seats and now appears moribund.

City of Montreal

Prior to the 1950s there were no organized municipal political parties in Montreal. Nevertheless, there were many recognizable factions, most members of which could be clearly identified with federal or provincial political parties. For example, Mayor Médéric Martin (1914–24 and 1926–28) was a well-known Liberal. Mayor Camillien Houde (1928–32, 1934–36, 1938–40, and 1944–54) was actually leader of the provincial Conservative party during part of his first term in office. After bitter wrangling with Duplessis prior to World War II, Houde became a firm ally of the *Union nationale* premier afterward.

Municipal Parties No Longer in Existence

Civic Action League: The league was formed prior to the 1954 municipal elections by Alderman Pierre DesMarais and other opponents of Mayor Houde. Its candidate for mayor was Jean Drapeau, who had become well known as lawyer for the Caron commission investigation of civic corruption. Drapeau won in 1954 but lost in 1957. In 1960 Drapeau left the Civic Action League, and it never recovered. Even during Drapeau's term as mayor, the league never controlled the Montreal city council.

Greater Montreal Rally: This group was sponsored by Premier Duplessis to counter the Civic Action League in the 1957 municipal elections. Its only real success was in electing its mayoral candidate, Sarto Fournier, who ironically was a Liberal senator in Ottawa. Following its defeat by Drapeau in 1960, the Greater Montreal Rally faded out of existence.

Front d'action politique *(FRAP):* With strong support from trade unions, this left-wing group contested many working-class wards in the 1970 municipal elections. During the crisis provoked by the *Front de libération du Québec* in October 1970, some of its candidates and organizers were arrested and imprisoned. None of its candidates was elected, and it never again contested an election.

Existing Municipal Political Parties

Civic Party: This is Jean Drapeau's personal party, which he established after leaving the Civic Action League just prior to the 1960 municipal elections. Drapeau and his hand-picked Civic Party candidates have won the mayoralty and virtually all council seats in every municipal election since 1960. The only serious threats came in 1974 (when Drapeau won only 55.1 percent of the votes for mayor and 36 of the 55 council seats) and 1982 (when he won 48 percent of the mayoralty votes and 39 of 57 council seats).

Montreal Citizens Movement (MCM): A coalition of left-wing groups formerly associated with FRAP and of English- and French-speaking reformers and conservationists, the MCM met with remarkable success in 1974 at its first municipal election. Its candidate for mayor, Jacques Couture, won 39.1 percent of the vote, and 18 of its council candidates were elected. Three years later the coalition split apart, with the more moderate, electoralist wing of the party no longer tolerating the socialist ideology adopted at many official party meetings. In 1978 the MCM mayoral candidate, Guy Duquette, won only 12.5 percent of the vote, and the party won only one seat on the council. With labor lawyer Jean Doré as its leader in 1982, the party experienced a resurgence: Doré won 37 percent of the mayoralty vote, and 15 MCM councillors were elected.

Municipal Action Group (MAG): Consisting primarily of the moderate group that broke away from the MCM, MAG contested its first municipal election in 1978. Its candidate for mayor, federal Liberal MP Serge Joyal, won 22.5 percent of the vote, but only one council candidate was elected. With former MUC police chief Henri-Paul Vignola as its candidate in 1982, the party won only 15 percent of the mayoralty votes. Three councillors were elected.

Index

Compositor: Huron Valley Graphics
Text: Melior
Display: Melior Bold